# THE HIDDEN LIFE OF TIROL

# THE HIDDEN LIFE OF
# TIROL

MARTHA C. WARD

*University of New Orleans*

WAVELAND PRESS, INC.

Prospect Heights, Illinois

For information about this book, write or call:
Waveland Press, Inc.
P.O. Box 400
Prospect Heights, Illinois 60070
(708) 634-0081

For information about programs sponsored by the University of New Orleans in Innsbruck or Brunnenburg, write to:
International Study Programs
University of New Orleans
New Orleans, Louisiana 70148

The publisher and author gratefully acknowledge the Austrian National Tourist Office in New York for supplying the black and white photography used in this volume. 



ISBN 0-88133-737-4



Printed in the United States of America

7 6 5 4 3 2 1

This book is dedicated to all the
Innsbruckers and all the Brunnenburgers,
past, present and future.

*The Heart of Europe*

# Acknowledgments

I want to thank the following people most earnestly and profoundly:

Dr. Gordon "Nick" Mueller whose vision and energy founded the International Study Programs at the University of New Orleans.

Carl Wagner and Margaret Davidson, whose calm and competent administration makes everything work and whose company I treasure. Günter Bischof and Alea Morelock Cot, both of whom helped me more than they know.

Erich Thöni, Anton Pelinka, Frederick Luhan, Georg Lamp, Fritz Kraft, Franz Mathis, Max Preglau, Klaus Frantz, Walter Freitag, Inga Fink, Eva Mayr and Joe Gott, friends and colleagues from Innsbruck.

Julian Pleasants and Paul Magnarella, colleagues from the University of Florida who have contributed many summers of work and dedication to making our programs work.

Mary de Rachewiltz, a continual inspiration. Siegfried and Brigitta de Rachewiltz and their sons for the food, the friendship, fellowship and the fun of Brunnenburg. And Philip Leist for his help.

Carol Peebles, student, assistant and artist-in-residence for the UNO International Study Programs. She drew the charming illustrations for the cover and throughout the chapters.

Peter McLean and Carla Gallo, travel experts who always get us there and back.

Ernst Riffeser, of ANRI in the Grödental, for the tours for my students and family.

Konrad Kressley, who taught me to hike. Joseph Logsdon, David Sandburg, George Gmelch, John Cole, Peter Petschauer, Steven Ambrose, Eric Wolf, Thomas Schlunz, and Peggy McDowell, American colleagues who encouraged me and helped me see what I was looking for.

Allen H. Chappel, University of New Orleans, translated the poems of Oswald von Wolkenstein. The poems are from a collection at the University of Innsbruck.

Dr. Ahmad Massasati, Department of Geography, University of New Orleans, for the maps and the fun of making them.

Kenneth Lacho Jr., Computer Genius Extraordinaire, for keeping me up and running through the worst.

Connie Phelps and the competent, friendly, fabulous staff of the Earl K. Long Library at the University of New Orleans.

Rainer Fadinger and Meg Hanks, who supported and translated.

Tom Curtin and the staff of Waveland Press, the best book publishers-editors I ever had.

Joel Simpson, Marlowe Ward and Ted Coonfield who trusted me enough to follow me there. Once again, my mother, Moselle Coonfield, who helped me go and my father, Hugh Coonfield, who taught me about woodworking.

I also want to acknowledge the Italian and Austrian students from the University of Innsbruck (all of whom claimed Tirolean citizenship) who lived with me and my family during our UNO Austrian-American Exchange Programs. Their stories have found a home.

I require my students in Innsbruck or Brunnenburg to keep a journal of their daily experiences and observations. This basic anthropological activity yields substantial emotional and intellectual rewards. On occasion I quote from these sources. I would like to thank the following students for permitting me to quote from their journals and for letting me share their experiences: Patti Meyer, Marlowe Ward, Andrew Wehle, Jeanne Whitson and Maggie Tiblier.

To thank properly all these good people, I borrowed a Tirolean saying, *Vergelt's Gott*. Loosely translated it means "Your golden deeds will be returned to you." *Herzlichen Dank*. My heartfelt gratitude.

# Contents

CULTURE AREA OF TIROL

# Introduction

*A rough peasant smock, but it warms well.*
—A tribute to Tirol from Emperor Maximillian I

This book was written for students and travelers in mind, imagination or memory. It is about an old and vivid folk culture called Tirol. Split between the modern nations of Austria and Italy, the "holy land of Tirol" sits in the heart of the spectacular Alps, astride the mountain passes which link the edges of Europe. My goal is to make sense of and define how the history, geography, politics and rootedness of community life in European Tirol fit together. In this ethnography of a culture area, we will use conventional anthropological categories: earning a living, getting married, inheriting property, staging religious festivals, telling stories and raising children and cows. We ask basic questions: How have people adapted and adjusted through time to an extraordinary environment? Do they transform the environment or does it profoundly shape their lives? What are the core customs and habits that define their identity as Tiroleans?

The study of European folk life and cohesive communal societies has particular relevance for us. We are drawn to traditions, rootedness and the community life we feel in places like Tirol. We want to be a part of it even as we worry that the very qualities which attract us are being altered, even destroyed, by time or tourists. Sometimes we have a sense of nostalgia for or resonance with Tirolean folk life. At other points we feel we are in a primitive country.

Yet the real life of Tirol is often hidden. Beyond the tourist facade and the scenery is one of the most vivid, accessible and integrated culture areas in all of Europe. My intent is to illuminate some of the patterns of culture woven into the tapestry which is Tirol. Four major themes or golden threads link all the chapters in this book.

Tirol is beautiful. The tourist brochures use the words: magnificent, extraordinary, breathtaking, awe-inspiring. As the poets say, every vista pleases. In fact, new adjectives fail after a while and only clichés become possible. So, throughout this book

I will frequently refer to mountains and valleys. Assume each time that I am acknowledging the beauty. I have my favorite places in Tirol (generally the last place I have been), but I have yet to see any that were not magnificent, extraordinary, breathtaking and awe-inspiring.

Tirol has peasant farmers. By this I mean rural cultivators, families involved in agriculture and animal husbandry for many generations. The people of whom I write are also villagers, Europeans, Catholics and Italians or Austrians. When I was growing up in Oklahoma we used the term "peasants" to insult each other on the playground. But the term is not a put-down here. It is simply a word to describe a comprehensive and complex way of life, a way to earn a living, bring home the bacon and put bread on the table. It may also be the chief observation to make about the people of Tirol.

Tirol is divided. One culture area with a common history in an alpine environment is split into two political parts. The map shows the nineteenth century borders of the culture area and the current configuration of its parts. Since the end of World War I, the northern half is the Federal province of Austria called Tirol or Bundesland Tirol. The southern half (or a little over half) belongs to Italy. German speakers call this Südtirol; Italians usually call it Alto Adige. How this split came to be and what it means is an integral part of this story. In a world where ethnic groups and ethnic tensions dominate the news, Tirol is a story of how people worked out their differences. They adjusted, they changed. How did they do it? Are there lessons for the rest of us?

Tirol is about tourism, the place people visit most in Austria. Tourists choose that country and its neighbors, Italy and Switzerland, as the paramount travel destinations in the world. Tourism is one of the three leading industries on the planet. So Tirol sits at the intersection of place and purpose. It is one of the sites where tourism started and where the very definition of what it means is continuously invented and reinvented. Tirol is also a localized and specialized story about environment, ecology, economics and the future. Can their success last? How did it happen? What can we learn from their experiences?

## Serendipity and Anthropology

I am regularly asked: Why is an anthropologist writing about Tirol? Don't you people do excavations or fieldwork in exotic or at least uncomfortable places? How do you manage to spend so much time in such a wonderful place? Can I carry your bags?

The University of New Orleans, where I teach, conducts a large and successful summer school program in Innsbruck, Austria. In 1979 I asked the founder and director of the program, Nick Mueller, to put anthropology courses on the curriculum and to send me to teach them. I loved teaching American students in Innsbruck and living in Tirol. I am eternally grateful for the opportunities, friendships and stimulation these programs have given me.

I struggled to make sense of what I saw and heard in Austria. Each village or chapel was more picturesque than the one before. Everything looked like the *Sound of Music* or *Heidi*. Restaurants had a realistic crucifix flanked by a stuffed bird, rabbit or deer head with antlers. The tourist in me loved every meal, however hearty, and every souvenir shop, however tacky. The anthropologist in me worked to put names on things, to see how they fit together and to understand. But I could find few materials to use in teaching students. There are fortunately some classic studies on Europe peasant societies; these gave us a comparative view. Unfortunately, there was little available or accessible about Tirol. I began as systematically as I could to collect experiences and materials.

In 1981 I signed up again to teach and in 1984 I went back to Innsbruck as director of the summer program. Part of the success of our programs (and I am very proud of them) is that we orient our courses to the local environment and to the European setting. We are constantly learning from and teaching each other. For example, a colleague, Günter Bischof, took students in his history classes to Südtirol. He made important contacts for the program and persuaded us to pay closer attention to the cultural riches of Italian Tirol. As a result of his influence, Nick Mueller and Carl Wagner of the International Studies Program called me with an idea. "Would you go live in a castle in northern Italy and teach an anthropology course there next summer if we made the arrangements?" But of course.

In the summer of 1987 I took a group of students to Brunnenburg Castle above the city of Merano, Italy. The ordinary reality of Brunnenburg is richer than any fantasy I ever had. The place and the people will appear at key moments throughout this narrative. Brunnenburg is a reconstructed twelfth century stone castle with a seventeenth century farmhouse, a vineyard and other rural features. Perched symbolically on the shoulder of Castle Tirol, it is linked to the village of Dorf Tirol with a very steep path. After World War II, Mary de Rachewiltz, the daughter of poet Ezra Pound, and her scholar-archaeologist husband, Boris, purchased the ruin from the Italian government. Their son, Siegfried de Rachewiltz, a scholar in comparative literature and ethnology, built there a museum dedicated to the rural economy and farming culture of Tirol. Brunnenburg radiates with the history and ethnography of the region. It also has the requisite spirits and ghosts.

The successful Brunnenburg summer developed into a field school for anthropology. Once again, my problem was fitting all the pieces together for myself as well as finding reading materials for American students. European scholars tend to write for each other; brilliant works are often out of print or too difficult for introductory students to read. Very little research is in English. I grabbed at bits and pieces: a few articles, one excellent book, my own experiences as an anthropologist, field trips and lectures from professionals like Dr. de Rachewiltz and colleagues at the University of Innsbruck. German was not the language I learned for my research projects; the closest I got to Italian was high school Latin and the number of dialects in remote mountain valleys is daunting even to linguists. The tourist offices of these two countries produce a staggering number of publications to entice and engage you but they explain little about the patterns of culture or what I think of as the real or hidden life of Tirol.

I have since returned to both Tirols. I have lectured on traditional culture, organized field trips throughout the region and traveled to many places where tourists do not go. These experiences and my continuing appreciation and fascination for the culture area convinced me to write this book. I had also failed to persuade my colleagues to write one themselves.

This book grows out of the craft of anthropology and the intuitive arts we practice when we participate in and observe another culture. Yet it is not an ethnography in the common anthropological manner. I did not live for a year or two in a village and immerse myself in local ways. Neither is it the kind of ethnography in which I make claims to interpret or reveal the thoughts, feelings or mind of a people different from myself.

The viewpoint is unconventional. As an anthropologist I hope to take you on a tour of a region often visited and highly visible but rarely studied in this fashion. It is my own way of making things clear about an area of the world I respect and want to tell others about.

Writing and publishing this book is also an act of presumption. I am an academic who treats the region as an anthropological unit of analysis similar to the unfamiliar, even so-called "primitive" cultures anthropologists have regularly studied. Worse, I have fallen into the classic trap that is the curse of Tirol, an outlander who writes yet another traveler's account. To be a woman in such a manifestly patriarchal culture has been a fascinating and trying experience. It is sometimes difficult to find evidence of women's lives. It would be easy for an American feminist to decry the strong male bias which so permeates Tirol. At the same time I believe that being largely invisible and an outsider has allowed me to see more.

I am not a Catholic, yet it feels familiar to me. I am not a farmer, but the values and consequences of agrarian lives resonate in my own culture and background. It is important to me as an anthropologist to understand and put these facets of social life into appropriate contexts.

I have enjoyed many unusual sources of information and enlightenment. I used the reactions and experiences of students, myself and other fellow travelers. I am entranced by and deeply grateful to the writings of people with singular connections to Tirol. Some were fostered into peasant families; some were born into the local aristocracy and others made journeys there which patently changed their lives. I found common ground in travelers' accounts; their stereotypes, awe, innocence and acute observations often parallel ours. Scholars in comparable alpine areas or peasant communities on other continents as well as colleagues at the University of Innsbruck have shared their insights generously with me. My university sponsors a number of international seminars in which scholars present their research. I have brought to bear my own fieldwork experiences from other parts of the world. I have borrowed ideas from any discipline I could find and from any source that made sense, primary, secondary or experiential.

## Words and Spellings

Because Tirol is divided, place names in the Italian part are a ticklish, even sensitive subject. Until well into this century most place names were in German. As part of the political and ethnic discord, Italians changed place names in Südtirol into their language. Now both names are used, but this is a bit awkward. I am keenly aware that my choices for place names imply that I have taken sides in old controversies. I would like to think I have a coherent and objective strategy, but mostly I use the older, German nomenclature. Often in the text I point out the changes or historic implications of place names and I have included a list of places in the appendix.

Two words in German for place names are helpful to know. *Schloss* means castle as in Schloss Tirol, the Castle of Tirol. The suffix *-tal* means valley, as in the Pustertal, the Puster Valley or the Grödental, the Gröden Valley. It will also be helpful to know that nouns in German, whether common or proper, are always capitalized.

I use the spelling that Tiroleans gave to their land. Over the years they courteously edit the publications that go to England or to America because they know that we spell the name—Tyrol.

Writers in English routinely argued about the spelling. "The fact that a number of geographical names have undergone in this half-century precisely the same change as the word Tyrol, and that the 'foreign' letter 'y' is hardly ever used by Germans, does not render the spelling of the word Tirol correct," says the Austrian-born W. A. Grohman in 1878.

The opposite opinion is equally firm. "It is most natural to adopt a country's own nomenclature; and in Tirol, by Tirolean writers, I have never seen the name spelt with a *y*," writes Rachel Busk in 1874. "We do not say 'the' France or 'the' Italy; even to accommodate ourselves to the genius of the languages of those countries, therefore, that we should have gone out of our way to say 'the Tyrol' when the genius of the languages of those countries does not require us so to call it, can have arisen only from a piece of carelessness which there is no need to repeat."

These days most anthropologists choose to follow the spelling and other terminology of the people we write about rather than using ethnocentric, even colonial, usages. I have preserved the Anglo-Saxon spelling only for quotations and citations. The Germanic-Tirolean spelling is older and in more common use. More to the point, I fell in love with posters that said, "Hier ist Tirol."

# 1

# The Roof Garden of Europe

## Places and People

*The journey up into the mountains from Innsbruck becomes more and more beautiful—no description can pay it justice. By well-prepared roads one climbs up a gorge which sends water down into the Inn, a gorge which offers the eye the most incredible variety. When the road passes right up close by a rock face or has even been carved out of it, one can see on the opposite side gentle slopes which are used for farming. Between fields and hedges on those high and broad plains stand villages, houses and huts, all painted white. But soon the picture changes: fields become meadows, until they in their turn merge into steep slopes . . . Now it became darker and darker: the individual details lost themselves and the blocks became larger and more magnificent; finally, when everything before me seemed like a deep, mysterious picture, I suddenly caught sight of the snowcapped peaks, illuminated by the moon, and now I wait until the morning brightens that ridge which divides the North from the South.*

—Johann Wolfgang von Goethe 1786

Imagine we are standing somewhere in the Alps. We look up and see mountains, hillsides, peaks and valleys. We are awestruck by their majesty. In Tirol mountains also determine and shape how generations of people will live and die. This chapter is about slope, disasters, beauty and other fundamental features of the particular geography of Tirol. Here we will also set the stage for time and place and introduce a cast of characters: peasants, travelers, journalists, anthropologists, writers or residents, historians and other scholars.

Everyone has heard of the Alps, the highest and most famous mountains in Europe. They are a unique ecological zone spanning four countries: France, Switzerland, Austria and Italy. The western

Alps in Switzerland have the highest and most narrow valleys, deeply incised with large remnant glaciers. The eastern Alps, which include Tirol, have broader, longer valleys which generally run along from east to west and lower peaks which rarely exceed 3000 meters or about 10,000 feet.

The heart of Tirol is the Brenner Pass, the great north-south route connecting Italy and the Mediterranean cultures to the south with northern Europe. The long curves of the Brenner Pass link the Austrian and the Italian halves of the ancient land of Tirol. At about 4500 feet or 1375 meters above sea level Brenner is carved by the tributaries of the Inn river flowing off the northern slopes and the Eisack flowing to the south. As traveler Ludwig Steub said in 1875, "The roof of the Brenner Post House is the watershed where drippings from one gutter flow to the Black Sea and from the other gutter to the Adriatic."

People and ideas have always passed freely through the mountains. Although the eastern Alps may appear forbidding, they have never served as a barrier to movement and change. The many low passes provided easy access to invaders, traders and others. Roman legions marched through on their conquest of Europe beyond the Alps. A few centuries later, Germanic tribes moved through the same passes to attack and end the Roman Empire. Even today Italians who live south of the mountains refer to them as "the magnificent Traitors"; they only look like a protective border.

The word *Alp* translates as "high meadow," a tribute to why and how people lived in such trying beauty. An alp or an *Alm* is a field where cattle are pastured or hay is harvested. The high pastures that circle the valleys are the grazing zones for dairy animals. At the core of Tirolean traditions and hard work are the high mountain meadows which feed the cows and therefore the people. We shall discuss this in more detail in chapter 3.

Scholars often refer to "the culture of Alpine continuity." They mean the conservative and specialized peasant cultures that developed in these mountains and still includes Tirol, the Grisons in Switzerland, Liechtenstein and Voralberg, the westernmost province of Austria. All these valleys have a common solution to earning a living: for thousands of years they have raised cows.

But within the broad Alpine ecology are regions that have a flavor all their own. Tirol is probably the quintessential example of this: it is what anthropologists call a *culture area*. That means that the life of the valleys and cultural traits in them are more similar to each other than they are to ideas or traits in adjacent regions. In chapter 2 we discuss the unique history and the feeling or identifications which people of the region have for each other and for the land.

## Ice and Sun

In the past, frozen rivers of ice covered all but the highest peaks. Some of my favorite photographs show valleys filled with morning fog; that is what the ice would have looked like. As the glaciers moved, pulled by gravity and their slippery underbellies, they ground out the softer soils and left the harder rock beneath exposed. The massive glaciers scoured the wide valleys which lie on an east and west axis; the valley of the Inn River is a prime example. As the forward edge of the glaciers melted, they dumped their loads of dirt and rocks. The melting and movements of the glaciers formed the current beds of the rivers and the hillside terraces.

People settled first on these sunny terraces, up from the dangerous valley floors and below the tree line, the altitude above which vegetation is sparse. The villages, fields and farms on those slopes are the classic image of Tirol. Valley floors, typically waterlogged and swampy, were poor places for human habitation. By contrast, wild animals and birds thrived in the marshy areas. Fall rains and spring snow melting from the mountain peaks meant annual flooding. Only when residents learned to drain the marshes could they build the lovely cities on the valley floor such as Innsbruck, Landeck, Brixen, Lienz or Merano. Modern highways run through the now safe valleys, but travelers by foot or cart in the past stuck to the hilly terraces.

By contrast, valleys that run on a north and south orientation were not eroded by glaciers. These transverse or hanging valleys produce deep, narrow canyons or gorges at the point where the tributary streams fall into the broader, lower longitudinal valleys. The landslides, avalanches, snowslides, and flash flooding which characterize these areas are the raw material of legend and defensive strategies. With natural barriers and quick disasters, people did not move easily or settle in large numbers in these remote high valleys.

How valleys orient to the sun determines how humans can use them. The north sides of the longitudinal valleys, those running east and west, face the sun. There you will see many fields and villages; the snow melts first there so the grasses grow best. The south side receives far less sunlight even at the height of summer and may go for days in the winter without sunlight. Crops planted there will not grow or only poorly; hence these slopes tend to be rugged or heavily forested. In the valleys oriented on a north to south axis (the transverse valleys) both sides receive an equal amount of sun. However, neither side receives as many hours of direct sunlight as the favored north side of a longitudinal valley.

The south-facing hillsides with the right amount of slope soak up the best sunlight. In the warmer regions, grapevines will grow there. The patterns of melting snow or the sections of a road built and rebuilt after a hard winter also graph how sunlight falls. Strategic sunlight, or insolation, determines the choice of a settlement site or what crops will reward the work of planting. Through centuries of trial and error, people have distributed themselves, their houses and their crops carefully in the path of potential sunlight.

In some areas, residents claim, sunlight determines marriage patterns. After all, it may be "shady characters" who come from the darker and less productive side of the valley.

## What Goes Up and What Goes Down

The culture of Tirol is an adjustment to slopes. Many material objects and everyday customs are about having to go up and down hills with a load. Most tools are adaptations to carrying things. Aprons are a good example. Americans assume that women wear them to protect the front of our dresses as we cook or clean. Before paper products, we wiped kids' noses with the corner or dried our hands on them after washing. However, in Tirol the traditional blue apron also belongs to men and men's work because it is the most practical and ready way to carry things.

Human backs and legs do most of the work in Tirol; this hard labor produces the pain and stiffness Tiroleans call "a hangover of the muscles." Museums in the region display an impressive array of carrying instruments, wooden backpacks, yokes, leather straps, buckets, baskets and equipment for leveraged lifting and balanced carrying for which we have no equivalents. The forked stick, *Ferggl*, is used for lifting hay; there is a children's version and one for wooden planks. There are tools for carrying hay, grain, soil, milk and other liquids, wooden planks, whetstones, manure, scythes, bread and babies.

Carrying heavy loads up steep mountains is crucial to survival and probably fosters the emphasis on male strength, heartiness and solidarity so characteristic of Tirol. Men typically carried hundred pound loads in long workdays of twelve hours or more across entire mountain ranges. Carrying weight is a way of proving a man's masculinity and his ability to take care of his family. It is no wonder that tests of men's strength and displays of male prowess are part of courtship rituals or that men in legends had to perform heroic deeds before winning the hand of a fair maiden. She wanted to be certain she and her children would eat well in a sturdy house. Folk sayings, poetry and songs are about the beauty of working outdoors and the pride of arduous hiking and carrying.

In Tirol, the work of carrying is often associated with play. Sleighs or sleds with runners are for carrying heavy loads as well as for children's play or contests and competitions. Carrying has a different symbolic value in flat lands. In Italy, by contrast, carrying is not considered dignified. A carrier or *facchino* has the lowest status of all and the worst kind of work for Italian men. This may be related to the work of women who carry heavy loads more often on flat land than in mountains.

Slopes create another problem—erosion. The primal method to slow down the loss of precious earth is to gather and carry it back up the mountains in the springtime. In alpine regions farmers used leather ropes, pulleys, carts and baskets. These organized "thing-movers" are the forerunners of the funicular railway and the lifts and cable cars so basic to our tourist experiences and to local economies.

A related problem is water—too much or too little and often in the wrong places. Sharing water to make crops grow or controlling it with dams, irrigation or other public work projects is thought by some to be the very origin of civilization itself. The earliest written laws in human life were supposed to solve the problems of equal

*Cable cars and chair lifts carry people and other loads in all seasons.*

distribution of water, of who controls it and who benefits from it. Types of water and definitions vary. Village councils must devote much of their governing energy to water management. Agriculturalists must consider the time of year, the time of the day, the potential usefulness and presumed fertility of the water. Farmers may have to get up in the middle of the night to take care of their turn for the water. Students are amazed to see irrigation systems operating in the midst of a rain; the system of taking turns is not altered by weather. The schedules of water distribution are set and the pipes are too complicated to turn on and off like a garden hose.

Most of the cultural features of the alpine regions are conditioned by or subordinated to slope. Here an observer in the nineteenth century describes the village of Wild-Schönau in Bundesland Tirol where most of the houses

> are built on such steep slopes that a heavy chain has to be laid round the houses and fastened to some firm object, a large tree, or boulder of rock, higher up. In many of the side valleys of the Pustertal manure and earth, the latter to replace the poor soil exhausted in one or two years, have to be carried up the precipitous slopes in large baskets, or *Kraksen*, on the backs of men. In one village off the Pustertal, and in two others off the Oberinntal, many of the villagers come to church with crampons on their feet, the terrible steep slopes on which their huts are built, somewhat like a swallow's nest on a wall, require this precaution (Grohman 1878:17).

The crampons of which he speaks are a nineteenth century version of sensible shoes. The iron soles with six or eight inch-long spikes jutting out are fastened to shoes with leather or cord straps. These are still used in mountain climbing. Sensible shoes for walking, hiking and climbing are another cultural adjustment to mountain slopes. I have often heard guides on the hiking trips out of Innsbruck tell lurid stories about "tennis shoe death." These cautionary tales tell of tourists who wear slick-soled shoes and slip on wet paths or rocks. Those who do not die gruesomely may have fractures or other injuries. In fact, the various Alpine Clubs value shoe safety so highly they often loan proper footwear to their customers.

A farmer on steep slopes anywhere in the world must solve the same problems. What can he do? Let things fall freely. Carry things up or use the incline in clever ways. Sleds for winter go down easily but they must be hauled up. Horses are not well suited to the terrain or to mountain climbing. Mules must be fed precious fodder. Alp dwellers have used innovative methods for thousands of years. Here is a description of a nineteenth century farmer taking a load of wood down the hill on a work sled or sleigh [sledge is the British usage]. Sleds or sleighs are light vehicles on runners for snow and ice; they are designed to be drawn by humans or other animals up the hill in preparation for sliding down it.

> Leaning back upon his cargo, his feet well forward and armed with crampons, he holds on to the two "horns" of the sledge. To one who has never watched a descent of this kind, it seems utterly impossible for a human being to slide down a narrow cutting at a gradient of fifty or sixty degrees, with a huge load of wood behind him, and not be dashed to pieces long before he reaches the bottom. Though severe accidents do sometimes occur, the prime fun of the expedition will outweigh your fears (Grohman 1878:345).

This and the following description are in the spirit of doing work is having fun. The author describes another daring adventure he had while tagging along with a party of young peasant women. It was their turn to bring the hay down to the barns from the high pastures. This is considered light, even light-hearted work. In the scene he describes, snow had already fallen at the higher altitudes when the girls, wearing trousers and crampons, hiked up the mountain hauling their sled behind them.

> The hay, packed in nets of strong cord, is tied down on the sledge; and then lighting their pipes, and making the valley at their feet ring with their merry yodeling, each girl placing herself in front of the sleigh, on which, towering far over her head, the huge bundles of fragrant Alpine grass are lying, sets out on her dangerous descent. . . . Your breath is taken, your eyes blink, now you imagine nothing can save you from dashing with fearful violence into a boulder the size of a moderate house, while a slight touch of your crampon-armed foot will guide the sleigh to the left. With dismay you see a couple of huge trunks of trees lying athwart your course; but it is too late! Then the steerswoman, when about to crash against the huge beams, lifts the front of the sledge, and you and the bundles pass over them in safety (Grohman 1878:345).

All this death-defying bravery comes from people this author calls "blushing lasses." Today many of these activities form the basis of Olympic sports and other competitions. Now mechanized vehicles and lifts do much of the work of hauling and carrying.

Hiking up the hill from our castle residence to the village above is one of the first and most intense adjustments my students and I make to the field school. Many of us come from flat lands or paved urban areas where such daily climbing is not necessary. Students say, "Even the toddlers and really old people walk faster and easier than we do." "I had no idea that walking up and walking down were two completely different movements. I ache all over." "This climb brings a whole new meaning to words like erosion, incline or steep." "I have to stop halfway up, sit and gasp for breath." The cultural adjustment to slopes and most of the examples of that concept I have used here are from the extraordinary lectures and demonstrations of Siegfried de Rachewiltz. His wife, Brigitta, provided me the best advice for going up the hill: "It's best to walk up very slowly and very deliberately; it gets easier."

Other anthropologists in Alpine ecologies have observed the same imperative of cultural adjustments to slope. John Friedl did fieldwork in a peasant valley in Switzerland. He summarized the principles well. The valleys of Tirol are like the valley in which he worked.

> Vertical movement is frequently the single most important factor in planning and executing many tasks in the agro-pastoral economic system of the Lötschental and other alpine valleys. Transportation and transit affect land use, the annual cycle, patterns of cooperative labor, location and use of buildings—in short, movement is a fundamental consideration in the evolution of the valley, and we can expect it will continue to be (1974:46).

## Dangers and Disasters

One of the major consequences of slope is avalanches. In 1483, a Dominican monk named Felix Faber traveled by foot through Tirol and wrote this letter home; he was a flatlander awed by the powerful forces he had witnessed.

> In this mountainous region there are awe-inspiring summits, and in Winter, especially when the snow melts, the passage through them is very dangerous, since great snow-masses break loose from the higher slopes and on their way down into the valley they grow into colossal avalanches, which roar down with such force and with such deafening din that it seems as though the mountains are being brutally torn apart. Such an avalanche drags away with it everything which stands in its path: rocks are seized, trees uprooted, houses demolished and sometimes whole villages are buried (Myss 1973:57).

Avalanches are always a threat. I have seen a wide section of the Brenner Pass closed by a mudslide. Traffic was backed up for miles and slowed down for days. In winter the local newspapers and television report roads, passes and narrow valleys blocked or closed by slides and other hazardous conditions. Travelers may, in most seasons of the year, face diversions, detours or dangers from the slopes.

The dangers of the slopes are omnipresent. Snow accumulates in winter, rains soak the earth in summer. Some areas are avalanche-prone; disaster may be an annual event. Other avalanches wait for a bad year when the accumulation of mass, moisture, temperature and gravity provoke a gathering momentum. Only standing forests are strong enough to hold back the snow and mud. This explains why villages are often clustered or huddled together on the spine of a hill. Some villages have very sharp edges next to rocky channels and houses built too close are in danger of destruction.

Centuries of experience and disaster have molded human habitation. Many avalanche channels have names and a history of activity as they follow the paths of streams or rivulets down the mountainsides. Experienced guides to the mountains will often point out the path of a slide and explain how to determine when it happened.

In 1867, Heinrich Noë, a linguist and prolific writer, observed an avalanche which covered the new railroad tracks through the Brenner Pass. Stopped there he began to chat with others to find out what was happening. He jotted down the following description in his journal.

> This is indeed a goods train which has been walled in by an avalanche and now blocks off the track to all traffic. The situation would not be too grave if it were only a question of clearing the line. But whilst those who drove the now wedged-in train escaped to safety long ago, those whose task it is to dig it out again are in a state of deadly danger which demands that they concentrate more on the terrifying slope than on their work. For the avalanche is now followed by a persistent stream of stragglers. Yesterday one such rolling bundle threw half a dozen people down into the village; although they could be freed, their broken arms and thighs act as a warning for everyone. Up there, there also hangs a snow-cornice, and if that breaks away—something which the icy wind could bring about at any moment—then the people under it will never see the lights of another Christmas (Myss 1973:72).

What could those beneath the threatening overhang do? Workers outfitted a special locomotive with a plough and a particularly shrill whistle. The vibrations bounced against the gorge and lured down the great masses perched above; the locomotive's daring crew navigated to safety and the exercise was repeated until no more masses fell.

Throughout Tirol and the rest of the alpine areas are many examples of public works projects to manage the ever present inconveniences and outright dangers of avalanches, mud slides, running water and gravity. Engineering practicalities in Tirol make travel by car, train, bus and foot easier and safer than in the past. I have seen wire baskets holding rock slides away from the road, side road turn-outs for vehicles with brake failures and tunnels, bridges, and hairpin curves of amazing ingenuity.

Mountain paths and roads are often scary and dangerous. Accidents happen. I am rarely reassured by the number of wayside crosses and memorials erected to victims of the terrain. I stop obsessively to read them and heed them. Such memorials catalog the dangers of sudden snowstorms, the randomness of lightning, flash-flooding, out-of-control vehicles or a careless placement of boot against rock.

> "Here a Kind and Decent Man was carried away by the waters of a stream."
>
> "Here was the Honorable Peasant N.N. trampled by a run-away wagon."
>
> "On that rock yonder perished the virtuous and honored maiden, Maria Nauders, in her twenty-second year. The kind wanderer is begged to release two doomed souls from the tortures of hell. This wench was with child."

## Odd Mountains and an Ancient Language

The first time I taught in Innsbruck, I yearned to see everything. I had just been to London, Amsterdam and Paris and was ready to take off for Vienna, Venice, Munich, Florence and other great cities of Europe. When I asked the director of the program where he planned to go on our free weekends, he answered casually, "Where else? I go into the Dolomites at every chance." I thought how silly an idea that was; how could mountains compare with famous cities, museums, parks, theatres and other urban amenities. Then I saw the Dolomites.

A part of the Alps tucked into the corner of northeastern Italy, this mountain region is different from the rest of Tirol and simultaneously an accentuation of the region. The startling rock walls of the Dolomites explode suddenly from pastoral valleys. Romantics in every century have loved the dramatic shapes, the brilliant colors and the deceptive contrast between wild and tame.

What distinguishes the Dolomites from the rest of the Alps and indeed most mountain areas of the world, is the juxtaposition of two types of rocks, dolomitic and volcanic. The pale towers of dolomitic rocks were once islands and reefs in a warm sea. Today there are fossil remains of algae, corals and marine invertebrates in rocks even on the summits. Later volcanoes erupted into this sea; molten lava filled in the deep-water basins between reefs. This dark brown volcanic rock is visible on terraces and pastures such as Seiser Alm, Europe's largest meadow. As the millennia passed, this vast tidal flat accumulated layer upon layer of rocks. After about a hundred million years of quiet accretion, the continent of Europe collided with the continent of Africa. This collision deformed, crumpled, compressed, folded up and lifted up the ancient sediments in complex and unique patterns. The great glaciers of recent geological time scoured and carved the valleys and gorges. The ice rivers erased the softer rocks first and carried the silt down into the Italian plains.

I treasure the following description from the journal of an English traveler who rode a mule through the Dolomites in the 1860s. She echoes my own feelings.

> The new and amazing forms of these colossal mountains; their strange colouring; the mystery of their formation; the singularity of their relative positions, each being so near its neighbour, yet in itself so distinct and isolated; the curious fact that they are all so nearly of one height; their very names, so unlike the names of all other mountains, high-sounding, majestic, like relics of a prehistoric tongue—all these sights and facts in sudden combination confuse the imagination, and leave one bewildered at first by the variety and rapidity with which impression after impression has charged up the memory. It was therefore almost with a sense of relief that, weary with wonder and admiration we found ourselves approaching the end of the day's journey (Edwards 1873:43).

Most of the Dolomites are geographically and culturally Tirolean. However, Italian language and culture become more pronounced in the southern reaches of the chain or lower in the valleys. Like the rest of South Tirol the signs and the languages are in both German and Italian. However, the Dolomites are home to a fascinating ethnic, linguistic and historical complication. Between forty and fifty thousand people speak a Romance language called Ladin.

A thousand years ago across central Europe a belt of cultures used a language we call Rhaeto-Romansch. This belt stretched from eastern Switzerland to the Adriatic coast. But as Bavarians moved south through the Brenner Pass and Venetians traveled north, they cut this language swath into three separate areas. The people who spoke Rhaeto-Romansch were separated from each other by politics, religious customs and physical barriers. The languages changed as languages always do. Time left three groups: the Swiss canton of Grisons, Friuli near Udine in northeastern Italy and the Italian Dolomites.

Ladin (the name of the Rhaeto-Romansch language in Tirol) is concentrated in three valleys which radiate from the mountain plateau of the Sella Gruppe: the Grödental, the Gadertal and the Fassatal. Within valleys the distribution of Ladin seems random. For example, near St. Ulrich in the Grödental, people living in the tiny section of Pontives speak Ladin while their neighbors a few hundred meters west speak only German. Meanwhile, it is quite difficult for outsiders to see cultural differences; the mountain ecology has forced characteristic adjustments which we know as Tirolean.

Most travelers are surprised to find these archaic languages not only surviving but flourishing along the highways that link the modern countries of Europe. Today the Italian government has granted certain official and administrative recognition to Ladin speakers. There are Ladin newspapers, radio stations, TV programs, instruction in some primary schools in the Dolomites, cultural institutes and an overt determination to preserve the language. All road and path signs in the Ladin-speaking valleys use three languages. This way to Selva Gardena/Sëlva Gherdëina/Wolkenstein.

The key to linguistic preservation is each new generation of children who speak it as their first language. This means couples who themselves speak Ladin marry and their children hear it in the neighborhoods, schools, churches and the radio or television. This reinforces its use. The Italian government would not be able to revive Ladin by fiat were it dying. The isolation of these valleys preserved the language and cultural revivalism insures its survival. Those who want good jobs will speak German, Italian and English, Spanish or French in addition to Ladin. This is a sociolinguistic rule of thumb. People in isolated ethnic groups or small countries have to communicate outside their own boundaries; therefore people will easily and early learn the languages of the larger or more dominant cultures in which they live. American visitors to the remote valleys of the Dolomites are amazed to find many people who speak four or five languages.

## A New Meaning to Participant-Observation Methodology

Something happened to me as I began to listen to what Tiroleans thought was important, to observe simple features like roofs or windows and to participate in activities that revealed the fabric of social life. For example, eating in a restaurant forced me to think about the meaning of food. I witnessed village councils leading their cows to high pastures. This led to chapter 3 on how people earn a living. I had not realized that mountain hiking was so unlike taking a walk through an American park. It is a totally different sensory experience, both cognitive and physical.

Consider wild flowers. Tourists and Tiroleans alike spend serious energies and love in finding, identifying and just admiring the Alpine flora. On one level wild flowers are a cliché of Tirolean folk arts and one of the images we already associate with the region. I never expected to fall for or fall into some of what I used to regard as one of the profound clichés of being a tourist. I never expected to be the kind of person to wander mountain paths with book in hand searching the ground for a wild flower I had yet to see. Of course, I knew that wild flowers have inspired travelers, artists and poets both to artistry and excess. Anthropologists usually consider that our participant-observer methods are about people, cultural events or other such phenomenon. Now I am a convert to such things as wild flowers.

One day a companion and I stopped the car to admire and photograph a hillside of flowers so red they looked like moving flames. As we walked closer, an enormous trailer truck passed, stopped and laboriously parked in the small space along the roadside. Two large and very tough-looking men jumped out and began to run toward us. They gestured frantically and began to yell at us in both Italian and German. As they raved, I realized we had nothing to fear. They only wanted us to understand how privileged we were to view the rare mountain lilies which grow only on a few south-facing hillsides during the height of summer. They produced their collector's notebooks and reverently entered the time, date and place of their sighting. They offered us coffee and cookies as a celebration. Since many species are protected, even endangered, just seeing them counts as a significant event.

On another occasion I was with a group of students on Seiser Alm in Südtirol's Grödental. This is the largest meadow in Europe. We had taken a lift up to the spectacular plateau and walked to a high point to admire the views and to find snow. Flatlanders and southerners like me consider snow, even in the summer, a special treat. Naturally this amuses those who have their fill in real winters. We played in the snow and then began to walk down. An old couple in full hiking regalia spotted my wild flower book and stopped me. They were so excited I had trouble following the conversation. Gesturing and talking all at once they asked me to take their photograph, then they took mine; we compared our books and they helped me identify pressed specimens I carried with me. The focus of their excitement was trumpet gentians, an entire field of purple-blue wild flowers they came every year to see. Linked forever by this shared beauty, we exchanged addresses. They invited me to their home in Germany.

Short summers with long days and ideal conditions of drainage, moisture and terrain produce extraordinary wild flowers. Some flowers grow in rock crevices where their insensitivity to cold, wind and lack of moisture permit survival. Some flowers prefer scree, the steep mass of rocks and debris washing down on the side of a mountain. There they creep and wander, sending down the taproots which are the first step in stabilizing the slope against slippage. Some dwarf plants spend the winter beneath the snow only to bloom briefly; others like mosses, marsh marigolds, saxifrages, and sedges seek out springs or spongy ground. Various kinds of meadows and thickets or well-fertilized and overgrazed grasslands produce flowers found only in that specialized ecology.

Edelweiss, the floral symbol of Austria, blooms and grows only

*Mountains and mountain hikers.*

in high alpine grasslands. Because the leaves protect the moisture in the ground from evaporation and the roots keep fragile soil from washing away, it is entirely protected. This national conservation policy means that these plants must not be picked, damaged or destroyed. No part of the plant may be picked, transplanted, purchased, transported or sold. Austrians take Edelweiss as well as other wild flower species very earnestly indeed.

Hiking is one of the most important activities anyone who hopes to understand Tirol can do. Walking, like carrying, is both work and play. A highly organized activity, it is viewed as a national pastime. There are rules and public manners to observe while doing it. I am still chagrined to remember the lecture I rightly incurred when I tramped across a hayfield leaving the grass flattened in my path. I thought only to take a shortcut down the mountain; now I understand about haying rights, feeding the cows through the winter and husbanding resources carefully. I have learned to use and appreciate the trail maps produced for local areas. The trails are numbered, marked and carefully maintained. I know now it is necessary to observe the local regulations about seasons, what to pick, how much and where it is safe to walk.

I have learned to look for many cultural features. For example, eagles are the national bird and the enduring symbol of Tirol. Sighting a genuine specimen is difficult; but spotting the cultural renditions of this bird is a relaxing hobby. Eagles are everywhere, black, red, two-headed, one-headed, golden, in military or in aristocratic regalia and rendered in every medium.

I am also a barn and village fancier (I discuss my barn-watching addiction in chapter 3). Some villages are densely concentrated with houses, barns, chapels and shops built closely together. Others have dispersed and scattered homesteads. Social scientists discuss very seriously the meaning of these patterns. Some say that tightly packed villages reflect a Mediterranean penchant for sociability and isolated farms more a Germanic tendency for privacy. Others say that the patterns reflect different adjustments to terrain. Eric Wolf, who studied Tirol, believes that the different patterns reflect when the settlement occurred more than who founded it. The valleys colonized in the Middle Ages have dispersed homesteads. In areas settled earlier people concentrated their buildings.

Fortunately for me, I have regularly encountered colleagues who have encouraged or forced me to see what I was looking at. One friend, a geologist, hopped off the trains to look for fossils in the station floors or darted into banks because he had spotted fossil-bearing facades. One collected sightings of St. Sebastian and another cherished Rococo chapels. I picked the brains of several who loved architectural history.

They pointed out to me that many cities in Tirol retain an old town center with Habsburg architecture, a cathedral, narrow stone streets, often a palace, museum, gate, tower or monuments. The bay windows alone are architectural delights; called oriels, these vivid windows are often cantilevered or corbelled out from the wall or corner of the building. Sometimes two-sided, sometimes three-sided, they often bear painted frescoes of the Virgin, Saint George with his dragon, St. Florian, St. Christopher, Adam and Eve, the birth of Jesus, Andreas Hofer or other religious or historic subjects. Sometimes the oriels are delicately carved in stone. In later times painters outlined the doors and windows with frescoes and paintings to look like stonework or wood carvings. These can be very convincing. Churches and chapels often have columns and paneling of wood painted to fool the eye into believing they are made of marble. In fact, most of what I see in Tirol is a feast for the senses and an inspiration to learn more.

## How Do We Know What We Know about Tirol?

Tirol has inspired few American investigators. It is easier to find an analysis of Australian aborigine kinship or social change in South American villages than a basic ethnography about the culture area of Tirol. I have used the works of anthropologists, geographers, historians, political scientists and other social scientists where I can find them, but I am particularly indebted to the following colleagues.

Eric Wolf, already famous in anthropology for his work on Mexican national identity as well as other fieldwork and research, grew up in Austria with German as his first language. Wolf started fieldwork in 1960 in a valley south of Merano, Italy; he wanted to know how people lived and worked on the ethnic frontier between two radically different cultures. But his background was similar to the people he wanted to learn from. Could he be properly objective? To enlarge his perspective he teamed up with John Cole, then a graduate student. Both had experience in the area as soldiers for the United States military.

Cole wanted to study ecology and how people earned a living in mountain environments. He worked in the Nonsberg or the Val di Non from 1965 to 1967. Their collaborative book, *Hidden Frontier: Ecology and Ethnicity in an Alpine Valley*, and the articles which grew out of this field research are the best primary anthropological writings about Tirol in English. Their comparison of two peasant villages on different sides of a major cultural divide remains a serious contribution to the scholarship about ethnic and peasant communities of Europe.

John Cole took his wife and two young daughters. His wife was criticized in the village for serving an American-style light lunch at noon. Finally they adjusted; she prepared a heavy repast at midday. When they returned to America his older daughter spoke German she learned in the village and Italian learned at school. The younger one wondered where the cows were.

Other ethnographers, Raoul and Frada Naroll, worked in a village in the Kaunertal, a high valley on the Upper Inn River. When they did their fieldwork in the late 1950s, the area was on the cusp of the economic changes which swept through Tirol after World War II. These developments are elaborated in chapter 6. The Narolls reported on community structure and occupational change at what we know was a pivotal moment for the region.

Peter Petschauer is a historian who sometimes thinks like an anthropologist. Although he now teaches in an American university, he grew up Tirolean. At the height of World War II his German parents sent their two small sons to be fostered by a peasant family in Afers, a village in the Dolomites outside Brixen. Safe from the traumas of war, Peter and his brother, who died of diphtheria, had been "farmed out." They had been abandoned for their own good into a strange culture whose economic life and childrearing styles were rooted in eighteenth and nineteenth century peasant life. His lived experiences coupled with his historic training give us a remarkable, even unique, perspective of Tirolean life. He speaks the local dialect but understands the connections of the village to the rest of European history. Since 1969 he and his wife have returned regularly to the village. He is still linked to his adopted family and has watched the twentieth century arrive in Afers.

The American poet, Ezra Pound and virtuoso violinist, Olga Rudge, sent their infant daughter to be raised by a peasant family on a farm in the village of Gais in the Pustertal above the town of Bruneck. Though the child of unmarried, expatriate artists and intellectuals, Mary grew up as a proper Tirolean peasant, raising her sheep, attending Mass and reading the only two books in her home: *The Life of Christ* and *The Lives of the Saints*. In her autobiography Mary de Rachewiltz tells stories from her childhood and recounts the extraordinary events which lead her to Brunnenburg. Although Mary is revered in literary circles for her stewardship of the Pound legacy, it is her poetic and participatory connections to Tirolean culture which have influenced me.

Her son, Siegfried, picked up the torch in the museum at Brunnenburg, the programs at Schloss Tirol and his ethnographies of Tirolean peasant life. The best insights in this book come from his lectures and running commentaries about what things really mean and how they fit together.

## Travelers' Tales

You will notice many quotes from travelers who visited Tirol. In the main, these accounts are from the pens of literate elites. Tirol has been for several thousand years an area through which to pass on the way to somewhere else as well as an exotic sojourn that inspired travelers. Visitors generally write rhapsodic paragraphs on the beauty of the scenery. They include predictable tourist episodes, heavy luggage to pack, transportation difficulties, processions, hiking expeditions and the experiences of inns, music, crafts, eating and drinking.

From our contemporary vantage point, we can see how educated Europeans came to terms with "the Other," with people and customs radically different from themselves. This is before university classes or a mass media brought home the fact that the world is populated with many kinds of people and cultures.

Anthropologists have learned to appreciate gifted amateurs and their talents for participating in and observing other cultures. Sometimes their books are the only source of understanding we will ever have for times and places we can never visit. One of my favorites is a man named W. A. Baillie-Grohman. He was a sportsman, bookworm and an upper-class leisured Austrian whose English mother settled the family in the castle of Matzen in the Inn Valley. Educated in England, he spoke four languages and dedicated his books to good friends like Teddy Roosevelt, president of the United States, Queen Victoria's brother-in-law and husband as well as other members of European royalty.

In his long life he traveled widely and wrote many successful books. I quote regularly from his *Gaddings with a Primitive People: Being a Series of Sketches of Tyrolese Life and Customs*, published in 1878, and *Tyrol* (1908). Other books dealt with the history of aristocratic residences, chamois-stalking and other Alpine sports and cowboys of the American West. He collected what might be called Early Tirolean antiques and hunted big game in the mountains. Among his other adventures was a winter ascent of Gross Glockner. This is the highest mountain in Austrian Tirol; it was a very severe winter and his account of its perils is still engrossing. But his peers claimed he was the first person who ever climbed that Austrian Alp in the cold season. Being first to do something for the sheer fun of doing it was a favorite conceit of Victorian gentlemen.

For decades Grohman spent most of his time with Tirolean friends at all kinds of events. Judging from his accounts they climbed, hunted and drank together in cheerful fellowship. He attended innumerable weddings and reported them in detail even as he staunchly disapproved of the brides having captured his drinking comrades. As a frequent guest in homes and inns, he witnessed and participated in many episodes we now call male bonding rituals. This is anthropological observation of the richest kind. He spoke as an ethnographer when he said:

> Nothing aids one's efforts to penetrate the outer coat of reserve, and at the same time to gain a true insight into the lives and characters of this people, so much as assimilation to their habits, customs, language, and dress. (1878:19).

He loved living in Tirol passionately and wanted to explain the region to others. His greatest fear was that "high pressure civilization and that curse of modern creation, the traveling tourist, are rapidly dismantling Tyrol of the charm of primitive seclusion."

Although Herr Grohman had little framework or cross-cultural perspective for his experiences, he was open about his prejudices. He was horrified about the "intolerant and overbearing Catholic Church" and the dreadful influence they exerted upon "the lower orders of society." The Tirolean "race," he notes, is known for its "upright and manly qualities of character," national qualities blemished only by "bigotry and laxity of morals." Grohman also thought Tirolean men treated women better than British men of his day did; at the same time he was astonished by how different English women and Tirolean women were from each other. His books are some of the best accounts we will ever have of Tirolean life in the last half of the nineteenth century. I am grateful for his frank style and keen eye.

Another Victorian traveler, Amelia Edwards, penned an often reprinted book about her mule trip through the Dolomites, then a primitive country to the English. Edwards was already a journalist and author of novels, poetry and art criticism when she decided to break away from the typical mode of travel for Victorian ladies. The journey through the Dolomites, recounted in *Untrodden Peaks and Unfrequented Valleys*, changed her life. What she called a ramble through mountains "impassible except by foot or mule and so relatively uncharted as to make the provision of food and shelter a triumph of ingenuity and good humour" (1873) inspired her. She then went to Egypt, traveled its far reaches, published more travel books and became a famous archaeologist and Egyptologist.

A feminist who preferred the company of other women, Edwards led a richly independent life outside of England. On this trip she took with her an equally capable companion known only as Miss L. The latter had an unnamed maid with no social identity who was left behind in remote inns whenever Miss Edwards and Miss L. took mule trips deeper into the mountains. Craving adventure, Edwards would not be constrained to suitably feminine pursuits as embroidery, sketching and vapid social formalities. Although the wealthier parts of fashionable English society took "grand tours" through Europe regularly as part of their education in humanities and class conformity, women did not go unchaperoned or to rural Tirol.

She also knew Italian art intimately and traced the life of the Renaissance artist, Titian, as a sidelight to the trip. She remembered all of his paintings, those attributed to him and those he painted only parts of, and what leading critics and art historians thought of each. She visited his birthplace and bedroom in the Italian Dolomites. I mention this only because traveling, writing and participant-observation became so much richer and deeper an experience for me when I started to look for something I care about, know about or want to find out about. This quality characterizes all of the travelers I have included and is available to the rest of us wherever we go.

Another intrepid traveler is Rachel Harriette Busk, a prolific writer in the British Romance tradition. She wrote a number of books, one about the folklore of Rome and another about what British travelers in those days called "the Far East" (meaning that it was farther from London than "the Near East"). She stayed strictly in the valley towns and traveled by the best conveyance she could find, preferably what she called "an organized service of carriages." Occasionally, given the quality of Alpine tourism at that time, she was reduced to a one-horse vehicle on bumpy roads. She complained loudly at these moments. Like many young women of her class she spoke fluent German and Italian and devoted herself to "high culture," churches, museums and art.

Although she rarely ventured into the countryside, she had an exceptionally good anthropological ear. She listened to folklore, stories, place names, Catholic mythology and iconography and compared them to theories and knowledge then fashionable in her intellectual circles. Her two books, *The Valleys of Tirol: Their Traditions and Customs and How to Visit Them* and *Household Tales from the Land of Hofer* contain her translations and collections of many of the legends and folktales I have used.

Travelers like Grohman, Edwards and Busk had many of the same personal reactions of culture shock and ethnocentrism that students and tourists today experience when we travel in body or imagination to a new land. For many Europeans, Tirol was as foreign a place as they would ever visit. In the Victorian era, people from the English educated classes often espoused narrow views, what today we might call racist, sexist, classist or provincial yet arrogant. They used to say, "God is an Englishman." They meant the Church of England and the men they went to school with were ordained by the only deity that mattered to be at the top of the world's pecking order.

At the same time, many travelers wanted to understand and explain what their money and privilege allowed them to visit. They loved the thrills of vicarious participation in another culture and the acceptance, even friendship, of people different from themselves. The roaming romantics of the nineteenth century left us a specific and very important experience of Tirol. Their viewpoint bears comparison with ours and, in fact, has probably subtly contributed to our beliefs about the world. We will discuss the development of tourism as an industry in chapter 6 and the anthropology of tourism and the experiences of being a traveler in chapter 8.

In the past, travelers followed a rich tradition of keeping journals and left written records. I suspect that my students and I fall short of their high standards. As we read them we see that their experiences as tourists and visitors often parallel ours. One intoxicating June morning in 1858 Karl Alexander, the Grand Duke of Saxony-Weimar, ate breakfast at a country inn outside of Merano (then Austria, now Italy). Looking up he glimpsed Schloss Tirol and convinced his companion to accompany him there.

> I longed to get up to that castle. I had been extraordinarily attracted to pictures I had seen of the panorama which surrounds it. We climbed up a bad, crumbling path between vineyards and their white walls. The air was filled with the aroma of the South. We walked past fig trees, under shadow roofs formed by overhanging vines, then back on the open rock-path or past picturesque chapels and houses. Only in Italy have I ever seen such perfect beauty. The old Schloss Tirol stands right in the middle of this glory on that point where the two valleys of the Etsch meet at an angle. It was once very extensive, for its walls used to stretch right down to the ruin which is called Brunnenburg. It was in the sixteenth century that a cloud-burst destroyed the connection between the two parts and also tore part of the mountain down into the abyss. What remains of the castle is of no particular value, but it can by no means be called uninteresting, when one views the marvelous carvings on the entrance doors of the Great Hall and the Chapel, an astonishing mixture of paganism and Christianity, which, I am sure, suggests the time when the rule by the Goths ceased, in other words, before Charlemagne. The underground passage leading down to Meran is also a ruin, for half of that too was destroyed by the cloud-burst which I mentioned before. We descended to the town by one of the steepest paths I have ever seen, passing through

> a very badly paved village, the Dorf Tirol. In the Gasthof Post we found good accommodation and a splendid table d'hôte (Myss 1973:80).

Or consider what Hans Christian Andersen, the famous storyteller observed about the premier city of Tirol in 1840. Writing down our impressions and comparing them to other systematic observations is a way of learning about different cultures and people. American college students and other visitors to Innsbruck often report the same observations as did Andersen.

> Shall I paint a picture of Innsbruck? First comes the rushing river with many timber rafts, each steered by two or three men; I must include some robust, wooden bridges, some crooked streets with shops tucked into the heavy arcades, but one street must be broad and imposing, the sun must shine here onto the balcony and there onto the golden moon-pedestal which carries the Madonna. I must give some indication of the hustle and bustle. Tyrolean women in their local dress, slim Austrian officers and travellers with books in their hands must meet one another. And that would be our picture of the town. But the surrounding frame is even more magnificent: high mountains, which look like threatening storm clouds that draw away above us, give our picture relief (Myss 1973:27).

## Time

Anthropologists often speak of habits and customs in the past as though they still exist. This is called the ethnographic present. It gives unequal weight to time. I am emphasizing two historical moments. The first is a kind of baseline or ordinary peasant village culture which most historians believe stood fully rooted by the eighteenth century. This rural and communal life endured well into the twentieth century in most areas. The nineteenth century accounts of observers like Grohman are particularly valuable. The twentieth century experiences of Peter Petschauer or Mary de Rachewiltz growing up in peasant villages tap into a culture whose basic forms lasted over two hundred years.

The other historic moment I emphasize is what we call "modern times," the places and experiences which you and other now-living people can feel. In Tirol this period started after World War II. We will talk about other eras and other influences but these two points in time are privileged.

We apply the concept of time unevenly. For example, peasants are often called backward or stuck in the past. This is because their lifestyle tends to persist as other worldviews change around them.

For example, Tirolean culture remained essentially as it was in the eighteenth century until halfway into the twentieth century.

Chapters 6 and 7 cover the changes since the end of World War II. I have taken the view that much of what we embrace or lament as change is just another phase of cultural, physical and economic adaptation to the special environment and history that is Tirol.

## What Are Peasants Like?

In the musical *Camelot* the question of King Arthur's poignant song is: "Oh, What do the Simple Folk Do?" From the king's high position of restrictions and responsibility, he wonders if common folk play games, fall in love and smell the roses. Most of us are many generations away from farms and farmers. Or we are by personality unsuited to the rural life. So the life of rural cultivators and cattle watchers is as alien to us as to King Arthur. It is therefore important to discuss what peasants and peasant life are like.

Those outside the tight world of peasant societies often see the people there as backward or insular, country bumpkins. It is said that peasants don't "take to strangers" easily. They consider themselves superior to city folk whose immoral ways they delight in discussing. They value hard work, honesty, communal spirit and the religious life. In no way would they consider themselves poor or needy.

From inside the narrow valley, peasants see strangers from different religions, from urban areas, as people who come to look down on and criticize them. Outsiders are people to blame for the economic ills of peasant life. John Friedl talks about and summarizes a kind of psychology of isolation which he sees as growing out of the concentrated lifestyle of a high mountain valley. Peasants want others to grant them the same social status they give to each other within the valley system.

> At times this quest for social status approaches a point of almost blind bigotry as a means of reinforcing the tenuous positive self-image. Yet considering the types of contact an inhabitant of the Lötschental has with outsiders, this attitude is not altogether unaccountable. When he deals with them outside his home area he is often confused and taken advantage of. When, on the other hand, they come to the Lötschental as visitors, he is shocked by their ignorance and insensitivity to his way of life. He develops a negative image of all foreigners, and transfers his frustration and anxiety to those most vulnerable because of their economic situation or their religion, such as the Italians or the non-Catholics (Friedl 1974:75).

Outside observers, whether anthropologists or not, feel free to comment on what we might call "national character" or the personality structures of peasants. Austrian-born Grohman lived in Tirol and knew that he would never be a peasant. Nonetheless he believed that his special knowledge added to the debate about the nature of culture and personality in the region.

> If, with regard to the Tyrolese themselves, the experience of many years spent in Tyrol gives me a right to express an opinion varying somewhat from those of many authors, I must say that I have found the Tyrolese in matters of daily life a highly intelligent, bold, and excessively hard-working people, distinguished, even from the inhabitants of other mountainous countries, by great patriotism and by an innate unquenchable love for their native soil, enhanced by strangely chivalrous feeling of manly independence. Regarding their warlike spirit,—fostered, to a great extent, by their strong attachment to the Hapsburg dynasty,—we need but refer to the endless wars in which the Tyrolese were involved from the earliest times down to the present day (Grohman 1878:7).

He continuously made basic anthropological arguments that cultural traditions ran deep and strong and were ultimately understandable. In the following episode Grohman has given in to the urge to tell some peasant friends how to change their habits in order to be modern and progressive. The subject is whether ringing the village church bells, the *Wetterglocke*, will forestall the dreaded and destructive forces of lightning. He argues from what we call science. His Tirolean friends counter his suggestions for innovation with the weight of tradition. They say "My ancestors did so and so and so much for this or that purpose, and I'll do the like."

> To swerve from a time-honored practice, be it ever so ill-adapted to meet the demands of civilization, be it ever so disadvantageous to their interest, is contrary to the nature of the more remote Tyrolese. Their ancestors, their grandfathers, and their fathers tolled the house-bell when a thunderstorm was approaching, to ward off the lightning, and they'll do it too: it does no harm, at any rate, and one can't tell if it may not do good. In vain you argue that it does no good whatever, but on the contrary it may do a great deal of mischief. An incredulous smile will be the answer. (Grohman 1878:135).

The tolling bells held a particular fascination for travelers to Tirol in earlier centuries. They are one symbol of how outsiders interpret other peoples' customs. Victorian travelers collected folk beliefs and what they called "superstitions." They were bothered about why peasants rang bells to alter the weather. The bells also kept them from sleeping when they rang through the night. "Thunder had muttered all the evening among the porches of the hills; and in the middle of the night the blessed sleep was broken by the loud clangour of the church bell, followed soon after by so blinding a glare, and a crash bumping the floors up and down, that the whole village was immediately astir. Shutters banged and voices called. But without pause the bell held on, resounding through the midnight storm" (Gilbert and Churchill 1964:138).

Traveler Amelia Edwards reported many nights in which the clanging bells kept her awake. She offers her explanation, a collection of what she calls "superstitions" in relation to class structure.

> The poor, I found, believed that this pious exercise dispersed the evil spirits of the storm; while the better sort conceived that it occasioned some kind of undulation in the air, and so broke the continuity of the electric fluid. Who would have expected to find these exploded superstitions yet in force in any corner of Europe? It was like being transported back into the Middle Ages (Edwards 1873:173).

She too tried to explain to the locals the sensible explanations from science and the rational Enlightenment which seemed obvious to her. She was rebuffed but undaunted in her certainties. "Your Tyrolean peasant, however, is not easily disabused of ancient errors" (Edwards 1873:25).

Tiroleans often emphasize local variations to me. Sometimes I want generalizations about Tirol and they want to tell me about highly particular habits or customs in a hanging valley above the Pustertal or in the Passeiertal. They often comment on these local distinctions which seem invisible, indeed irrelevant, to outsiders. As one author remarks,

> In no other European country is there such a variety of temperament, dialect and landscape in such a small space. Despite these frequently marked local distinctions, the Tyroleans are proud of their patriotic sentiments towards the province; these rise above local rivalries and are only rarely subordinated to feelings of national patriotism (Caramelle et al. 1987:39).

The descriptions and explanations Tiroleans give in describing themselves have a remarkable consistency and integrity through time. Here are the phrases German-speaking citizens of Südtirol used to characterize themselves to a German psychologist during the time of ethnic and political troubles in the 1960s. He wanted to elicit the psychological and emotional correlates of nationalism. So he asked them to define themselves in a few sentences (Doob 1962). They told him:

> "We are a peasant people and therefore very conservative."
>
> "Everywhere in our country people use every square meter of fertile land."
>
> "The higher one goes in the mountains, the more silent the inhabitants become."
>
> "We are industrious, independent, patriotic and conservative."
>
> "We can be very proud of our ancestors. We must never forget our history."
>
> "Our land, mountains, churches and castles are very beautiful."
>
> "We cling to the loneliness of scattered farms although life there is so very difficult."

These same phrases occur in historical and literary accounts by Tiroleans since the early Middle Ages.

Such sentiments also take the form of sayings or aphorisms. Growing up in Afers, Peter Petschauer heard similar phrases which people employ to justify and explain themselves. Sometimes the sayings help children or foreigners understand how the texture of daily life is defined.

> "Our valley, you know. That is how we are."
>
> "A farm has to look this way."
>
> "It has always been this way."
>
> "God does what He does."
>
> "Children need to learn to obey."

When Petschauer describes the peasants he grew up with, he uses words like resiliency and stability (1990:731). The phrases which villagers of Afers use are not clichés, but daily discourses which affirm simple truths about working the land to survive. Yes, life in the mountains is hard. But the inhabitants have learned "to live in affinity with the given." As the farmers say in their dialect, "Woaschö, ändern tuat sie nöt viel." (*Weisst Du, es ändert sich nicht viel.*) You know, nothing much changes.

# 2

# Fires of the Sacred Heart
## A Short Cultural History of Tirol

*. . . . Peasant of the Alps,*
*Thy humble virtues, hospitable home,*
*And spirit patient, pious, proud, and free;*
*Thy self-respect, grafted on innocent thoughts;*
*Thy days of health, thy nights of sleep, thy toil*
*By danger dignified, yet guiltless; hopes*
*Of cheerful old age, and then a quiet grave*
*With cross and garland over its green turf.*
—Lord Byron [*Manfred*]

The summer of 1991 was unusually hot in Tirol. Those who watched the retreat of the glaciers deeper in their mountain abodes blamed the global warming trend. Others, tired of the winter cold, appreciated warmth from whatever source it came. The newspaper in Innsbruck featured a story about two climbers found forty years after they had vanished in a sudden mountain storm. The hot weather had melted the snows that covered their bodies and records kept of those lost in the mountains revealed their identities. So hikers who came across yet another body at an altitude of 10,000 feet were not surprised.

But this was not an ordinary hiker lost in the Alps. The wind, cold and sun turned him into a mummy. Then ice encased him, preserving bones, hair, even fingernails, heart and genitals. He carried a copper ax with a flanged head, a leather quiver with twelve arrows, a long bow and a flint-bladed knife. Such a find is rare but revealing, so scientists flocked to the discovery and the media named him the "Glacier Man" or "Ice Man." Soon we learned from the radio-carbon dating and other analyses that he was between twenty-five and thirty-five years old when he perished in a sudden summer snowstorm between 3500 and 3000 B.C. Archaeologists call this period the Early Bronze Age. It is important to note that both Italy and Austria claimed the body.

The clues he left point to a life of herding cattle. His tanned and tailored leather clothes were carefully cut and sewn to fit. Despite the climate he wore no woolen clothing; this suggests he tended cattle rather than sheep or goats. He carried weapons; bears and wolves probably threatened his herds. His shoes had three pieces, a bottom sole, an upper flap and a net sock stuffed with grass which probably insulated his feet from snow and ice. The original construction and some repairs on his leather clothes had been done with exceptionally fine stitching using sinew thread. But subsequent patches were sloppy, done with grass fibers. This clue suggests that the man had been gone from home for some time and had to make temporary, even clumsy, repairs himself.

In the millennium before this man's solitary death, people had started to settle down in parts of Tirol. Studies of pollens found in ancient swamps show that about 5000 years ago early settlers had burned parts of the forests in the Tirolean Alps, presumably to create meadows for their livestock. Just as they do today, herdsmen grazed their flocks in lower fields in the spring and drove them up to fresh fields as the summer progressed. Shepherds would leave their settlements near the valley floors in June and return in September when snow covered the grass in the high ranges of the mountains.

The first people in the region hunted and gathered food. They stalked deer, chamois, goats, rabbits, elk with giant horns and other wild animals. The hides of these animals provided leather and fur for clothes, containers, tools and trade goods. They caught trout and birds, collected bird eggs and honey from bees and dried plants for herbal teas and medicines. In the summer and fall, wild fruits and berries grew in profusion.

At some point people started to grow crops and to keep domestic animals. This radical change in the way human beings relate to the environment is usually called the Neolithic Revolution. People in Tirol did not just stop hunting wild animals or gathering wild foods. Leather, honey, fruits, and wild game are still part of contemporary lifestyles. As in many areas of the world, they added a food production complex which turned them into settled villager farmers. The Neolithic cultures of Tirol with their cattle tending, hunting, gathering and crops have cultural similarities to archaeological sites on lakes in Switzerland and sites in the Po Valley of Italy.

The pioneers of Tirol were also miners drawn to the copper deposits and other valuable ores in the mountains. Bronze is an alloy made of nine parts copper and one part tin. Because it is tough, easily formed and holds an edge, this metal gave its name to an entire period of history. Expanding civilizations in the Mediterranean region demanded raw materials and fueled an expansion into the mineral-rich Alps.

Mining is a theme which links many parts of Tirolean history. In the first millennium B.C., groups from the Danube valley in eastern Austria, expanded dramatically. Early Iron Age cultures such as Hallstadt built their lives and cultures on mining salt and iron ores. Hall im Tirol was part of this economic complex. Hereditary chiefs governed them. A class structure and specialization in jobs and crafts added social complexity. Salt may seem a humble base for the growth of a culture as dynamic as Hallstadt; but salt, essential to life and to food preservation, developed into a form of exchange or currency in the Hallstadt era.

## Anthropology and the Meaning of History

As I wrote this book I kept hearing voices. They reminded me of a place, a person or a period, something I had witnessed or felt while living and studying in Tirol. They said, "Don't forget the altarpieces, that treaty, silver mines and Rococo cows!" "How can you make sense of economic development, land tenure and inheritance or the culture of tourism if you don't tell about the history of Tirol?" They made me write this chapter. Some of the voices were friends and fellow academics; many were historians. Some were Tiroleans I met on hikes, in trains, restaurants, inns, homes or classrooms.

One set of voices came from a skit my students wrote about me. In their portrayal I wore a floppy hat, sensible shoes and lectured about everything we saw or did. I pointed out details and made nonstop connections about time, place, people and history. I discussed the Council of Trent over dinner and the Biblical themes embedded in pastel frescoes while hiking. Apparently, I did not need to convince them. The setting did that for us. Student journals and evaluations include comments on the feeling of history they have in Tirol: "I believe anthropological study *demands* a historical perspective in order to understand why things are the way they are *today*." "History makes sense to me now that I'm in the middle of it. I'm amazed with myself—I want more; I have questions all the time."

Anthropologists sometimes omit the past from our ethnographies. The cultures we study may have few records of that past, so reconstructing is extremely difficult. The culture area of Tirol, however, is so full of its own history and the echoes of European and world history that I have trouble absorbing it. My personal roots go back only three generations to pioneer Oklahoma. There are few buildings over a hundred years old there. I am always amazed by the depth of time in Tirol and the enthusiastic participation of ordinary people in their own living history. I am also grateful to those who helped me see the present rooted in the past. I have even converted a number of very good historians to the anthropological study of Tirolean life.

This chapter centers on what we might call the growth of Tirolean identity. How and why did these groups of people living in remote valleys forge a communal personality? What are the predominant qualities or features which characterize the culture area of Tirol? At this point I will apologize to historians whose work I deeply respect. But I am going to rudely summarize complicated events, give unequal weight to others, and ignore whole eras in European history which did not affect Tirol. I want to keep in mind what ordinary people living in the high mountains are doing. In the last chapter we talked about the sense of place that is Tirol. In this chapter I want to talk about the sense of time that is Tirol.

## From North and South They Came

After 15 B.C. and until about A.D. 400, the Romans and their mighty apparatus of empire moved into the alpine regions from the south. They called the area Rhaetia and the people barbarians. The Romans believed they had a colonizing mission to the primitive peoples living there. Traces of Roman influence in roads, place names and architectural remains are still visible throughout Tirol. Romans built primarily on strategic hills and secured transportation routes to their outposts of empire in the north and northwest with roads through the Brenner Pass and the Reschen Pass. The Latin accounts from this period reveal the Romans' amazement at the practical ingenuity and adaptations of the mountain people. They admired crafts such as making or coopering barrels. They traded for honey, furs and the resins needed to make Roman ships water-tight. But Roman ways and customs did not penetrate the deeper, higher mountain valleys.

At the same time Germanic tribes from beyond the Rhine and Danube rivers started to move south into what is now Austria. From the north these tribes of Celts and Teutonic peoples began to hassle the Romans on their northern frontiers. Celtic culture lives on in the grains they cultivated, the herds they loved, the jewelry they crafted, the tales they told and in many other fundamental ways.

Meanwhile, a small cult which originated in Israel appealed to many people living under Roman political rule. Converts to this sect began to move throughout the empire in a rather subversive fashion. Gradually this movement expanded and found political favor. In A.D. 313, the Emperor Constantine legitimized this new and growing belief system and declared Christianity the state religion. In one of the complexities of history, monks from Ireland, the edge of the Celtic world, carried early forms of Christian practice and worship into Tirol. As we shall see, the Catholic religion which grew from these diffusions of ideas is one of the bases of Tirolean identity.

The people expanding into mountain areas spoke an earlier version of today's German language. Empowered by new farming techniques and by burgeoning population growth, they gradually moved beyond the original terrace settlements above the valley

*A monument marks the path for travelers on the old Roman road.*

floor and higher up the slopes. They consolidated some of the classic patterns of Tirolean life—the farming system, independent households and inheritance standards. This prefigures the contemporary situation in Südtirol. Italian-speakers are concentrated along the lowland transportation routes and the towns that link them just as the ancient Romans were. But higher up the slopes cultural life is based on German language and rural traditions forged in mountain terrain.

## Early Medieval

As the Roman Empire disintegrated, small states to the north began forays into the mountain regions. Bavarian nobles enlarged their perimeter of influence. By A.D. 1000 these Bavarian families were married to and living beside the descendants of the original settlers. They formed the basis of a local aristocracy.

The rising nobility marked their ascension with castles, cathedrals, palaces and town centers. Südtirol alone has more than four hundred residences built for the elites of the Middle Ages; a tourist official told me there is one castle to every 18 square kilometers. A conspicuous focus of the landscape, the monuments testify to the dynamism of this period.

The premier example is Schloss Tirol situated at an extraordinary and strategic spot in the Adige valley. This sheltered valley with its rich soils and botanical diversity has been called "the balcony of the Habsburgs overlooking the corridors of the sun." An exception to other east-west valleys of Tirol, the Adige opens itself broadly to the south. At its northwestern reaches the valley of the Vinschgau and the Reschen Pass formed the gateway to medieval Europe. The castle located at a crossroads also had access to the Jaufen Pass and the Brenner Pass to the north.

It is little wonder that the Counts of Tirol picked this strategic spot to build the administrative center of their holdings. The broad terraces are elegantly poised to receive a maximum of sunlight. In ancient times it made a perfect site for a village, off the dangerous plains and with plenty of upland pastures. In the Middle Ages, powerful families set up command centers in various castles. Acting as military commanders and governors, these petty aristocrats had power to try court cases, make laws and collect taxes, dues or tributes. The first written records for the construction of Schloss Tirol date to A.D. 1140. Eventually the Counts who administered the budding civil and military district centered in this castle complex gave their name to all of Tirol.

As the Catholic church consolidated its fortunes, it began to build edifices of power and worship. Ecclesiastical organizations sponsored cathedrals and seats for the ruling clergy. For example, the town of Brixen still bears elegant witness to its centuries as a Bishopric, or bishop's seat. The builders had only ingenious and simple technologies, many dependent on the strength of men and ropes. They had to marshal and store the raw materials and find or train the skilled craftsmen necessary to construct such enormous undertakings. They controlled a work force who had to climb sheer cliffs carrying heavy loads and carve bay windows or arches which hang thousands of feet over rocky gorges. The fundamental feature about the cathedrals and supporting architecture, nunneries, monasteries or palaces, is what they reveal about the social organization of power.

Meanwhile, other entrepreneurial and hard-working families colonized new farming settlements on available land. They remind Americans of pioneers on the western frontier. While these homesteads and villages were linked in complex ways to nobles, landlords or clerical control, they were not organized along feudal principles. Political, legal or economic repression by the upper classes which characterized other areas of Europe was largely absent in Tirol. Although contracts, rents, tithes, land leases and other laws reenforced the structural position of the nobility, the peasantry was still what we can call "free." The independence of peasant farmers as a social class is one of the consistent and remarkable features of Tirol.

Tirol blossomed after A.D. 1000. The valley floors were the thoroughfares of an unfolding Europe. The old roads through the Brenner and Reschen passes carried cotton, silk, spices and glass north from Venice. Merchants went south with linen, wool, furs, dyes, iron tools and precious metals. Armies marched through. Frederick Barbarossa in the twelfth century commanded 100,000 men, 15,000 horses and the political and religious agendas of the early Middle Ages. Crusaders, traders, Gypsies and the germs of the Great Plague of 1349 crisscrossed the region.

How did the people of this rural, free, food-producing, German-speaking mountain culture adjust to sitting astride the major trade routes of the Western world? They started what is arguably the earliest example of organized traveler-care in the world.

First, they built taverns and hostelries to feed and house people and their animals. They developed crafts and technologies which supported traders and travelers: smiths who worked iron, coopers who made the barrels and boxes, wainwrights and carters who put together the wheeled vehicles. Craftsmen in wood, leather, silver, pewter and other trades supported them. They transformed little settlements into towns centered on commerce and transportation.

Then they set up internal markets for the food produced and processed in the countryside and developed currencies for international commercial transactions. Thus were peasant farmers even in the remote high valleys linked to urban centers such as Venice, Florence, Augsburg, Munich, Vienna or Paris.

The transit trade of Tirol also promoted the unification of the region, one of the earliest manifestations of representative government in medieval Europe. After 1415, peasant farmers voted in a Tirolean assembly, collaborated with the Counts of Tirol in local government and allied themselves to the ascendancy of the Habsburg empire centered in Vienna. A traveler-care industry produced by a spirited and independent peasantry has been a mainstay of Tirolean economics for more than a thousand years. Today a tourist publication for Südtirol claims a hotel for every 80 inhabitants and more than 3 million visitors a year.

## The Glories of Gothic

In the late Middle Ages Tirol was to German-speaking areas what Burgundy was to France: wealthy, stable and independent. True, Tirol was not a kingdom; it had no king. But there were dukes and Tirol was a duchy. People lived decently and well.

Margaret Maultasch—Pocket-Mouth Meg or Drooping Mouth Margarethe as she is often referred to in history books—was Duchess of Tirol in her own right. From the time she lay in her cradle, her father stayed busy with matrimonial projects to enrich himself through the numerous wooers who sought the hand of the rich heiress. The husband her father finally picked for her was not only foreign-born, but younger and as the stories hint, weak in body and mind. Even before the marriage could be consummated they were fighting. Margaret intrigued to rid herself of this encumbrance. One day she barred her husband from the castle as he returned from a hunting trip. He returned to his own land.

The following year she decided to wed a more suitable man. But the Catholic church had taken a dim view of her severing nuptial ties in such an informal fashion and banned their priests from performing another ceremony. For this escapade and other love-thirsty adventures, she, the last of her line, has been the subject of gossip for 600 years. Some stories concern her nickname and memorable facial features. Others deal with her temper, sexual exploits and zesty lifestyle.

In 1342, Margaret Maultasch and her new husband, Ludwig, issued the oldest known ordinance in Tirol. Called the "Grand Proclamation of Freedom," it assured equal political rights for all communities and individuals. And in 1363, a year faithfully commemorated in Tirol, the only son of Margaret Maultasch died. With no heir to her domain she ceded the duchy of Tirol to the duke of Austria, Rudolph IV. From that time until the breakup of the Austrian kingdom at the end of the World War I, Tirol was part and parcel of the Habsburg dynasty.

The land of Tirol glowed in the waning years of the Gothic Age. The Habsburgs were prolific and well connected to the ruling houses and powers of Europe. The glory days were capped by Maximillian I who is fondly remembered as Max the Knight; he reigned from 1479–1519. Innsbruck was his favorite place to hunt, hike, eat, carouse, rest and relax. There he set up an administrative structure, organized the local militia and consolidated territorial borders. He ordered built a gun foundry, court armory, public buildings and a spectacular tomb and permanent memorial, the famous Hofkirche in Innsbruck. Although he is not buried there the remarkable iron statues he commissioned are a monument to the achievements of the Gothic period. "Maximillian burned to represent the whole of his world, his ancestors, his conquests and all his pride of possession. In the court church just across from the palace may be seen his tomb, with the accompaniment of twenty-eight larger than life-size figures, his most noble actual or reputed relatives—including King Arthur of England—without doubt the finest group of Renaissance sculpture of this kind" (Kates 1963:59).

The late Gothic in Tirol was a period of integration and political unity. The advances and achievement of its artisans, craftsmen and artists were admired and emulated over all of Europe. From public architecture to armor and altars, Tiroleans left a lasting and unique legacy.

> In Mühlau, a suburb of Innsbruck, a colony of metalworkers, armorers who were really artists, also turned out examples of superlative craftsmanship, renowned not only for their elegance, but also fabricated with alloys of unusually resistant metal. Every prince in Europe was glad to possess a suit; and examples were sent to such sovereigns as Henry VIII (today one can be seen in the Tower of London). Armor at its best . . . is really a subtle form of functional, mobile sculpture (Kates 1963:30).

Churburg Castle in Südtirol has a world-famous armory, the finest private collection of armor in Europe. Commoners might take the view that armor is another form of container, technology for carrying things, in this case people. Elites might view armor, as in the above quote, as an art form, a kind of specialized sculpture. Military historians note that as standards of warfare changed in this period, armor no longer served a useful purpose on the battlefields of Europe.

In the middle of the fifteenth century, artists in painted wood sculpture took the old folk customs and elevated the craft of wood carving to the highest levels of art. The greatest Tirolean-born master was Michael Pacher, born near Bruneck about 1435. Trained in both painting and sculpture, Pacher learned from the great Italian masters of the Renaissance like Donatello. Later, he studied in Germany and the Netherlands. Pacher's studio produced other carvers-painters who carried out many large commissions for Tirolean churches. His style reflects the local intensity of religious creed and, in its turn, has shaped subsequent generations of Tirolean artistry.

Legends say he carved with a brush. Pacher's altarpiece in the parish church of Gries epitomizes the union of painting and sculpture in Tirol in its fullest flowering. "It is large, complex and magnificently composed. All of its parts are in harmony and each carved figure is superbly delineated" (Plaut 1984:6). The pieces he painted look like richly sculptured carvings and the themes are those which engaged fertile imaginations of his time. One altarpiece depicts the Coronation of the Virgin and another, the Devil tempting St. Augustine. His paintings show "a world-wide, emphatic realism in the great precision of the forms with a refined linear feeling, an agitated, almost self-sufficient flow of drapery and luxuriant ornaments with an expressive beauty" (Goldberg 1982:242). Pacher died in 1498; his works can be seen at the Alte Pinakothek in Munich and, of course, all over Südtirol. With the death of Maximillian and Michael Pacher, the glories of the Gothic Age ended for Tirol.

## Mining and Religious Protest in the 1500s

Tiroleans had problems by the start of the sixteenth century. Peasants produced many children and, as the population grew, each new generation needed work and food. The most serious questions for Tirol during the four hundred years to follow were crystallized in this century. How could people earn a living when land was finite but the birthrate was not? Where were the jobs to support growing families? Even with a high death rate, similar to the rest of Europe at this time, the population outstripped the resources.

A mining boom for silver and copper blossomed dramatically. Money and jobs opened up for thousands of workers. During this short time the mines of Tirol financed in large measure the pan-European expansion of the Habsburg dynasty. The bonanza brought early forms of capitalism, wage labor, specialization and economic sophistication to Tirol. Commercial expansion, the transit trade and the rise of towns lured laborers into the region.

*Details of the memorial to Max the Knight in the Court Church of Innsbruck.*

Schwaz, outside the city of Innsbruck, had the largest silver mine in the empire. Ten thousand miners plus auxiliary laborers, craftsmen and their families came from all over Europe, bringing new and threatening ideas. Mining as an industry required huge amounts of charcoal, wood, leather and iron while dependent on transportation lines, food supplies and capital. As the mining boom declined in the early 1600s a growing population outstripped the agricultural productivity.

Other than farming, men could practice a craft, cut wood, hunt, smuggle or leave the region to find work. Crafts and cottage industries such as weaving, hat or basket making, embroidery on leather, artificial and dried flowers, woodcarving or distilling were not sufficient ways of earning a living. There was not and would never be in Tirol the kind of industrial development that occurred in northern Europe.

Foreign financial interests like the Fugger family from Augsburg controlled most of the ore mines. Foreign workers gradually excluded Tirolean miners from their ancient guild privileges. The competition of miners and other common laborers who moved into Tirol angered and frightened people, already suspicious of outsiders. The initial promise of mining gave way to subtle but frightening forms of social dislocation, aggravated by the religious turmoil of the Protestant Reformation.

Threatened people form social movements of protest or they hope for a new religious order. The Peasant War of 1525–1526 in Tirol matched other uprisings in conservative German-speaking areas of Europe. Prosperous peasants did not like the foreign financiers who manipulated much of the commerce and mining. They resented the influence of Spanish nobles who had married Habsburg aristocrats; they dismissed such outsiders as smelly, heretical or Jewish. The Catholic clergy who came from the upper classes themselves were also offensive to them. Tirolean leaders wanted a peasant republic without kings, nobles or clergy, far from the destructive influences of financial institutions and urban centers. Their leader, Michael Gaismair, gave his life for a peasant republic without cities; the Habsburg rulers ordered him assassinated in 1527.

As the peasants revolted, the great smelting works around Schwaz, which were famous for the latest scientific methods of treating ores, stood unused. Pockets of ore were impossible to reach and the deeper levels filled with water which pumps could not drain. A great plague and an earthquake in the following century completed the disaster. Armies passing through during the Napoleonic wars in the beginning of the 1800s sacked and burned the town.

By the end of the mining boom Tiroleans had lost their economic edge and the leverage to influence the affairs of the empire. Henceforth, they would define themselves and be defined by others as rural pastoralists, farmers, conservatives and Catholics. Marginal to and shielded from many of the great events sweeping Europe, they would forge a durable folk culture in the Alpine ecology centered on emerging concepts of what it meant to live and die as a Tirolean.

## The Fires Start

One of the keys to this identity was religious. It is not enough to say that Tiroleans are Catholic, pious and observant. After all, they had chances to become Protestants; other groups of hard-working farmers from German-speaking areas did. They could have become nominal or "cradle" Catholics, paying lip service to the conventions of the Church of Rome. There are, in fact, many ways to be Catholic. This is not to say that everyone who lives in the Tirol is a serious religious person or that Catholicism is as fundamental in the cities and towns as in the villages and farms. This is to claim, however, that the Tirolean brand of being Catholic is the golden thread which stands out against the tapestry of cultural life. Like the tall trees they cut for timber, Tiroleans sawed and planed their own version of Catholicism.

We see the roots in the shifts of history we call the Counter-Reformation. You will remember that the German monk, Martin Luther, started a reform movement challenging some of the theology, practices and social policies of the Roman Catholic church. This resulted in the Protestant Reformation, much of which was a struggle between classes and powerful political or economic interests. The emerging Protestant sects in northern Europe appealed to the lower estates, particularly farmers. The Protestant call to a rationalist and personalized religion free of state controls understandably threatened the Habsburgs' court in Vienna. With their wealth and power they mobilized against any of the nobility, burghers or peasant movements who left the fold. This was called the Counter-Reformation.

But the Counter-Reformation left two forms of Catholicism in Austria. The first centered in the cosmopolitan court life of Vienna where religion was international, upper class, worldly, aristocratic, bureaucratic, Latin-Mediterranean and dominated by the clergy. Many of the Habsburgs had married into the Spanish aristocracy; some were even rulers in Spain. The Vatican in Rome controlled the clergy and the religious orders. Much of the art, architecture, music and intellectual life we associate with Austria in this period grew directly or indirectly out of these international connections of religion and dynasty.

Folk Catholicism was the second shape of religion in Austria. Strongly rooted in the land, this religion drew specifically from German values and customs of hard work and communal commitment. Like folk religions anywhere, the practitioners were suspicious of the bad influences of cities, foreigners or innovations.

Sometime in the eighteenth century Tiroleans committed anew to being Catholics. Although the first records date from 1796, the revivalistic spirit had probably been building for some time. Their new devotional unity recreated Tirol as a holy land which had a special covenant with Jesus. The devout began to light fires on the third Sunday after Pentecost across the mountaintops of Tirol. Pentecost, also called Whitsunday or the seventh Sunday after Easter, is associated in Christian theology with spirit visitations or visions of a supernatural world.

The fires of the Sacred Heart on a summer's eve amidst spectacular mountain scenery are among the most profound anthropological encounters I have ever had. Some of the flames are shaped like a heart with a cross on the lower right hand curve. Others are bonfires or beacons balanced on the ridge joining two peaks. These dramatic flames are visible from several intersecting valleys. Men carry firewood up the steep mountains in preparation and stay through the night to tend the fires. I will not swear the same religious impulses that motivated their first lightings are still alive or that the hard labor of hauling fuel for the fires up the steep mountains will inspire more secular generations of the future. I do know the fires have little to do with tourists or the tourist industry. I have never met a traveler who knew anything of their background. The fires of the Sacred Heart remain a quintessential expression of Tirolean folk religion. In my opinion, visiting Tirol on the third Sunday after Pentecost is worth the trip.

Other manifestations of this recommitment include many beautiful churches and chapels that date from this period. Artisans made an extraordinary variety of crafts based on religious themes. Itinerant messengers spread the word through villages where devotions to the Virgin Mary and the prayers of rosary beads soared to heaven. Throughout the Alpine regions devout villagers staged Passion plays, dramas which take the crucifixion of Jesus as the script and elaborate on themes of suffering, salvation and faith.

Religious revivalism went hand in hand with increased social controls and conformity at the village level. For example, priests mandated church attendance. Today in Tirol people often march in ceremonies and processions by gender, age and marital status. Organizations, clubs and sodalities center around unmarried people, married people, males and females. Subtle markers indicate the marcher's social class and degree of integration into the village hierarchies and the life of the parish. In the aftermath of the Counter-Reformation new forms of worship and piety were coupled with the social restructuring of peasant villages. We shall return to these themes again.

## Architecture and the Religious Spirit

Tirol, "the holy land," is often said to be the most Catholic part of Germany. In the Austrian Tirol today there are 536 churches, 46 cloisters, 2000 chapels and more than 10,000 minor monuments, shrines, memorial tablets and statues of saints. Architecture blossomed during the reign of Maximillian I and again during the time of Maria Theresa. The drama of Baroque and Rococo artistry captured the imagination of Tiroleans and other Austrians. In the seventeenth and eighteenth centuries Austrians built new edifices or went back and added architectural elements to the older chapels, churches and palaces. The upper classes and the Vatican had the financial resources to indulge their artistic fantasies. This outpouring of Baroque was not just religiosity but a reflection of economic prosperity.

The sheer density and focus, the communal outpouring and concentrated themes, continue to amaze us. The wealth of forms, the soft colors, the lightness, naked babies and even plump cows floating through clouds, silken scarves and garlands of flowers are the hallmarks of these two periods. The continuum from folk traditions to high art is especially clear. The wood carving that so marks the mountains is still there beneath a coat of gilded paint in the Baroque chapels. Three of the great northern Tirolean abbeys (Wilten, St. Georgenberg and Stams) are only wearing Baroque clothes; the original layout is Romanesque.

Grohman, traveling through Tirol in the nineteenth century, complained endlessly about the excesses of the late Baroque. He calls Rococo renovation of the older Gothic structures in the eighteenth century another example of "Jesuit vandalism."

> The outward signs of their age have been ruthlessly ravaged by the iconoclastic improvers of the last century. The disastrous preference for *rococo* stripped the majority of Tyrolese churches of the pure severe lines of the Gothic and of the rich but no less pure details of the early Renaissance ornamental designs that adorned their interior and exterior, and metamorphosed them into the highly inartistic structures that pain one's eyes (1878:160).

He bemoaned the pink and blue ceilings, gilt painted over wooden altars, countless pot-bellied angels and oak paneling stripped and lost. On the other hand, many good historians claim that Austrian identity is rooted primarily in the imagination of the Baroque period. I have also spent many happy days visiting these sites and listening to Tiroleans or other Austrians pay homage to an architecture they consider one of their highest achievements.

## Ordinary Peoples' Times

Sometimes we concentrate on wars, elitist art styles, technological revolutions or philosophical differences in the great sweep of history. We may forget about what time feels like or what history is for ordinary people. Peter Petschauer details five intrusions that changed the little eighteenth century village of Afers. He notes that the dynamic reign of Empress Maria Theresa, in the final analysis, produced less real change in peasants' lives than might be suggested from her memorials.

At the opening of the eighteenth century a priest arrived in Afers. Through him, villagers were bound more closely to the rest of the continent. The changes he introduced began to multiply. He kept records of the births, deaths and marriages at which he officiated. He installed a clock on the steeple of the then-Gothic chapel. Clocks and the meanings of time were a major obsession of urban Europe in this period. While peasants continued to attend services at the sound of the bells and sleep or plant on the sun's schedule, the clock connected them to Enlightenment social philosophies. The fourth priest assigned to the village built a new parish church.

> The new church highlighted in the village what architectural innovations tended to accomplish on a grander scale for the more powerful, be they prince or bishop, outside the village. Here, too, a newer and grander structure enhanced the status of the priest and altered religious and secular development. With the approval of his superiors, or at their behest, the priest had the new church built on the foundation of a smaller Gothic church and near his residence. By doing so, he infused a European trend in architecture and confirmed the shift of the village away from one set of its roots. Aside from the building of a road in 1917 and 1918, and the introduction of radio, telephone, and television in the 1970s, this change was the singularly most important event in the history of the village. At the very least, with their new church, the villagers achieved linkage with the most fashionable architectural trend of their time. Simultaneously the new church stood for the last phases of a renewed and vigorous Roman Catholicism that spread its teaching, architecture, art, and music to the furthest corners of Europe after the Council of Trent (Petschauer 1990:724).

The villagers of Afers in the 1780s retained the Gothic steeple and sacristy of the older structure when they built their new church. They adopted the late Baroque traditions then current in southern Germany and Austria and added to them the Tirolean penchant for decorating with bright colors, flowers, hearts, flowing ribbons, birds or other favorite, sentimental motifs. The decorations in the chapel imitated the folk art paintings on armoires or blanket chests.

Other conventional traits of religious life remained unchanged. Priests spoke in Latin, popular prayers were in German. "Just as important, men and women continued to kneel separately in their respective pews; the women on the shadier and colder left, the North side, and the men on the sunnier and warmer right, the South side"

(Petschauer 1990:729). The villagers probably felt more connected to the burden of debt than to the sweep of European history. The increased dues and tithes to pay for the new chapel extended for generations. Parishioners would have spent more time cutting wood and feeding the workers than praying in the new chapel.

From Vienna, rulers Maria Theresa and Joseph II introduced educational innovations, a type of civic reform. By the time the grand plans from the capital had been translated into local action, Afers had a rudimentary primary school. An untrained and unmarried village woman taught a part-time elementary class in one room. However, going to school and having a clock means an involvement in time, space and citizenship beyond getting the cows in before dark. Literacy and schedules linked villagers to other Austrians and other Europeans.

The final transformation in the village during the eighteenth century was the new custom of private ownership for the forests. Eventually the reverberations of this change restructured sex, sleeping arrangements, and the meaning of modesty. But that is a story for the next chapter.

## Eddies in Time: Economic and Political Decline, 1700–1900

As villages and folk religion grew powerful, Tirol as a political entity waned. The transit trade from south to north through the Brenner Pass dwindled as traders and travelers looked westward toward the Atlantic and the Americas. Tiroleans were minor players in the wars of succession sweeping Austria. Few invaded them or even wanted to exploit them. They were an economic backwater. Such woes as heavy taxes, military conscription, loss of land holdings, serfdom, industrialization and economic bondage to one's betters affected the rest of Europe but left Tirol strangely untouched.

This isolation only accentuated the traditional freedoms of Tirolean farmers. Every male could carry weapons and serve in the local militia or shooting companies. Each landed peasant jealously guarded his right to pass on an undivided land holding to a designated heir. This custom, one of the bulwarks of Tirolean identity, is discussed in chapter 4. Noble families in the region were merely first among equals; they were not the worldly aristocrats of other countries. They, too, worked for a living.

The class structure of Tirol during the 1600s, 1700s and 1800s centered on prosperous landed families be they mountain burgher or village gentry. The differences between them were partially erased by the common grounds they shared: Catholicism, patriotism, land and inheritance. Peasant barns were as big and as well constructed as the three-story townhouses were. The silver bowls of the gentry cost more than the pewter ones of the peasant households but served the same purpose.

At the ends of the class structure a few people contrasted more obviously. Some peasant families had more children than cows, chickens or goats. Servants, day-workers or itinerant laborers came from these families. At the other end of the social spectrum were the nobles at places like Schloss Ambras in Innsbruck with links to court circles throughout Europe. But when the University of Innsbruck was founded in 1669, the sons of peasant families were admitted as equals to the sons of the urban middle classes or the nobility. Families of all social orders aspired to send a son to study for the priesthood. And on the entrancing ceiling of the Riesensaal in the eighteenth century Hofburg palace in Innsbruck, cheerful peasants cavort with half-naked gods and goddesses as the nobility watches.

The fate of Schloss Tirol is symbolic of the decline in this period. The great wars of the late Middle Ages, assorted conflagrations, earthquakes and landslides left it a mere shell. Robbers and housebreakers had started to strip it of stones and old iron fittings. In the aftermath of the Napoleonic battles in the region local authorities in Merano auctioned the castle for only £ 200. A few citizens scraped together funds, purchased and saved the historic ruin from certain destruction. Today the castle is a major museum and a place of pilgrimage for those who celebrate the history of the region. That is why I framed the chronology or historical chart in this chapter with the arched stone windows of Schloss Tirol.

Traveling through Tirol was easier for everyone after 1772. The first road in the Alps accessible to carriages went through the Brenner Pass. For a thousand years numerous towns along the Brenner highroad had grown prosperous from the traffic. The trade between Italy and northern Europe employed thousands. Wagons, carts, pack trains and those who drove them needed nightly accommodations, food and drink. So the road was lined with commodious inns and extensive stables. Even with the carriage road, travelers had to stop frequently along the way.

But in 1867 the construction of a railroad through the Brenner Pass radically altered the ancient traffic patterns. The railroad was an engineering triumph: seventeen tunnels totaling almost three miles, eleven bridges between Innsbruck and Bozen, on time and under budget. Railroads eventually replaced water transport. Forwarding goods by rail was cheaper and faster than by boat. The Inn River, which had once carried Tirol's chief exports of salt, wood

*A pen and ink drawing of the ruins of Brunnenburg by a traveler to Tirol in the nineteenth century.*

and ores down the Danube to Vienna and around the world, was no longer the primary transport route.

Travelers and transit commerce no longer needed way stations to rest along the long road. The trains crossed the Brenner Pass in less than a day. It bypassed many villages which had existed primarily to serve the slow transit trade across the pass. These little places languished economically. Providentially, they retained the charms of a vanished era and in this century have attracted a new wave of travelers.

Just as Tiroleans appeared to turn inward, nineteenth century European travelers with easier access discovered the region. Adventurous Victorians wanted to climb remote mountains and hike or ride mules through what they imagined to be valleys untouched by civilization. They wrote best-selling guidebooks for the next wave of wanderers. Youthful elites touring France, Italy and Germany passed through Tirol. They left diaries, journals and endless sketches of happy peasants and soaring castles. These roaming Romantics celebrated innocence, fantasy and the "primitive" or "the Other." The poem by Byron at the beginning of this chapter is an excellent example of this fascination for what intellectuals saw as the simple life. According to this sentimentality, peasants are patient, pious, humble and face death cheerfully. One of the themes in this book is the recurring intersection of travelers, tourists, art, kitsch, economics and folk life in the culture area of Tirol. In hundreds of other ways outsiders opened, discovered and claimed Tirol for themselves during this period.

## The Peasant Patriot

The major event of these two centuries of insularity was the existence of an innkeeper named Andreas Hofer. When I want to begin a conversation with a Tirolean, I ask about him. Hofer's picture adorns the frescoed sides of guest houses, murals in tramways and ski lifts, museums and souvenir shops. He is the omnipresent hero of Tirol.

What did he do to deserve these honors? In April of 1809 he led small groups of Tirolean militia to rebel against the godless and revolutionary French and their allies in southern Germany. The French-influenced Bavarian occupiers (read foreigners again) wanted to impose taxes, conscription and their own bureaucracies over free Tiroleans. Their ultimate crime, however, was to introduce the ideals of revolutionary rationalism and to wrest control over secular life from the clergy. Hofer and his contemporaries saw their freedoms threatened. Although these episodes are only a footnote to the saga of the French revolution and Napoleon's rise to power, they have achieved enormous mythic significance in Tirol.

Hofer and his compatriots won three battles at Berg Isel outside of Innsbruck. They lost the fourth. His enemies betrayed and captured Andreas Hofer; they executed him on February 20, 1810 in Mantua on the Italian plains south of Tirol. Some say the emperor in Vienna abandoned his loyal subjects whom he had incited to rise against the foreign invaders. Others say that Tirolean militia never had a chance against the outsider armies of Napoleon. Still others maintain that Hofer's little band of armed farmers saved Tirol from tyranny and foreign domination. The death of Andreas Hofer confirmed a Tirolean brand of liberty and religious conviction. Backed by the power of myth, the innkeeper armed with a pitchfork remains the premier folk hero of Tirol.

After the death of Andreas Hofer, Tirol played only a marginal role in European politics. This is ironic: to that point the region was surprisingly "modern." Peasants had relative political independence and economic freedoms rarely witnessed in Europe. Early experiences in capitalism and a prosperous yet agrarian middle class might have predicted a wider world involvement. When the revolts and organized discontents failed

> to create an autonomous, egalitarian, peasant republic in the Alps, it was transformed into a conservative and encapsulated component of a cumbersome and hierarchically organized polity that bent Tyrolese aspirations to its own economic, military, and religious ends (Cole and Wolf 1974:48).

## The Tug of War Starts

In the 1800s Italy decided to become a unified country. In a process called the *Risorgimento*, Italians consolidated their national territorial aspirations. They pushed into the mountain regions of the north and challenged the once-mighty Austro-Hungarian empire on its vulnerable edges. The regular Austrian army activated the Tirolean militia.

Meanwhile to the north, Germany was growing stronger, testing its own boundaries and national strengths. Beliefs and values taking root in Germany tugged at the heartstrings of the Tiroleans. They listened to talk of unity for German-speaking peoples within a *Reich*. Tiroleans had long feared strangers, those from other ethnic minorities and their precarious position within the Empire. They were responsive to the appeal of anti-Semitism as they felt the dislocations of urbanization, capitalism and industrialization. Students at the University of Innsbruck and cultural societies in the German-speaking islands of Südtirol basked in the sentiments of pan-Germanism. Intellectuals and politicians in the 1900s and at the turn of the century began to flirt with German nationalism.

World War I started in 1914. Italy sided with the Allies. In 1919 the victorious Allied powers signed peace treaties ending the war. Germany and Austria had lost and Italy claimed the territory, whether German-speaking or Italian-speaking, up to the peaks of the Brenner Pass. As part of the end of hostilities and the spoils of victories, the Treaty of St. Germain split the historically integrated culture area of Tirol and gave the southern part to Italy. For Tiroleans, the Treaty of St. Germain was the watershed of the twentieth century. I have attended ceremonies in Innsbruck which included a moment of silence in memory of the loss which still rankles and pains.

The end of the war brought serious ethnic and class conflicts to Italy. The Fascist government decided to change South Tiroleans into Italians. They systematically passed laws to eliminate the visible and invisible markers of non-Italian culture. After 1922, they outlawed schools teaching the German language or curriculum and required Italian to be used. Appointees from a central Roman bureaucracy filled key political offices and eliminated free elections for the positions. They obliterated many political boundaries and folded old communities into bigger bureaucracies.

The first battle zone was language. All places were assigned Italian names. The last names of families and the names of farming estates were ordered changed to Italian ones. Tombstones were not exempt; they, too, had to be rewritten. Even the name Südtirol was banned. The new province became Alto Adige, named after the river which originated at the new border and flowed south into Italy.

Anthropologists have seen entire cultures destroyed or altered beyond recognition by outside interference in one of the key ideas or institutions that glue the parts together. The Germanic tradition of land tenure and inheritance was one of the cornerstones of Tirolean family life and cultural identity, as we shall see later. Moving to suppress Tirolean culture, the Italian government revoked the right of impartible inheritance, that is, the custom of passing on land holdings intact to one heir. The belief in the holy covenant between Jesus and Tiroleans was another such tradition. So the Italian government banned the fires of the Sacred Heart of Jesus and prohibited Südtiroleans from lighting the ritual fires.

Symbols of cultural life became contested arenas. Ordinances forbade men to come to town wearing their bright blue aprons, the uniform of the proud upland farmer. The *Schützenkompanie*, the community militia which had fought against outside invaders, lost their rights to carry arms. As Hofer had proved, even pitchforks could be dangerous in the hands of nationalist and outraged Tiroleans.

The Italian government planned to colonize the mountains. They sent Italian workers out to farm and Italian priests into valleys where villagers spoke only unwritten dialects of German. They gave incentives to Italian workers to relocate, buy land, build businesses and take government jobs. They assigned military units from other parts of Italy to Tirol. Heavy industries like car manufacturing and metal processing (steel, aluminum and magnesium) moved into Bozen, renamed Bolzano.

This was a frightening time for people whose cultural and ethnic identity had been uprooted. Austria could no longer come to their aid or bring pressure against Mussolini's Fascist policies. As part of resistance, both passive and overt, educated Tirolean clergy and other leaders operated clandestine or "catacomb" schools and German-language presses. In a time-honored Tirolean tradition, smugglers carried such contraband as sugar, tobacco and flints across the mountains from Austria in defiance of the edicts against them.

One form of resistance came from the growing Nazi movement in Austria and the northern half of Tirol. This part of regional history has some understandable sore points and many may be tempted to judge Tiroleans harshly. For them, the growth of national socialism meant a focus for patriotism and resistance to Italian domination. They participated in illegal youth organizations whose appeal was centered in Catholic identity, pan-German ideologies and increasing obedience to Hitler's new fatherland. Tiroleans living in Austria had their own reasons for an attraction to this ideology.

Ultimately, the Italian government had bigger problems than linguistic and ethnic conformity in Alto Adige and less power to change such fundamental culture patterns than they believed.

## War Again

Once more I offer apologies to my historian friends. I am aware of the momentous and complex set of events we call World War II. But I want only to sort out its effects on this group of people whose war was different from the rest of Europe and who are peripheral to the accounts that make our history books.

Adolf Hitler did not give a shilling or a lire for Südtirol. His plans included a world-class alliance between the Fascists of Italy and the national socialists of the Third Reich. No mediating groups should come between them. In his view, expounded forcefully in several publications, the troublesome Südtiroleans could choose: if they wanted to be Germans, they could relocate in German-held lands. If they wanted to remain in their ancestral areas, they could learn to be Italians. So, in 1939, a vote or plebiscite (called the *Option*) forced difficult choices. Between the leavers and the stay-at-homes, it was a civil war without the bullets.

> The plebiscite itself unfolded in the most tense atmosphere of political pressure and counterpressure. The National Socialists developed a masterful and harassing propaganda that equated the retention of German identity with a "return" to the *Reich* . . . The conflict between *Optanten*, those voting to depart for Germany, and the *Dableiber*, the stay-at-homes, divided whole villages and families; the hatreds, recriminations, and mutual suspicions engendered by the plebiscite have remained alive to this day (Cole and Wolf 1974:61).

There were rumors, typical of these supercharged episodes. Südtiroleans would be relocated to southern Italy, Poland, the Crimea, even to Ethiopia. Everyone had complex motives for a vote. Those who voted for Germany may have feared Italian policies more; perhaps they hoped to participate in a victorious and powerful Teutonic empire. Those who voted for Italy may have judged their footholds on the land worth an accommodation or feared the godless and impious Nazis. Given the opportunity, Südtiroleans would probably have voted to restore the status quo before the Treaty of St. Germain.

As it was they voted narrowly for the closest option, return to a *Reich* from which they never came. But relocation was fragmentary at best. There was, as Americans say, a war going on. The logistics and expense of such a population transfer even without a major war are daunting. The passive-aggressive resistance of landed Tiroleans also brought the intrinsic worth of the idea into question.

In 1943 Italy collapsed. Allied armies pushed north. The severed halves of Tirol were briefly reunited. True, it was a unification imposed by the Nazis under the gathering clouds of German defeat. But this short burst of sunshine revived Tirolean spirits. Patriotism surged once again.

Once again the great powers left the battlefields victorious. They redrew the political boundaries of Europe for the second half of the twentieth century. They ignored the ethnic aspirations of little regions like Tirol. Halved again, its parts returned to Italy and Austria, the story of Tirolean unity thwarted and ethnicity resolved continues in chapter 7.

## A Story Told by a Young Patriot

The division of Tirol after World War I was not just a decision made in the international halls of power. The Treaty of St. Germain and the actions of the Italian government altered every portion of cultural life in Südtirol from public ceremonials to school uniforms. In her autobiography Mary de Rachewiltz recounts what happened to her when Südtirol became Italian. She was a young schoolgirl in Gais in the Pustertal. She and her peers had been automatically registered as Fascist party members. Most, however, refused to pay the five lire for the party card or to wear the Fascist uniform. And in the manner of spirited children everywhere, she and her friends engaged in telling acts of rebellion against authority.

> When I came home with the circular requesting that schoolchildren whose parents had sufficient means be provided with a Fascist uniform, Mamme [her foster mother] merely said, *Tumma Tanz*—nonsense. And, anyway, she had no money to throw away and it couldn't be made out of some old dress. . . . We had to stay after class on Saturday to learn the *giuramento fascista* and songs, "Giovinezza," "Sole che sorgi"—the oath and the anthems. But we had learned at catechism—the only lesson still held in German by the priest, thanks to the Concordat in which Mussolini had granted the church freedom and

> autonomy—that to swear a false oath is deadly sin. So, sly brats that we were, we slipped in a *non* as a private reservation. "*Nel nome di Dio e dell Italia giuro di NON servire fedelmente la mia patria.*" —In the name of God and Italy I swear *NOT* to serve faithfully my country . . . At the *non* we gulped, looking the teacher straight in the eyes. We considered it daring and fun. We also had to learn how to march and to command the rest of the school when marching. *Attenti! Riposo! un due, un due, dietro front front.* This was called physical education, two hours, twice a week, back and forth in front of the school and, when, in spring especially, grown-ups passed by, they fumed: such nonsense, wearing out their shoes instead of letting them go home and give a hand where they are needed (1975:71).

Mary's American parents living in Venice sent her an Italian uniform. The white blouse and black pleated skirt seemed more a fashionable delight than a political statement to a young girl on a mountain farm. Her foster mother had also sewn a *Dirndl* with all the trimmings, the traditional Tirolean costume for young girls. The family conspired to hide it from the probing Italian police. Then to a procession in honor of the Bishop's visit she proudly wore her new Dirndl with a cockade of red and white feathers, colors of the flag of the undivided Tirol.

Her actions dared the Italian occupiers to act. They often confiscated small items which suggested hostility or nostalgia. Probably more symbolic than provocative, Mary's patriotic fervor escaped detection. It seems quite clear, however, that Tirolean consciousness below the Brenner had never been higher. As Mary de Rachewiltz, young patriot, notes on page 74 of her autobiography:

> Being jerked between the two factions—Italian Fascists and Tyrolean Nationalists—because I owned their respective uniforms, did not disturb me. I don't think I ever gave it any deep thought, since my loyalty was undivided: it was everything Tyrolean that made me bubble over with enthusiasm and excitement.

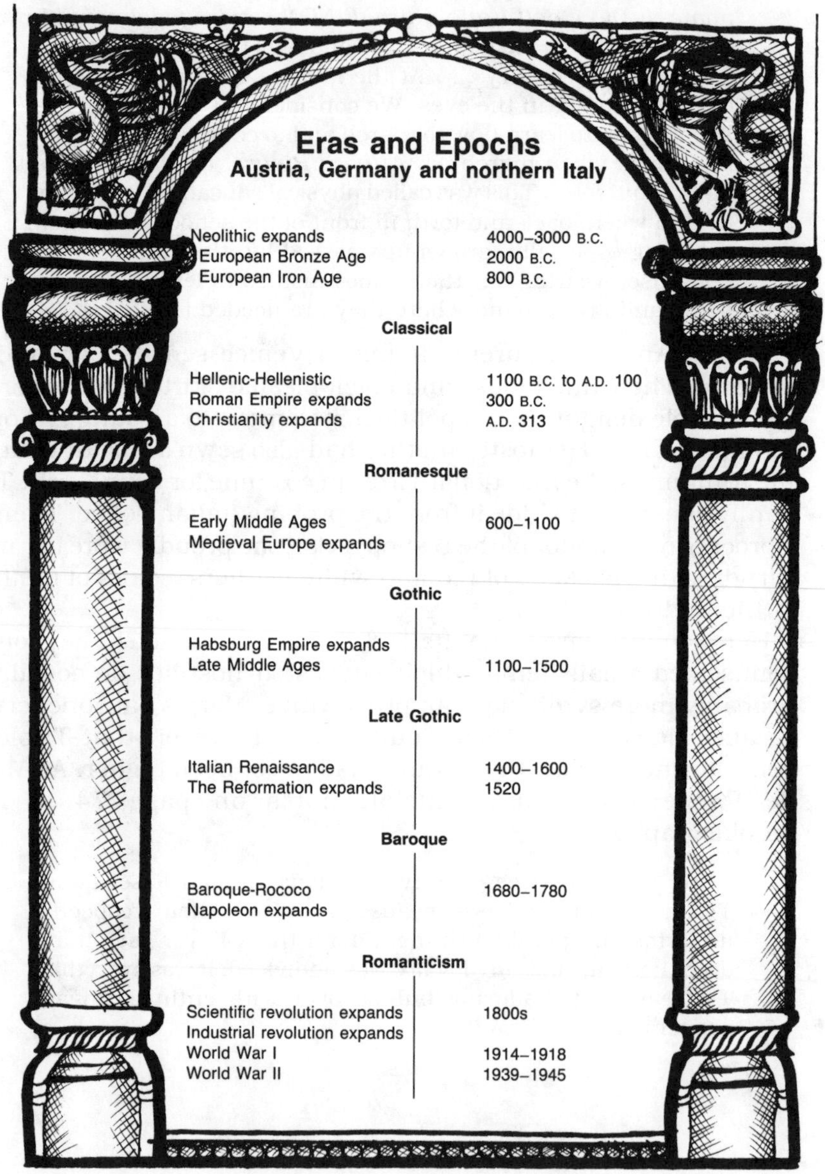

## Eras and Epochs
### Austria, Germany and northern Italy

| | |
|---|---|
| Neolithic expands | 4000–3000 B.C. |
| European Bronze Age | 2000 B.C. |
| European Iron Age | 800 B.C. |
| **Classical** | |
| Hellenic-Hellenistic | 1100 B.C. to A.D. 100 |
| Roman Empire expands | 300 B.C. |
| Christianity expands | A.D. 313 |
| **Romanesque** | |
| Early Middle Ages | 600–1100 |
| Medieval Europe expands | |
| **Gothic** | |
| Habsburg Empire expands | |
| Late Middle Ages | 1100–1500 |
| **Late Gothic** | |
| Italian Renaissance | 1400–1600 |
| The Reformation expands | 1520 |
| **Baroque** | |
| Baroque-Rococo | 1680–1780 |
| Napoleon expands | |
| **Romanticism** | |
| Scientific revolution expands | 1800s |
| Industrial revolution expands | |
| World War I | 1914–1918 |
| World War II | 1939–1945 |

# 3

# Give Us This Day
## Agriculture, Pastoralism and the Annual Cycle of Work

*Nothing is as positive as bread.*
—Dostoyevsky

*The ground grows rocks more easily than grains.*
—Folk saying

This chapter begins with a Tirolean meal in the *Stube* or the dining room of the Hotel Post. First we will order *Knödelsuppe*, a heavy, fist-size dumpling in a broth. The rye flour dumplings may have liver, ham or bacon in them. Then we might have the *Bauernschmaus* or "farmer's delight," smoked pork, grilled beef, sausages, sauerkraut, boiled potatoes and perhaps another dumpling. Or we might try *Tirolerleber*, calf's liver in a thick gravy, or a cold cut plate with local cheeses, cabbage salad or *Speck* (the famous smoked ham of the region). We can also eat *Gröstel*, fried potatoes and cold cabbage salad, or variations of dishes with local trout, chicken or wild game. For dessert we will definitely order *Apfelstrudel* (apple pie) with ice cream. We can drink mineral water, a local beer like *Adambräu* or a Südtirolean wine like St. Magdalener. A small glass of *Schnaps* will complete our meal.

The menus in village restaurants are a good starting place to understand how people of this region live. The servings are hearty and the ingredients underscore the farm heritage of the region. One of the first questions anthropologists ask about any group we study is: What do people eat? We need to know how groups make a living and how they solve the inevitable problems of food-getting.

In this chapter I want to show how the quest for food shapes daily life, architecture and, ultimately, the fabric of social relationships. We will discuss the management of cows, the central role of bread, the annual cycle of work and the nature of workers and work places in Tirol.

## The Cows in the Pasture: Transhumance Pastoralism

Tiroleans favor a diet heavy in bread, meat and dairy products such as butter or cheese. Raising cows, feeding them, milking them and processing them to eat is the most important work in Tirolean peasant culture. Raising crops feeds both animals and people. Most recipes start with poultry, beef, pork, wild game, grains and diary products. The recipes say "take three pounds fresh sausage" or "one pound of butter." They should say, "first feed a calf, slaughter a pig and milk the cow."

The mountain pastures, the *Almen* or *Alpen*, are too high for farming. So the cultures of Alpine regions of Austria, Bavaria, Switzerland, Italy and France evolved a very specialized and unique way of earning a living called transhumance pastoralism. This means that Tirolean farmers and people like them practice a seasonal migration with their livestock, moving them in gradual stages from winter barns and pastures in the lowlands up to summer mountain grazing areas. Unlike nomads who must move from place to place, the pastoralist has a permanent and well-built home for the winter. They move their cattle to follow the grassy pastures as they mature through the summer months.

As the snow melts in late spring, farmers drive their cattle into the high mountain pastures. Through the summer season herders live in small huts, milk the animals and make cheese or butter to be sent into the valley for storage or marketing. Each pasturage has a hut situated about an hour's walk up the mountain. As grass grows scarce on the lower slopes, the cattle move higher and higher until the highest pasture is reached in the warmest season of the year, July. Rich peasants may have three or more huts.

In the fall, communities bring their cattle down from the pastures to be housed for the winter in their barns. There cattle eat the hay or fodder the family harvested and stored through the summer. Farmers in Tirol tell stories about the anxiety of stretching out hay supplies until the meadows are ready to graze; they say that in the past they had to carry the winter-weak cows from the stables and lay them in the grass.

Up in the pastures the herders milk the cows and make cheese. Cheese is easier to carry down the mountains than milk or butter. It is portable, nourishing and stores well. The hard work of tending cattle in remote places is offset by magnificent scenery, singing,

Staggered Systems
3000 meters
tree line
2000 meters
Alpine Pasture Zones
1500 meters
Meadow & forest Zones
1000 meters
Village & farm Zones
600 meters
Valley & towns

yodeling and the visits of family and friends. Courting in high pastures is said to be one of the benefits of this work. The cows' tasks are to grow fat, mow the grass and simultaneously fertilize the mountain pastures. Manure may seem a small contribution but the grasses that grow as a result hold down the poor soils in the rocky heights and thus prevent erosion.

The late September homecoming from the alpine meadows is a celebration. Bells, often named and valuable, emerge from their storage places. The large bells on embroidered straps are the pride of farmers, inherited through many generations and reminders of legendary cows and farmers of the past. Garlands of flowers and grasses decorate the triumphant animals and the lead cows wear elaborate headgear. Fall foliage drapes balconies, wayside crosses, statues and the altars along the processional routes. Priests lead and bless the proceedings. Church bells ring. The next morning's church attendance has doubled for the services of homecoming and thanksgiving.

Not all farmers or rural dwellers practiced transhumance pastoralism. Some households did not keep cows or did not need to send theirs to the high pastures. These exceptions notwithstanding, these fundamental practices through time and the culture area are basic to understanding Tirolean consciousness and ecology. This system of transhumance pastoralism has more than ceremonial importance. The *Gemeinde*, or local government, must decide the most propitious time for the spring migration. Too early and snows may yet prove dangerous; too late and the cows will not have enough time to grow fat. The rights to pasturage are communally and carefully managed. Tiroleans are quite articulate about this landscape management system. In both Austria and Italy formal laws and strong local customs buttress the annual movements of cattle to pasture.

Policy makers worry, with justification, that skilled young people will not be willing to do this kind of work in the future. They worry, with even more justification, that failure to take the cattle to the high pastures will cause serious ecological problems. Fragile soils of the mountainside will erode leaving only barren rocks. After all, erosion was one of the forces that created the valleys and hillsides. The beneficial interaction of ecology, cows and human maintenance helps explain odd public policies. Local and national governments have price supports for homemade cheeses and programs to attract young people to jobs tending cows in summer pastures.

Hikers into the mountains during the summer will hear the distant sound of cowbells and the soft lowing of feeding cattle. They can stop on occasion and drink warm, fresh milk from a wooden cup. These are some of the many delights of summer hiking. But this is not *Sound of Music* sentimentality. These habits are not just a Heidi-like preservation of a traditional lifestyle. This is an ecologically balanced system which has supported humans, animals and the mountain environment for thousands of years.

## Our Daily Bread

At the southern edge of Tirol runs one of the most significant cultural divisions in all of Europe. We call this border "the bread line." South of the line people love light, white wheat bread; north of the line they eat dark, heavy breads made from rye and similar grains. At this point the line also coincides with the separation of Germanic and Romance languages. So bread becomes the symbol of ancient differences. This line actually determines marriage and career choices.

People in the areas where wheat grows like its light taste and ability to rise; they grow up thinking this is the way bread is supposed to taste. The nutritious breads made from the grains of the colder climates are dark and heavy; people who grew up in northern Europe eating rye bread may look down on white bread eaters and vice-versa. The cultures of bread do not easily mix or convert because what they eat is the direct result of how land is inherited and social class is structured. Latitude, terrain and plant genetics configure beliefs and history.

Barley and rye are heartier grains than wheat and grow well in cooler climates; they can even grow in marginal areas where rainfall is scarce or the soils are poor. Indeed, rye was a weed in wheat fields before it was domesticated. Oats and barley may be used as livestock feed or in soups and porridges. These food-growing complexes are ancient. People in central Europe have been planting grains for about five thousand years.

Breadmaking in Tirol was not a daily kitchen task. Bread was baked only a few times a year at most. The ovens were hard to fire and to handle. Rye flour does not rise easily like wheat flour. The sourdough was heavy; only the strongest people in the family could knead and lift it. Men had to mix the sourdough in great wooden buckets, shape the patties by hand, dip them in flour, place them on long wooden paddles and shove them into the hot open oven. Baking meant lifting, carrying heavy loads and hot dangerous work. The ever-thrifty Tiroleans saved fuel by doing it all at once and called in their neighbors to use the leftover heat.

The bread they made was hard, dark and flat. It stored and traveled easily and nourished families through the calendar and ceremonial year. Hard rye bread with milk, butter and cheese was the nutritious cornerstone of their diet. The meaning and making of bread went on all year. Firing the oven and stacking the finished bread was only the culmination of a year's labor in plowing, harvesting, loading, threshing, sifting, grinding and storing the grain.

Making bread was an intense family ritual; children participated at both symbolic and practical levels. Bread and the making of it was a sanctified activity. Every stage of bread production shone with folklore; every stage was blessed by the Church. Every household had special racks where the dried, flat bread was safe from rodents and bugs. Stored bread and the equipment to produce it carried special feelings of security and safety.

Bread is the perfect leitmotif of social life in Tirol. Everything about bread, including its shapes, is intimately connected to fertility and fecundity. The symbolism is hard to miss in phrases like "shot into the oven" or "a bun in the oven." Just talking about bread in Tirol eventually connects principles of increase, whether it is pregnancy, giving birth, tending animals or growing the grain.

Bread from each baking was shaped for ceremonial purposes. Special breads marked a child's birth, a marriage or christening; someone's death meant a half or broken loaf. Some breads revealed the village of their origin. Bread shaped into horses, chickens, cocks, rabbits or characteristic shapes with braids, ties or holes in the middle indicated where the baking was done. For example, the pretzel, a characteristically shaped hard, flat bread, came from a village of the same name.

It is obvious why most households in modern Tirol no longer bake bread for themselves. Most communities have bakeries which supply flat rye loaves, white bread baked with wheat flour, pastries, rolls and other delicacies. For many people, making bread and selling other food provides a livelihood away from the farm. It also means that mills, once a significant feature of rural life, are shut down and farmsteads are used for purposes other than food management. Now it is easier to buy bread than to bake it. Supermarkets in towns and cities and small stores in every village sell packaged food, snack foods, milk, meat, butter and bread.

The major ethnographic museums of Tirol such as Brunnenburg, Detenheim and Kramsach have elaborate displays of ovens, mills and other specialized technology for bread and food production. The first time I went to Brunnenburg I naively assumed that we would bake bread regularly, eat what we had produced and thus participate in traditional culture. I owe the above ethnographic insights and a more realistic viewpoint about baking to the research of Dr. de Rachewiltz. He has been exceptional in preserving and understanding this core pattern of Tirolean culture.

Potatoes and corn, valuable food plants, arrived after A.D. 1600 from North and South America where Native Americans of this hemisphere had domesticated them. Both of these crops are so important to the diet and economy that it is hard to imagine Tirol without them. Potatoes grow easily in the cool, cloudy climates. They produce large amounts of good, storable food for little expenditure of energy. Corn is an important cattle feed in Tirol. The word "corn" means any grain in European traditions; Indians called it "maize."

## "Life is Hard in the Mountains": A Tirolean Saying

While the mountains appeal to winter sports enthusiasts, writers, and nature lovers, peasants must wrest their livelihoods from this harsh land. To survive, they must live in intimacy with climate and topography and balance them with the needs of humans and animals.

For example, the higher the altitude the harder it is to grow crops. The cold weather lingers longer. Plants are slow to mature and yields decrease on the higher slopes. A farmer knows which slopes are best exposed to sunlight; but he cannot control which days the sun agrees to shine. He must also consider the slope, the types of soils and the amount and availability of moisture. He will worry about erosion and landslides. Truly level land is rare in Tirol.

Dozens of considerations enter his calculations: is this field on the windward or leeward side of the mountain; from what direction comes the sun? Which fields need careful manuring; such hard work is possible only for productive fields nearby or at low altitudes. In the end he can only lament the picturesque rock outcroppings or the shadow of a mountain falling on a strategic field. Even hard work will not alter the facts of geography.

The longer the farmer can keep his cattle in the high pastures the less food he has to collect for the days the cattle must stay in the stables. Indeed, in the modern market cattle which have been kept on alpine pastures in the summer fetch higher prices when they are sold. A farmer has to balance his needs, rotate his crop, protect the soil, cut enough hay to feed the animals through the winter and plant enough garden crops to sell. To provide for the farmstead through the winter he must decide the fate of each animal and carry out the decision. Above all, a farmer must manage his labor force, that is, his family and other household workers. Once snow falls the homestead will survive on the wisdom of these decisions and the hard work of everyone on the farm.

Rural residents long ago devised a system to make the best possible use of their limited land. The diagram at the beginning of this chapter shows this staggered or vertical system. Each ecological zone has a different economic potential. At the village level farmers have a wide range of agriculture, plow and meadow land. The middle zone permits communal and private pastures amid the scattered forests. In the highest usable zone the land is marginal, difficult to reach and available only during the high months of summer. Here cattle herds are pastured as long as the grasses last.

Part of the land stretching up the mountain is owned privately by farmers and the rest is managed by the village councils. Cole and Wolf talk about the vertical or staggered system of land management in the valley of Nonsberg or Val de Non where they did research.

> Each village controls land distributed over altitudes extending from 800 to over 2000 meters. Land use within this range of altitudes follows the general alpine pattern. The most favorably situated lands, relatively level and lying near the lower limits of the range, are in each case devoted to settlement, plowland, and meadow; fields at higher altitudes are devoted to forest and high meadows, and higher still stretch the summer pastures (1974:138).

Informed observers can easily see and understand the staggered system of land use on the hillsides. Knowing who owns what parcel of land and under what circumstances is much more difficult.

## "I Work for My Cows": The Annual Cycle

The most dramatic way to feel the true texture of peasant life is to trace a family through an entire year's work. The rhythm of a year starts slowly in winter, speeds up in spring, grows relentless in summer and eases in fall. The religious holidays of the calendar year are also part of the work of earning a living. They should be understood as the spiritual share of the economy, rather than as Catholic theology or ceremonialism.

The heavy work starts as soon as the first spring flowers push through the melting snow. This is soil grooming time. Farmers cart away the manure and spoiled hay from the winter barns, dump it on selected fields, and rake and turn them. Because the melting snow has carried topsoil down the slopes, the farmers must organize children, teenagers and womenfolk to load the dirt into baskets and haul it up again. On steeper slopes a rope relay for the baskets works best. March is spent manicuring the soil on valuable fields.

In April and May the meadows must be cleared of debris, plowed and planted. There will be extra time to repair fences or build new ones. Like Robert Frost, Tiroleans believe that good fences make good neighbors.

Farmers love an early spring. They will use any means to control what is essentially uncontrollable. That is why in olden days villagers cracked huge whips and noise makers to drive away winter or ignited wooden disks and balls of straw, rolling them down the slopes to melt the snow. Young boys ran through meadows ringing bells or making other loud noises to accelerate the growing grass. Young girls danced around a decorated May Pole erected in the village center; the symbols of fertility are obvious. Catholic Easter customs are probably grafted on to pre-Christian rites which celebrated a safe passage through winter, the coming of spring and the promise of increase and good health for people, plants and animals.

June, July and August are dawn to dusk labor for everyone. The chief task is haying. They say, "I work for my cattle." The hay is cut, turned, raked, loaded, transported and stored. The livestock will die in the winter months if fodder falls short. This backbreaking task is greater than all other agricultural activities combined. Everyone must pitch in. Even those in college or those with jobs must return to the farm and help with the work. They rise before sunup, feed the animals, clean the stalls, hurry through the household chores and rush to get out in the fields. Haying begins on the home meadows where the grass is richly and rapidly maturing. They follow the ripening hay up the mountains as summer progresses. They cut even the hay that grows beside the roads, in the marginal and rocky fields. Then there is the second cutting of the good fields. All pray for hot and steady sunlight and hope the sudden summer storms that flatten hayfields will strike elsewhere.

When there is spare time, the farmers hoe the potato fields planted in mid-April. They harvest the winter rye and plant oats, cabbages and garden crops. If it rains on Sunday they take half a day off to attend church services; if it rains on other days they will clean the barn, repair equipment and attend to other chores.

Late spring and early summer are the times of processions in Tirol. The priest strides through the town and countryside blessing the village and people. Villagers follow, praying and singing; they give thanks to God and ask for his blessing and protection. "From lightning and thunderstorm. Protect us, O God."

September, October and November present a potpourri of small tasks. The kitchen garden will mature and need tending during this time. Nuts and berries can be gathered and the fruits of the orchard trees—apples, cherries, pears, plums and grapes—must be harvested. These must then be processed and stored carefully. They are important nourishment and a welcome addition to the diet. If they do not store well, they are canned, pickled or converted into jams and jellies. This process is repeated for vegetable crops. These may include turnips, peas, carrots, potatoes and cabbages. The sauerkraut made from shredded, packed and pickled cabbages will provide vitamins and minerals through the winter. The farmers collect, cut and store the firewood they will need to keep warm in the coming winter. They collect needles from larch trees which will be needed for litter in the stalls when the livestock is brought down from the summer pasture. The care of livestock, feeding and milking, whether they are in pasture or barns may still take four hours a day.

There is no time in summer for more than work, no time for celebrating until the crops are harvested and the cows driven down from the pastures. The harvest and slaughter festivals in October have, over time, been combined with the church festivals and services of thanksgiving and consecration. This is the best time of year for market days, themselves festive, if practical, days. Now the farmer and household members can go shopping. They buy necessities for the family and perhaps a small luxury for themselves.

"In winter," peasant families used to say, "sit by the fire and make sure it doesn't go out." But the relative leisure of the cold months involves no slacking in the work ethic or the long hours which peasants routinely serve. During the cold months of December, January and February they butcher pigs. The meat does not spoil in the cold weather and it is a good time to make sausages and hang bacon in the smoke house to cure. Cold weather is the best time to make things, mend tools, study, tell stories, weave, card, spin, tan leather and complete hundreds of practical tasks. Because the workload seems easier relative to the rest of the year, winter is the best time for weddings.

The intricately woven ceremonial and agricultural cycle is governed by a book, the farmer's almanac. In use since the Middle Ages for people who were not readers, almanacs used only signs and symbols: black triangles for weekdays and red ones for Sundays and holy days. The traditional almanac gave the sunrise and sunset, the stages of the moon, long-term weather predictions and a suggested annual agricultural calendar—when to plant, sow, cut wood or even when a farmer should trim his hair or breed his mare. The almanacs used well into the twentieth century had special days for 126 saints spread over the calendar year, called "Saints' Days." If a village or its chapel is named after a saint, that day (or the closest

*A scene from the celebratory descent from high pastures at the end of summer. The cows are ornamented for the occasion.*

Sunday) will be the day for a celebration in honor of that saint.

An almanac had astrological signs, signs of the zodiac. These came to have many meanings attributed to them: Cows calving for the first time in Gemini will always be good breeders. Children born in Leo are strong and healthy. Farmers kept notes in theirs; when saved they are an extraordinary compendium of knowledge and experience. Here is an excerpt from the almanac of Mary de Rachewiltz's foster father.

> spotted cow in heat
> sow littered 7, 3 dead
> rams castrated
> sheep shorn, 20 kg. wool
> the gray cow calved, 16 liters of milk (1971:32)

## The Business of Agriculture

The annual budget of a peasant farmer was extremely tight. Grohman collected notes for over a year for a household in the valley of Enneberg in the Dolomites (1908:38). Although the valley was high and had poor soils where only the hardiest grains would grow, it was still not the poorest in Tirol. The property was listed in the government's land registry in the value of £ 600. There were two mortgages totaling £ 300 on the land, representing the shares of brothers and sisters, on which the farmer had to pay 4 percent interest. The household consisted of six people, four of whom were capable of farm work. The farmer possessed eight head of cattle, twelve sheep and two goats.

In one year his income was listed at £ 184. The farm produced barley, beans, hay, milk, butter, three calves and three cows. He required for household use produce worth £ 136 of the above amount. In addition he had to spend cash for provisions he could not produce on the farm. These included clothes and boots for the household members, tobacco, tithes to the church, repairs, taxes, fire insurance premiums and seed; these expenditures totaled £ 47.

When we calculate his expenses against his income, the farmer is left with one pound for discretionary spending. Practically all the cash he saw in twelve months was from the sale of the three beasts. They were replaced by three calves. It is easy to imagine what the loss of even one from an accident or a disease would mean to a frugal family. It was little wonder that meat was reserved for special holidays and coffee and sugar were indulgences enjoyed only on Sundays. The tight budget which Grohman outlines gives us a baseline to compare with the present which I discuss in chapters 6 and 7. When I talk to people in Tirol about the relative prosperity today, they emphasize again and again how their families managed in the past, how hard they worked and how close to the edge they often came. They talk about the values of thrift and stewardship. They say "Can Do, Make Do" and "To Will It is to Do It."

## More Work

If the annual cycle sounds like very hard work for an uncertain return, it is. From my urban American vantage point, I am dismayed, even appalled, by the sheer physical labor of mountain farms. But the visible productive labor of agriculture is only the beginning. Women do the invisible work of maintenance and reproduction on top of the jobs outlined above. In the past, women did the family washing by hand, outdoors in icy water and cold weather. The corrugated washboard was once considered a major labor-saving device for housewives. Once the raw meat and vegetables are processed and stored, she had to prepare meals, make and mend clothes, carry water, scrub floors, tend poultry and pigs, milk cows, make cheese and butter. She tended the sick, the aged and the disabled. She may have had emotional responsibility for the family's spiritual life.

Here is a description of a housewife's summer day from Frau Maria Lechleitner from Pfafflar in the Lechtal. She was sixty years old at the time and still doing the work she describes.

> You get up at four, make a fire, feed the chickens, clean the stable, milk the cows, separate the cream from the milk with a centrifuge, wash the centrifuge, and cook breakfast, wash dishes, make the beds. Then up the mountainside to mow the fields, if the weather is good. If not, you bundle grass or bring hay home. At noon, half an hour for bread and cheese. More field work until six. Cook supper and eat until the cows come home at seven, do the milking, and out into the field again until it gets really dark at nine-thirty (White and Wentzel 1961).

Then there are babies. As is true for women's work everywhere, the demands of child care are added to whatever work earns a woman her living. Her life as a mother is adjusted to the demands of the agricultural cycle and the maintenance work she produces within the household. It is common for us to take the work of women in such societies for granted, to make it invisible. It is common for us to lament that modern women just don't do the work as well as their grandmothers did. We just as often overlook how many women and men it took to run a farm.

By the same token, so dependent are Tirolean farmsteads on the labor of skilled housewives (in the truest sense of that word) that young men cannot hope to succeed without a "good wife." Young women in Alpine regions today do not regularly volunteer for this kind of work. They laugh at a lifestyle of such unremitting (even unrewarded) labor. They seek the freedoms and comforts their peers in urban areas have. Young men resort to advertising in local newspapers for a prospective bride adept in the myriad technicalities and tasks of farm life. Ideas of romantic love are irrelevant when work needs to be done.

Later we shall talk about how marriage customs are shaped, even determined, by the work of farm and mountain life. All societies divide the work of survival by gender and by age. Tirol is no different; men and women work very hard, together and separately. But their work is not equivalent or equal. You might say that each gender does 100 percent of its own work rather than dividing up

100 percent of the work between them as American couples often envision. Look at their work as complementary. To survive, put bread on the table and raise children to a reasonable adulthood, women have certain tasks and men have certain tasks. That these jobs are rewarded and recognized differently is beside the point.

Making cloth is a good example. In Tirol in the past men did the shearing of the sheep, dying and weaving. Traveling craftsmen came to stay with the family, brought their own shuttles or other equipment and did the actual weaving on the heavy looms or loden cloth presses. As with bread, the heavy, dangerous or strenuous parts of the work went to men. Women carded, spun, loaded the bobbins and when the cloth was finished, they cut and sewed it into clothes. There are probably reasons beyond custom to account for these habits. The work of women had to fit with the physical demands of pregnancy or the myriad demands of tending small children. Men built the massive looms, threw down the sheep for shearing and carried the wool at its heaviest. Women and children fed the sheep and the workers. Like bread making, everyone had to pitch in because warm clothes and occasional cash from selling cloth in the market are crucial to survival; and like bread, the stages of cloth making are ripe with symbolism and meaning beyond the ordinary.

Producing flax, which looked like hair, became a symbol of seductiveness or sensuality; this was women's work. Linens were an inevitable layer in any hope chest and one of the symbols of a dowry a bride brought to her wedding. The famous loden cloth of Tirol is simultaneously woven and felted, so it is warm, waterproof and lasts forever. Producing and marketing the heavy cloth is another example of men's work.

## Other Kinds of Workers: Creatures Great and Small

Domesticated animals also work and contribute to both spirituality and survival. Sheep are sheared for wool and the young ones slaughtered and eaten. They feast on fallow fields leaving the meadowlands in hay for cattle feeding. On the Sunday after Easter in Matrei, a decorated unsheared ram is led through the village streets in gratitude for surviving the winter's threats of avalanches and illness. Then the sacrificial ram is auctioned off. The money goes to the church or to a local charity. Easter means chickens, rabbits, eggs and cakes in the shape of lambs.

Swine are particularly valuable; most of the pig can be eaten, roasted, salted down into ham, chopped up into sausages or rendered into fat. Pigs are practical; they convert even repulsive garbage into high-quality meat and clear the floors of forests by eating mast, the fruit of oak and beech trees. The famous ham of the region, Speck, keeps well without refrigeration and is also a seasoning for other foods.

A farmer's animals provide meat, milk, cheese, butter, manure for the fields, leather for clothes and tools and power to pull a plow. Oxen drag heavy loads (oxen are the castrated adult males of any bovine species). The domesticated animals of a Tirolean farm came from the early cradles of civilization in the Middle East, so they carry many deep biblical associations.

Ancient German laws counted bees among the domesticated animals of the farm. Honey is a classic sweetener and a major ingredient in brewing beer. Beeswax from honeycombs has a hundred uses, from making candles to smelting metals. So valuable are bees they have their own patron saint, Ambrose. Never mind that imported sugars have replaced honey and electricity is more efficient than candles. Bees remain one of the mascots of Tirol: like farmers, farmers' wives and their domestic animals, bees are known for their hard work.

## The Work on High

Meanwhile, up in the mountain pastures, those who tend the cows also spend their summer working hard. In the following description, a seventeen-year-old cowgirl named Kati has been sent to work in the high mountain pastures for six long summer months.

> This was her second season on high. Cut off from the world, rarely seeing a human face, she is left entirely to her own resources. She has to tackle the vicious bull single-handed; she has to tame the cow, no longer, since her calf was taken away from her, the docile creature that would come when she called her name. The fierce thunderstorm, the no less trying heavy fall of snow in September, the swollen torrent that threatens to carry away her hut, all have to be met by ready defense and prompt means of warding off the threatening danger. Heavy stones have to be piled on the shingle roof of the hut to keep it from being blown away; the snow, accumulated to an astonishing depth in the course of one night, has to be cleared off round the hut, and a path made from the cattle-shed to the water tank. Timber has to be felled to stave the foaming, angry watercourse. Sick cattle have to be treated with physic and poultices; the calving cow, the heifer that has broken its leg by an unlucky slip, have

> to be attended; the wild goats have to be kept from straying too far; and besides all this, her daily round of heavy work in the hut, milking twice a day some twenty head of cattle, churning, and making cheese, cleaning the shed, and keeping her milkpails, boiler, and churning machine scrupulously clean.
>
> And what does she get for all this, for six months of the roughest work and privations of all kinds, to be followed by the winter with various household duties in the peasant's home in the village? Why, two pounds in money, a pair of shoes, and two hempen skirts of the coarsest texture, per annum! (Grohman 1874:216).

This description from the nineteenth century vividly portrays the kind of work and responsibility of jobs in the high pastures. For all the labor, however, young people coveted the position for its freedom. In fact, the observer, Herr Grohman, has accompanied a friend who is courting Kati. Later in chapter 4 we shall return to this couple and the results of their courtship on the high pastures.

Not all of the hard work was in the past. Anyone associated with farming, animal care or large households works very hard. Modern technology requires its own kind of labor. The annual cycles of holidays in the Alpine regions, like other farming regions, still follow the old farmer's almanac and the dictates of the seasons. As we shall see in later chapters, there are still compelling reasons to move the cows to higher pastures in summer. Rural habits are still very much alive in Tirol.

## Many Mansions

The centuries of farm life and the specialized activities which grow out of transhumance pastoralism continue to mark every phase of public life in Tirol. Agricultural architecture is a good example. Farmhouses and barns have become a serious subject of research, nostalgia, preservation and cultural continuity. Some scholars of Tirol or house hobbyists can tell you exactly how many kinds of houses and barns are in each district, which features are dominant in each valley and where the best examples of classic highlights such as carved gables are. They collect old buildings like others collect antique cars or baseball cards.

> The arrangement of a farmhouse, the disposition of the living and working quarters, is a fundamental aspect of a farm and an important criteria of research. Two main types of farmstead are familiar in the Tyrol today: single farmsteads, the living-working quarters being joined beneath one common roof, and double farmsteads with separate living and working quarters (Caramelle et al. 1987:62).

Superbly adapted to local resources and climate, farmsteads have a unity of purpose; they are living and working quarters whose designs vary in only small ways from region to region and whose features have been sharpened by thousands of years of daily living. Even newly built houses in Tirol imitate in spirit and form the older models.

For many Tiroleans the big farm-barn complex is not just architecture; it reflects their deepest cultural patterns, myths and ideals. For example, because of the custom of passing on the estate intact to one heir the farmstead itself never "aged." The house-barn did not change its function as a generation of residents changed and died. Regardless of who lived there, it never belonged to a family; it was held in trust for the next generation. The functions of the farmhouse never varied: they always centered on food production and the care of livestock and babies.

I am a serious convert to house and barn watching. My first experience with this mild addiction involved Tirolean roofs. I frequently took lifts up the mountains. When I felt courageous enough, I looked down. Roofs are fascinating. I noticed curved metal flanges at intervals on some roofs. They keep the snow from sliding off. Snow on the roof provides insulation and is a sign that heat is not escaping wastefully. I also saw buildings with large rocks spaced evenly across the surface of their roofs. The rocks anchor the roof in high winds and against sliding snow. When I hiked down I could see how the roof fit the rest of the house and barns.

The classic roof in Tirol is a saddle-back; this means it has one central ridge pole and gables at either end. A saddle-back roof is a simple and efficient use of labor and materials. The wooden gables at the front of the building under the sides of the roof are often decorated, painted or carved. The pitch of the roof and the architectural supports under it must be strong enough to support snow that accumulates and high enough to leave storage and work spaces. This is one of the primary purposes of the purlin (or purline), a term from carpentry for the innovative and ancient kind of three-dimensional support for the roof structure.

It makes sense that traditional houses and barns in Tirol were made from wood—in the past most tools or equipment were wooden. Even as they cut the wood, the forests replenished themselves. But after the 1800s many men left Tirol to work as masons and plasterers; they returned with knowledge of other techniques. So new construction (that within the last 200 years) features wood, stone and stucco. Bricks are a still newer idea.

A visitor to a Tirolean home will enter a wide central hallway marked by heavy doors on either side. There is often a door at each end and stairs to the second floor. One of the doors will lead to the sunny corner room or parlor; other doors lead to the kitchen or other square, closed rooms opening to either side.

The heart of a home for all of Tirol is the Stube, combination parlor and dining room. Even in seemingly simple farmhouses the wooden ceiling and the wall paneling of this room are flawlessly crafted of fine wood. Buttery oak and larch pine, a light wood which darkens with age, are carved in patterns alive with Gothic memories. Windows take maximum advantage of the sun. The most striking and predictable features are the tile or stucco fireplace built out into the room and the square corner table and benches under a crucifix adorned with sheaves of wheat, corn or wild flowers—the *Herrgottseck* or Lord's corner. Also common is a carved wooden cabinet on the wall used to hold tobacco; wooden benches may line the walls.

> This room served as the center of most of the farm's domestic activities. Here most everyone was conceived, born, ate, worked, prayed, slept and died. Here the scythe was resharpened, the harness fixed, the wool spun, the socks knitted, and the dough kneaded once a year for the hard rye bread. Here the next farmer learned to walk, played with home-made toys, and dozed in the long winter months. Here, too, a rare guest was received (Petschauer 1990:717).

Even the aristocracy and upper bourgeoisie had a *Gute Stube* for special occasions and a living Stube for daily life.

## Practical Spaces

Staying warm and storing things shaped the architecture as much as did the materials available for construction. Rooms must be shut off from the drafty entrance hall with thick doors. The open spaces of modern living were not practical in Tirol. Most of the household space was devoted to storage of food and equipment. Feather beds, blankets, coats, boots, firewood—all equipment for staying warm—must be stored somewhere in the farmhouse. Young girls filled the painted cupboards and chests of Tirol with hopes and supplies for their bridal day.

The rest of the house was devoted to food processing. Milk, cheese, butter, bacon, ham, fruits, vegetables, potatoes and rye bread all required elaborate processing and storage facilities.

Modern cooks would find a traditional Tirolean kitchen smoky, dark and cramped. On the other hand, the actual work took place in many other areas. Typical meals were of bread, already baked and stored, cheese and milk; an ever-present porridge, dumplings or soup completed the evening meal. As Peter Petschauer comments about village houses in Afers:

> The kitchen, by contrast, reflected both the relatively little time spent in it and the different status and priority assigned to rooms associated with women's activities; it was stuck in the darkest and dampest corner of the house and often right next to the pig sty for ready access with the slop (1990:717).

The kitchen was smoky enough to preserve meat and turn it into bacon or ham. Women often went blind and ended their days stooped over as a consequence of the dark, smoky, low kitchens. The atmosphere probably did not help their complexions either.

The attic lofts or barns were filled with farm implements for the preparation of the meadows and fields in the spring and the harvests and processing through the summer and fall, as well as sleighs, sleighbaskets, plows, wheelbarrows and baskets in many shapes and sizes. Someplace there was probably equipment to distill spirits and make Schnaps. The frames for horizontal looms used in weaving cloth were kept in houses; all the tools for processing wool and flax. All the equipment necessary for milk, butter, cheese, drying, baking and a hundred other tasks had to be stored. Each task required special tools and equipment. The inventory for any farm estate was extraordinary: scissors, hammers, nails, plowshares, pickaxes, ax-heads, cradle-saws, buckets, measures and hundreds of other useful objects.

The alpine huts in the high pasture zones where cows and cowtenders spend their summer are also considered part of the farmstead. This description of Kati's quarters contains hints of what life for a teenage girl in earlier periods could be like.

> There, in one corner, is her berth filled with hay, bed we can hardly call the box-like inclosure, and one thick blanket for a cover. Underneath or rather beside it are ranged on a shelf half a dozen bottles. They contain her ready remedies for sudden sickness or accidents among her dumb charges. Beside them, nailed to the wall, is a crucifix, surrounded by a wreath of freshly-picked rhododendrons, edelweiss and the azure-tinted gentians of the Alps. On the footboard of her couch is fastened a tiny looking-glass, not more than two inches square; it is the only one luxury of civilized life we perceive in the hut. Beside it are a comb, kept perfectly clean, and a bit of soap—her Sunday soap—for on weekdays she makes a few handfuls of wood ashes do in its stead. A rosary and a much-worn old prayer book—not to mention the huge peasant's almanac with its red and black hieroglyphics—are all that remain to be mentioned. The deal box, very like a seaman's sea chest, containing her Sunday gown, the silver string of beads (the sole remembrance of her

mother), and the ring with a gaudy glass jewel in it, the gift of her lover. A change of linen, that is a shirt, is stored in her underground milk cellar, the only receptacle that can be locked, not so much on account of thieves, but on that of the goats who will stray into the hut in expectancy of their wonted handful of salt.

. . . . The fireplace, sunk lower than the floor, is surrounded by a trench; here one places one's feet, while the floor itself is the seat. The huge copper caldron, so necessary for cheese making, its outside crusted with soot, the inside bright as a mirror, hangs on a crane-like machine, enabling it to swing round when not used. The low door, provided with a wicket [small door within a larger one], gives ingress into the cowshed, where are ranged into two rows her charges. Such is the empire over which this lonesome queen exercises unlimited control (Grohman 1874:218).

Huts such as Grohman describes were simple shelters. They typically contained a fireplace, a wooden seat, a bed, a crane and a kettle or caldron for making cheese. A rock shelter kept the milk cool until it could be processed. The dairy areas had to be kept scrupulously clean, a special job added to the routine work of Alpine life. Huts such as these are still in service though they have more comforts now. In winter they become refuges and rest houses for those who work and play in the snow.

## Houses, History and Hygiene

Houses, tools, construction materials and the purposes they serve are like fossils or an archaeological expedition. We see the past in them. A tour of a Tirolean farmstead is a tour through European history. There are tools whose function harkens to the days when Tiroleans were gatherers and hunters: a comb and box for berry picking; shaking baskets and hammers for wild nuts like those from the chestnut tree; pounders for poppy seeds. Ground chestnuts served as food for poor people at various times; many people ate them during the times of privation in World War II.

The plows in the barns are another example. The asymmetrical ones with the molding board were a major medieval innovation. The ard, or Mediterranean plow, had only a symmetrical share which cut a furrow in dry soils, but the plow with a molding board is three times more efficient because it turns the soil over and breaks up roots. The ox bows and horse collars were innovations brought by Jesuits from China. They changed the distribution of energy; with them an animal does more work than the human. Every barn has

*This is the* Stube *or living room of a Südtirolean peasant family. Built in 1732, it is on display at the Tirolean National Art Museum in Innsbruck.*

scythes and sickles. What is the difference? Sickles spare more grain and waste less; but using them is very hard work. So scythes have been used since World War I because Tirolean farms lost so much manpower. So much on a farm must be measured or weighed. A farmer wants to buy or sell a bushel, a peck, a liter, a gallon or their Tirolean equivalents. Each new government imposes its own standards; establishing weights and measures is as important as irrigation. The names and substances may have changed, but the quantities and the necessities don't. For example, oats equal gasoline because gasoline equals horsepower.

The fireplaces in Tirolean parlors were another social and technological advance. Most of us take electric or gas stoves as well as other heat sources for granted and forget that cooking and heating with wood-burning fires produces smoke. People who live in smoke-filled rooms may develop breathing difficulties, eye problems or other ailments due to the unhealthy conditions. In Tirol, farmhouse parlors free of smoke date to before A.D. 1300. This is quite early for Europe and was regarded as a major cultural advance by grateful travelers. Since then no Stube is complete without its enclosed corner fireplace jutting squarely into the room. Made from tiles or stucco the fireplaces may have benches along the edges, places to sleep on the top or exquisite decorations.

With smoke-free parlors, family members could sit around talking, drinking and serving guests. Art, music and crafts were increasingly possible with such a cultural innovation. From the simplest farmhouse to the most elegant manor house, the fireplace served the same purposes. Before that time, lavish castles had been no more comfortable than simple farmhouses were.

In a more complex example of houses and history, Petschauer details a change in government policy about trees that ultimately altered how Tiroleans slept and conducted family life. In 1727 new provisions from the Austrian regime allowed farmers to partition and, in effect, to own forested land previously held in common and used by all. Because of the distribution of the communal forests, farmers could collect branches for firewood and needles for stable floors, and cut down the trees to sell as lumber. Suddenly more wood was available for building and rebuilding. Farmers enlarged or constructed new barns or stables. New technology in axes and planers, coupled with the availability of magnificent trees, allowed peasant estates to build new barns and remodel the insides of homes.

Their renovated Stube looked grand. In essence, farm families paneled the den and cleaned out the attic. They shifted all the stored materials and equipment from the upper stories of the house into the new barn and rearranged their bedrooms. Low-ranking household members moved into the newly freed space. The master and his wife moved into a master's bedroom. This was a major innovation because until the middle of the seventeenth century "men, women, servants, and children still slept together, often naked" (Petschauer 1990:726). As in many other peasant cultures throughout the world, one did not sleep, have sex, urinate or defecate alone or out of sight or hearing of others. The idea of wearing clothing at night in rooms designed just for sleeping was certainly novel, even radical.

It is possible to trace private ownership of forests to ideas of privacy and individuality. Prudishness and modesty were "modern" notions when farm families started sleeping in separate bedrooms and wearing night clothes in Tirol. Now such notions are just more evidence of how old-fashioned peasants really are.

Writing from the later part of the nineteenth century, Grohman supports Petschauer's analysis of architecture and morality and adds his own analysis about hygiene.

> Priests have told me that thirty years ago the custom of sleeping in an entirely nude state, and crowding all the members of the family into one bedroom, was the constant theme of their discourses from the pulpit; and even nowadays I have frequently listened to sermons of some well-meaning rural priest, the subject of which was the necessity of washing every day and changing one's linen once a week (1878:101).

Pastors also preached against the customs of male cowherders who proudly did not wash themselves or their clothes the entire five or six months spent tending herds in the alpine pastures. As one priest remarked, "How can a comely girl feel herself honored with the love of a man approaching her in dirt-begrimed clothes, emitting an effluvium sufficient to knock a man down at ten paces?" This appears to be the only occasion where Grohman agreed with village priests. Clean underwear, he maintains, are not just "domestic comforts necessary to the equanimity of the human mind. A dirty face and filthy shirt are obstacles in the path of true love" (Grohman 1878:101).

Bathing closets or small detached houses like Scandinavian saunas were a common sight in Tirol until the early 1800s. Some authorities were indignant about putatively immoral activities occurring in the bathing closets and passed ordinances to close them. This is one of the reasons nineteenth century travelers in Tirol complained about the smells of unwashed people and clothes. For another century practical families used the little houses to dry and scutch flax. [Scutch means to beat the flax plants to make the yarns or threads for linen fabrics]. Now flax is no longer cultivated and processed because fabrics are available from outside Tirol. Such is the irony of history that sauna and bath customs have been revived for the benefit of the tourist industry. Some people still suspect what goes on in the "little bathhouses."

Today in Tirol codes for new construction try to preserve the form and feel of farmhouse architecture. Not only have these buildings been honed by time and the elements but the aesthetic effect is enhanced by zoning and laws written with an eye to tourism. Government policy is still shaping Tirolean habits. Ironically, Tirolean farmhouses are widely imitated in mountain and ski resorts all over the world. The solid house and barn representative of unremitting work have become the international standard of what the architecture of leisure should look like.

## Not Just a Farm: The Estate and the Estate Manager

Our knowledge of what homesteads and farms are like in America or our fantasies about European customs may obscure the true state of affairs in Tirol. To begin with, a farm is a complex multipurpose, multistructure unit of production which is the work station of the rural middle class. Predictably the center is a house, living quarters for the domestic unit, and a barn, living quarters for the livestock. These can be on top of one another, side-by-side or separated.

Farm families needed a covered well, smokehouse, baking oven, hay drying racks, threshing floors, granary, work rooms, bath or wash houses, outhouses and beehives. Farmsteads often included a tiny chapel and what we would consider small businesses: a sawmill, a forge, a tannery, a flax-processing building, water wheels to produce power or a grinding mill. Most of these tasks needed fire or power beyond human muscle. Because Tirol has steep slopes and a strong flow of water, the Alpine mill was simple, effective and one of the hallmarks of rural life. One turn of the water wheel powered one turn of the grinding wheel. Before electricity, a *Stampfe* (stomper) powered by a water wheel pounded barley and bones or felted fibers into cloth. Stilts raised sheds or small barns for drying or ripening produce off the damp ground. The stilts are notched to prevent rodents and other pests from climbing up them and feasting off the fruits of hard work.

Given this description of a farm, it makes more sense to think of it as an estate. The term, estate, is a translation from the German *Hof* or the Italian *maso*. Cole and Wolf (1974) used the term to refer to the minimum domestic economic unit which manages resources, rights and responsibilities. An estate is not just a plot of ground with a family, a house and a barn on it. An estate is the exclusive right to specific parcels of land. These are not necessarily adjacent to each other. Also, the estate is the right to use lands held in common by the community.

Ideally, the combination of outright ownership and right to common use will provide the estate with a range of resources across ecological zones and altitudes. The estate needs cleared land near the village for plowland and meadows as well as clearings in the forest higher up the slopes for grazing. It needs access to forests for cutting firewood and lumber for construction, whether the forests are privately owned or held communally. The water rights, too, must be shared.

The holdings of an estate may be scattered across the landscape like a crazy quilt; a patch here and a patch there. Only careful surveys in each village would reveal which estate is linked to which parcel. Even more invisible are the rights to communal resources. However, I imagine that when an estate manager walks along a path, he sees time and space in ways visitors cannot see. I imagine he sees a checkerboard of ownership, generations of decisions about where to plant and where to fallow, entire genealogies rooted by the fences. All the episodes of community life are revealed: here a pig got loose, here a worker was seriously injured, here is a well-loved courting spot.

Each estate has a manager, usually the senior male. He has the responsibility to make decisions about crops and husbandry, to dispose of goods produced on the estate and to negotiate with the community. In fact, estates, not individuals, have rights, independence and freedom. Estate managers are more than just farmers; they are agrarian business administrators. That this relates to Germanic ideas about hierarchies, patriarchies and authority is no accident. As we shall see in the next chapter, these ideas about power and property have life-changing consequences for those who are born, live and expect to die on the estate.

# 4

# To Have and to Hold
## Inheritance, Land Tenure and Marriage

*My maiden bride,*
*Take heed of my advice:*
*Salt well thy cabbage,*
*But not thy husband's life.*

—Song for a Woman on her Wedding Day

Two stark facts stand out about life in Tirol during the last seven hundred years. First: peasant farmers have a great many children who must eat and find work to do when they grow up. Second: land is finite and cannot be divided as each generation of children comes of age.

In this chapter I want to show how Tiroleans have adjusted to this dilemma. We will look at the "whole house," the system of land tenure, inheritance, marriage, child rearing, household and work patterns which stem from how people earned their living in Tirol. We shall see what happened to those who did not inherit. I will generally remain in the ethnographic present; that means that I speak of traditions and patterns for the culture area of Tirol which began centuries ago, essentially lasted until the middle part of the twentieth century and still have enormous power to shape family and economic life. This approach sets a baseline or a foundation for talking about contemporary changes or modernization as we do in chapters 6 and 7.

The mountains may look untamed and wild, but they are treated in the same practical manner as all parts of the pig: processed and eaten, ears, tail, toes and tongue! Both farmers and anthropologists talk about how many people the land can "carry" or *tragen*, that is, the optimal point where the number of mouths to feed is equal to or exceeds the amount of food produced by their labor. "Hands" or workers are needed to produce food; yet the estate manager can not feed many extra "mouths." Many surviving children must be "farmed out"—sent to live where there are fewer stomachs to fill.

New adaptations relieved the pressure for a generation or so. Then the stresses built again. For example, peasants started planting potatoes as a new food crop after 1800. Potatoes grow well even in marginal fields, taste good, store well and sell for cash. Mountain farmers fed more people but could not indefinitely produce enough surplus crops to sell. So within three generations the crisis of overpopulation returned.

The paradox of limits is obvious. Land does not expand. It seems impossible to divide up land reasonably so each child can inherit a portion of it. How will new estates in succeeding generations have access to rich meadowlands as well as forested slopes and high pastures? How can new generations earn a living on ever-smaller parcels of land? Because Americans have the expanding frontier as part of our historic consciousness, we have to concentrate to imagine such stringent limitations.

The Tirolean solution, forged in the constraints of space and numbers, is to pass on the property intact to one heir. This core custom reverberates in every corner of their lives.

## Primogeniture and Impartible Inheritance

What choices does an aging estate manager have to pass on his life's work? He could give it all to one person. He could give the inheritance to sons and dowries to daughters. He could try to divide up unequal things; but many things simply cannot be divided. A barn cannot be divided and authority is difficult to share equally. So enduring and significant are these choices that nations, states and cultures do not leave them up to individual whim and agony.

Both custom and law in Germanic tradition favors the firstborn son. This is called primogeniture. When the land and the privileges of the estate go to one person and cannot be divided up or partitioned, the system is called impartible inheritance. Under impartible inheritance the entire parcel could theoretically go to any one person as long as it remained intact; the younger son, a middle daughter, or someone who worked hard and found favor with the estate manager. But Germanic emphasis on male lines—or lineages—and on hierarchies of age and gender favor the first son.

By contrast, Italian custom and law emphasize partible inheritance, that is, property can be subdivided and distributed to all the heirs. This is the legacy of flatter land, urban opportunities and a less hierarchical kinship system. In the mountain cantons of Switzerland, each heir, regardless of age or sex, receives an equal part of the estate. They believe that the division of land into many small pieces protects the individual owner from a localized disaster and elicits a high level of social cooperation. Each of these systems is only an ideal; in reality, there are strategies, family infighting and inevitable consequences. Each generation must negotiate within the patterns it inherits.

In Südtirol there is a long and technical history of the struggle between old customs and new laws. Tirolean customs in the last six hundred years have been based in impartibility. Italian laws since 1919 require partible inheritance. This rather fundamental difference in outlook about the world holds the potential for serious ethnic conflicts. The resolution of this seemingly unsolvable dilemma is that Italian laws leave a category of "closed holdings" and Germanic traditions allow flexibility for some land to be parceled out or sold. So the Tirolean norm of primogeniture and indivisibility finds space within the Italian preference for dividing up the property. The situation in the province of Bundesland Tirol is less complex because of the continuity of Austrian government and the stability of Germanic traditions.

## The Inheritors

Anthropologists tend to dwell on land tenure and inheritance patterns. Few subjects are, however, as potentially tedious. So I think of inheritance patterns as soap operas. Call them "As the Tirol Turns," "All the Farms of our Lives," "The Old and the Settled," "Father Knows Best," or "One Farm to Give." This approach tends to simplify a very complex historical and legal reality. But it does preserve the dramatic core and the very real human elements.

The first major theme of our soap opera is friction between father and son. Fathers are reluctant to give up control. Young men want to be independent; senior males demand obedience and hard labor. They will disagree and argue. Only death or disability forces a father to abandon the management of the estate. So the son must wait, chafe under his father's domination, and hope to hold out long enough to inherit. The heir apparent himself will age, frozen in time as a dependent, serving as long as twenty years before his father dies. To make matters worse, the son cannot marry because the estate is too small to support another family.

The estate manager has political clout in the village and a prominent place in ceremonials. He is lord and master in his domicile. Everyone who lives on the homestead—brother, sister, son, daughter and wife—is supposed to obey. As the anthropologists comment:

> As long as they stay on their natal holding, men and women are vulnerable to the whims of their father. He decides what is to be done in the fields on any given day and how to proceed. The purchase of clothing, and even the decision to attend a dance, are ruled on by the parent, to say nothing of permission to spend a day working for another villager, or to seek temporary work as an agricultural laborer in the lowlands. The individual who earns money by his own labor turns over his earnings to his parent (Cole and Wolf 1974:183).

The oldest son must balance his chances of inheriting the estate, marrying and taking his adult place in the community, with the reality of his father's age and temperament. The older his father is, the greater the likelihood that the son will actually inherit. A father is supposed to step aside when his children are grown, his wife is dead or they start to slow down. A homestead is a place for active adults to raise children and livestock, not a place in which to age gracefully. The land and the animals do not retire.

The estate can not support all the children of an average family when they grow up. Regardless of how hard everyone works, the land does not increase in size as pigs and people do. As the estate manager feels the weight of years, he wants to keep the holdings intact, see his daughters in prosperous marriages and tie his sons solidly to the land.

To add drama, brothers eye each other cautiously. Suppose the oldest son, despairing of the strategy of waiting for his father to die, leaves the village to find work somewhere else. Eventually a younger son, the second in line or even the third, will stand to inherit. The soap opera of Tirolean inheritance raises sibling rivalries to a new high. Brothers joust for favor and position themselves jealously.

It is easy to see why so many European folktales tell about a young man who must leave home to seek his fortune. Impartible inheritance, generational competition and ecological limits will force extra or unfavored sons out into the world.

## The Whole House

Consider a household as it unfolds through time. What we call a "family" will include a time in which the healthy parents and nearly adult children do all the work (a "nuclear family"), a time in which grandparents or aunts and uncles are living in the household (an "extended family") or a time when small children and heavy workloads necessitate servants. Families are really work units. It is no wonder that major ceremonials in societies like Tirol are family-oriented: weddings, funerals, births and transfers of property.

This is the "whole house" principle or, as others call it, a stem family (Berkner 1972). One child remains at home, marries and inherits the land. The other children can leave to set up a different life or stay in the household as servants and celibates. This practice is also reported for Ireland and other peasant societies. The family included all the people under the authority of the household head either by blood (children and siblings) or by law (wife and servants). Servants were not just employees; they were family members.

Take the case of Joseph and Anna Maria Pichler (of the province of Upper Austria). Having managed a large estate for many years, the couple decided to retire in October of 1784.

> They drew up a contract with their son Johann and his bride Gertraud, selling them their house and fields for 100 florins. Joseph deducted 20 florins from the price as a wedding gift to his son and asked that the rest be paid in installments of 20 florin every *Michaeli* (September 29). As a retirement settlement (*Ausnahm*) they reserved the right to live in the *Stübl* rent-free for the rest of their lives, the use of a small piece of meadow and a section of the garden to grow cabbage and potatoes, and a yearly supply of seven bushels of wheat, thirty-two batches of hay, and two piles of wood (Berkner 1972:401).

There may have been love, trust or mutual respect. But this is a legal contract which guaranteed the retiring couple food and a roof for their old age, a form of social security. Here is an economic, contractual and legal basis for the notion of respect for elders and taking care of the aged. When an aging estate manager could not work as hard as he used to, he traded his legal authority for security and a small income. His son probably chafed to marry and, in the manner of sons everywhere, believed he would do things better when placed in charge.

Inheriting was not always a blessing. The estate manager did not inherit outright; brothers, unmarried sisters, even nieces and nephews had legal claims against the estate. The inheritor often had to pay off heavy mortgages or debts incurred to buy out his siblings. For example, at various times and places in Tirolean history governments in power had the right to appraise the property for inheritance taxes. The new heir then had to pay off the government and the other heirs based on the appraisal. Perhaps he had to give away pieces of property, sell them or place a mortgage on the estate to pay siblings or other claimants their share.

Sometimes the landed estate was already entailed; this means that inheritance was limited in some fashion. The rights of a specified line of heirs could not be alienated or bequeathed in other ways. If the inheritor failed to juggle the mortgages or was a spendthrift, his children would have no inheritance. They were doomed to be paupers. So the estate manager's life was not just power, prestige and the coziest position to inhabit.

> Inheriting brought its own burdens. Andreas Mantinger's will of 1806 points to some of the disadvantages. Johann Mantinger, the oldest son, not only inherited three farms, but was also asked to take on the life-long care of his mother, provide substantially for his two surviving sisters, and be aware of the needs of the children of his dead sister (Petschauer 1990:719).

An estate manager was respected only as he managed his resources well within the harsh annual cycles and met all the legal obligations which high status brought him. In the example above Johann inherited the land and many other problems. Before his death he had lost two of the three farms his father willed him. Today only the historic particulars and the names of the people have changed. Land transactions within families and households are still governed by complex laws in both Italy and Austria. Contracts about estates, entailed or otherwise, partly determine inheritance and family relationships.

## Other Characters and Other Endings

The soap opera has female characters too. The oldest sister is filling her hope chest, saving money from her job and negotiating for a piece of land from her father's estate. A good meadow would be better than money. She has her eye on a young man across the valley. He stands to inherit his father's estate and land and an infusion of capital from a wife's inheritance will help. For now, they may court. Until his father dies or willingly steps down, they cannot marry. Furthermore, her fiancé's mother is still hale and hearty; she will hate to give control over the household to a daughter-in-law. As Tiroleans say, "There can be only one woman in the kitchen."

Other sisters may marry men who are not estate managers, brothers passed over in the inheritance or those who follow a craft or work for wages. If she marries an innkeeper or store owner, she will manage these businesses. In the past a girl could marry into the church, become a Bride of Christ, a nun or sister. In recent decades, higher education, job training, low wage jobs in the cities, migration or marriage to an outsider draw many young women out of the villages forever.

Sometimes a person can take his or her inheritance in the form of an apprenticeship, a college education, training for the priesthood or other trades, or help in establishing a business like an inn. Unmarried women and those without the aid of an inheritance became servants. Most households hired helpers at some point in their development cycle. The *Kindsmagd*, "child's maid," was nanny and baby sitter. She slept with the children and took care of them while their mother worked.

To remain in the village unmarried was a marginal existence for both men and women. An unmarried person could claim the right to be dependent on the family homestead. They were expected to work, but a roof over their heads, regular meals and security were one way to claim an inheritance. The estate manager was required to care for his siblings and, in effect, parcel out to them their part of the inheritance. This may be the origin of the idea of spinsters, originally a single woman who stayed home and earned her keep by spinning. Single men, as in the "lonely cowherd" or the taciturn farmhand, are also frequent images in peasant songs and folklore.

In one solution to the inheritance problem, a core group of brothers and sisters was left to manage the estate. This sibling set as a business and domestic unit was not uncommon. Cole and Wolf reported that such consanguineal teams held about 10 percent of the village holdings they studied. The soap opera heated up when one of the brothers decided to take a wife.

> The marriage of any man on the holding is therefore a threat to the security of the others. And since all are very directly affected by such a marriage, the courting process involves not only the mutual acceptance of bride and groom, but approval of the bride by the entire sibling subset. Long courtships result, during which the bride-to-be is gradually integrated into the social life and work routine of the household. The plans may come to naught, however, if frictions develop, as they often do—especially between the girl and her fiancé's sister. If such tensions can be avoided until after the marriage, by a diplomatic girl, or resolved by a man willing to put his sisters "in their place," the marriage will finally take place (Cole and Wolf 1974:193).

An unrelated woman with access to the special powers of matrimony may prove unsettling. The sibling set is, at best, an awkward and temporary adjustment to impartible inheritance.

It is extraordinary for a woman to be a primary heir or an estate's manager. As she transfers from her father's domain to her husband's, a daughter is typically treated differently than a son.

Under the laws of inheritance she will receive something, a cash settlement, a piece of land or some other benefit from the estate. She can remain under the family roof as a type of helper. Her fate, however, is partially determined by the intangibles of obligation and responsibility her father and brothers feel.

Even the best laid plans fall apart. Suppose the family has no sons. In this case a daughter's clever marriage to the right man (picked either by herself or by her parents) will keep the holding intact, ensure her livelihood and give the estate a manager. A woman may be widowed by a tragic accident or sudden illness. With the power and property of a widow, she would have serious options for controlling both her own life and the future of the estate.

Perhaps the estate is in debt. Its best prospect for salvation is a man with deep pockets who arrives to marry one of the daughters, pay off the debts and settle down as estate manager. This scenario is the dream of many a young girl—"Someday my prince will come." In fact, it is also the corresponding dream of many migrants yearning to return to the soils of their native land. Remember all the folktales that start with "The King had a beautiful daughter for whom he wished to find a suitable husband . . ."?

Each estate offers a continuing saga. The script is never finished. Villagers watch carefully and speculate about the motives and actions of the characters in the unfolding drama.

> Purely domestic in appearance, the inheritance process thus has vital public dimension: it continuously creates and recreates the conditions for the recruitment of the village core population, while creating the conditions for the development of a village fringe population and for the expulsion of supernumeraries. Above all, it creates a local "elite"—however humble in comparison with the elites of the world beyond the valley—an elite in control of the means of production. And it provides the elite with a labor force of disadvantaged siblings who work in exchange for little more than subsistence wages. The inheritance process is thus the key force in creating both the village labor market and the village order of social precedence (Cole and Wolf 1974:204).

Farm families collect these stories and repeat them as cautionary tales to their own children. Naturally, villagers gossip about each other.

Unlike most, our soap opera does not seem to have much dramatic sex. About a third to a half of all villagers in the past never married. Premarital sex was frowned on; adultery was a sin; family planning was officially out. There is little historical evidence for sex as recreation or fulfillment in the rural, conservative and Catholic villages of Tirol. However, people were definitely procreating. Then as now, babies were born without the benefit of wedlock or less than nine months after their parents' marriage. But art, songs, folklore and stories extol the beauty of the land, the virtues of hard work and the advantages of obedience to authority. We hear less of romantic love, passionately idealistic or individualistic. Such notions undermine inheritance and practical land management.

## Family Feud

What strikes observers is how fundamentally unequal household residents were to each other. In essence, each dining table held people from the lower class, middle class and upper class. Relatives were also servants. Apart from divine intervention they would not marry, have children or property to pass on, or decide how to plan a day or a life. The inheritors and the disinherited might work equally hard and eat the same food but they did not have the same life chances.

> The *Arbeitsgemeinschaft* [the estate or work and living community] was organized in an unusual hierarchical fashion. Generally the farmer made decisions about when to do what, where and how, and the others followed. While eating, he sat at the most prominent place in the *Stube* directly under the crucifix, and at night he slept on the most comfortable bench by the stove in the same room. Next in rank followed the first male hand or servant, the *erste Knecht*, and so on down the line through the male servants (if there were more than one), the farmer's wife, the female servants, and the male and female children (Petschauer 1990:718).

This is an unusual hierarchy. Ordinarily one expects that the status of farmer's wife would outrank that of male servants as it does in other peasant societies. But the erste Knecht may have been an unmarried brother or one who worked at the longest and hardest jobs on the estate. His tasks, kinship and gender allowed him a seat under the crucifix.

Women who served others lived a shorter life. Those who cooked in the smoky, damp kitchens and brought the food to the table, ate last and probably less. In times of food shortages, resources went to working men and growing children. Petschauer's analysis of parish records in Afers graphically shows these consequences of being female (1990). He found that women owned about 10 percent of the farms in Afers through widowhood or some other form of inheritance. These women generally lived longer. His theory is that they had someone to help them. Women with servants or men with

*A traditional cookhouse and smoking chamber. Meats such as* Speck *(smoked ham) are hanging from the ceiling for curing.*

wives could expect to live longer. They had more and choicer foods, nursing care and time to recover from illnesses. With repeated pregnancies, childbirths and the demands of rearing infants in a harsh environment, hierarchies and help made the difference between a full life and an early death. Tiroleans could hardly have been conscious that facing the crucifix to eat symbolized the subserviency which ended women's lives sooner.

Looking at the whole house from another direction we see how the system provided important social services. Many families had small children coming close together, a sick or disabled member, or someone who would never be able to learn much or to work independently. Estates always needed a strong hand to cut firewood for fuel, watch the livestock in the summer pasture and help with the haying. There were thousands of tasks to be done.

None of the research, however insightful, paints a happy picture of Tirolean family life in the past. Social life was hierarchical and authoritarian.

> Dissatisfaction shows up in folk songs in which the farmer complains of his servant's laziness, disobedience, and immorality and is answered by the servant's song complaining of the peasant's enjoyment of a comfortable life at his expense. The peasant's entire household may have looked like a big happy family, but it was held together by legal restrictions imposed in the peasant community and by the limited opportunities offered by the rural economy (Berkner 1972:418).

There was always hard work and often hard times. Peasant cultures in general and Catholic families even with late marriage typically produce many children. In the past parents had to send their children away to work outside Tirol. It did not matter if they earned only a pittance; they were not an extra mouth to feed. Surplus young men who would never inherit control of an estate apparently had strong feelings; exile and the longing for home and land is a poignant theme in their songs and poetry.

## The Second Son:<br>Or What Else Do Men Do Besides Farm

Not all of the men disenfranchised by the whole house inheritance system were secondborns; they would just never come in first. A second son might inherit something or might succeed in other arenas. But he would never become an estate manager, the model for a man in Tirol. As we shall see in subsequent chapters, one of the key economic questions for Tirol in the twentieth century grows out of what I call the dilemma of the second son. What will disinherited sons do? How could they marry and assume an adult place in the village if they could not support a wife and babies? The solution to these questions has transformed Tirol.

In the past, men who could not succeed to the estate often left Tirol to seek their fortunes. There are endless reports of Tirolean men traveling abroad as peddlers, musicians, writers, artists and cowherders. Some became wandering traders and hawkers of straw objects, carpets, musical instruments, wood carvings, gloves and other practical things made of leather or chamois skin. Some valleys produced Schnaps, *Kirschwasser* or farmer's cheese for their men to sell far away. Men worked as cattle drivers, miners or mercenaries. Others apprenticed themselves to various craftsmen. Itinerant weavers also moved about as needed. Village life required many kinds of workers: millers, priests, blacksmiths, teachers, postmen and others. Traveling cobblers moved into the household and made all the shoes they needed. One pair of boots took about one workday, twelve hours in those days.

The most common occupation outside of farming was cutting wood. The value of timber is obvious; the fact that this work was dangerous and difficult attracted reckless young men in large numbers. The votive tablets that line the country byways are all too frequently dedicated to dead woodcutters.

> "Johann Lemberger, aged 52 and 3/4 years. This upright and virtuous [unmarried] youth was squashed by a falling tree on the 11th December, 1849. Pious passers-by are implored to say Three Lord's Prayers to redeem his tortured soul from the fires of purgatory."
>
> "Michael Gerstner
> Climbed Up, Fell Down, And Was Dead."

Falling and being fallen upon were only the beginning of logging problems. Wood felled during the autumn and spring was floated or drifted down rivers to markets in June. Sometimes floating log islands blocked the watercourses at constricted parts of the valley. The resulting log jams took many lives. Men were often forced to climb out onto the jam and break it up with poles. This work was treacherous as a man could easily fall and become pinned between the rolling logs. "Crushed to a pancake," comments Grohman.

Smuggling was a popular occupation at various times for daredevil young men. When governments levied high taxes on essential goods, young Tiroleans had another major career choice. The Bavarians to the north wanted gunpowder, salt and kegs of distilled spirits, all products of Tirol. Tiroleans craved tobacco and silk. Smuggling these goods against all the dangers of weather, terrain and government border guards fit nicely into the Tirolean men's work patterns. They also liked defying outsiders, carrying heavy loads, climbing courageously and taking risks.

Such dangerous high-yield adventures were an excellent way to amass capital. A landless second son could buy land and marry well. He then stood equal to his brother and his father. Young smugglers called themselves *Schwärzers* because they put soot on their faces to avoid detection at night. Smugglers or free-traders enlivened many an evening of drinking telling their stories to their peers. Owners of inns assisted by hiding the goods. Others produced or packed the contraband articles for transport. Everyone knew what was going on. When the tax structure changed, many Tiroleans mourned lost career paths for second sons.

Oswald von Wolkenstein, from whom we shall hear more in chapter 5, was a second son. He wrote poems and songs about his life after leaving his Tirolean homeland. Note the themes of impoverished knighthood, near-death experiences, linguistic virtuosity and musical abilities. The eagle he served was, of course, the Habsburg rulers.

> With three pennies and a little piece of bread,
> I left home on my way into misery.
> I left many drops of blood with friends and strangers
> And I thought I was near to death sometimes.
>
> I was a messenger, even a cook and a groom.
> With the armies of two kings, with Sigismund, Ruprecht,
> Both with the sign of the eagle.
> I travelled in the service of love, but paid my own way.
>
> French and Arabic, Spanish, Catalan, German, Latin, Slavic,
> Italian, Russian and Ladin
> Ten languages I have used when necessary.
> I could also play the fiddle, the flute,
> the drums and the trumpet.

Such activities were always part of Tirol's history. But when the wanderers had accumulated a small fortune they returned, bought land and married their childhood sweetheart. This is the Tirolean version of lived-happily-ever-after stories.

## Child Rearing in the Whole House

As we have discussed, Tirolean families produced lots of offspring. Child rearing customs in peasant societies, as elsewhere, follow from how people earn a living. The habits of the whole house and the workdays of parents in Tirol determined how babies were dressed, played and survived the dangers of childhood. Infants died easily in the past. Parents could not invest much effort in that precarious first year. High infant death rates and the urgency of work schedules explain many customs which otherwise seem strange or neglectful to us.

Fortunately, Peter Petschauer who grew up in a peasant village brings a unique viewpoint to child rearing in Tirol. It is difficult to imagine how relentlessly work scheduled and shaped every minute. The easier winter months still meant working from six in the morning until seven o'clock at night. For half of the year the day started at four or five in the morning and ended only at nine or ten when darkness fell.

> However romantically some authors portray mountain farm life, it was as exhausting as the haggard faces and bent backs of middle-aged men and women show it to be. In an environment in which most hands were needed most of the time for chores in and around the house, swaddling seemed the best method for freeing women to complete their other daily tasks (Petschauer 1985:127).

In Afers, as in most of premodern Europe, caregivers swaddled newborns; they wrapped the tiny bundles tightly in three layers of clothing. An inner piece fitted into a larger cover resembling a cloth diaper and an outer wrapping held the other two pieces in place. These were changed perhaps once a day, more often in affluent or less busy families.

Initially the swaddling clothes restricted all the infants' movements. But the resulting bundle was easy to pick up and carry. After three or four months caregivers left the baby's arms free to move about. By twelve months the child was allowed out of swaddling cloths and dressed in skirts. Some people attribute this custom to a devout imitation of Jesus whom the Bible says was swaddled. Others claim it is a custom indicating a lack of care or even hostility for infants. Anthropologists have studied many cultures where babies are confined in some way. We have reasons to believe that swaddled infants did not smell very good but were probably comfortable and easy to handle by busy caregivers.

Paintings from these periods show boys and girls alike dressed in skirts. It was not customary for children to wear what we call underwear. This meant that small children could (and did) urinate and defecate standing up. Gradually the child learned to make more select messes in more select places and to approximate adult patterns. Toilet training was completed in a very different and probably easier fashion than we commonly think of and there were fewer clothes to wash. Certainly these customs made sense in light of the work schedule or even modern concerns about environmental sensitivity.

Tirolean children did not learn to crawl. They first used wooden walkers that looked like standing cages. When they had mastered upright walking with the assistance of the walker, they were put in skirts and turned loose. Why is this important?

> It is almost impossible to crawl with a skirt under one's knees unless one wants to end up either with one's face on the floor or with a torn skirt. Crawling is equally disadvantageous in view

*Children dressed in traditional costumes.*

> of the customary wooden floors, anyone who has had experience with splinters knows not to drag clothed or unclothed skin over weathered wood (Petschauer 1985:129).

A crawling child has much more potential to make messes (with feces or other materials) than a restrained child; therefore, a crawling child is more work for its caregivers.

Customs like lead strings, a form of harness or leash, also make sense under these circumstances. Like walkers, these restraints allowed the now unswaddled child to pull itself up, have mobility and still be protected from the ordinary dangers of the household.

Open hearths are perilous and even wood stoves have pieces that burn. Rocks, slopes and precipices in an average village made walking risky for toddlers who, therefore, had to be restrained. Playpens are an analogous form of restraint in American culture.

Babies ate on their mother's work schedules. New mothers on farmsteads in the past worked continuously. Even with the help of servants, they had very little time to nurse babies. In premodern times, women in Afers probably nursed an infant no more than six months. This is fairly short by the standards of farming communities around the world. In the last fifty years the nursing period has dropped to three or four months. Women from both urban and rural areas told Peter Petschauer that their milk just naturally dried up after that point (1985). He reasons that the more work women have to do the more they space out or shorten the baby feedings and the earlier lactation ceases.

Frada Naroll took her young daughter on a short field trip to the Kaunertal in the northwestern part of Tirol just as the changes after World War II were beginning to show. Her observations add to the picture Petschauer painted.

> Although the government of Austria has encouraged breast-feeding by paying nursing mothers a small allowance, the peasant women of Kaunertal make little attempt at it. Most of them who do breast-feed wean to the bottle by two or three months of age, using cow's milk, goat's milk, or a combination. When the infants are breast-weaned they get a mixture of half milk and half water with a little flour in it, called the *Pappele*. Until about twenty years ago mothers and grandmothers chewed solids, usually dumplings, for the infant, spat them out and fed them to him. In some families this practice is still followed (Naroll 1960:108).

All the older women Peter Petschauer interviewed told him that they had never used wet-nurses (1985). Hiring another lactating woman to nurse a baby is widely reported for the rest of Europe, in fact, for many peasant cultures around the world. If a new mother has no milk or dies, the baby is nursed by someone else. In Afers, however, women used large wooden spoons to feed infants water, milk and wheat porridge or cereal. This makes sense. In small and isolated villages in the past, very few, if any, women were nursing simultaneously. Even fewer could suspend their own heavy schedule to take care of another infant. Their time was already filled.

Placing one's children into other households to be raised is another widely reported European custom. Although reasons for this habit vary, in Tirol fostering children is one of the consequences of living against the margins and producing lots of babies. Peasant life was, at best, unpredictable. No one controls how many children a couple will have or how many will survive. Proper parents, even loving ones, would have to send children away when the farm could not carry them. Farms with more resources needed the labor. This ancient custom of fostering children was no longer needed as a survival strategy after World War II.

> Two reasons seem to account for the change; first, about thirty years ago modern farm technology and rising labor costs eliminated every single hired hand in the village; second, recent lower birth—and improved survival rates have led to a more profound emotional and financial investment in each child. Since love was definitely not missing from the relationships between parents and children of the past, in the pre-modern setting it may simply have lacked the ability to get away from tradition or, as farmers would have put it, required one set of actions while today's world allows for others (Petschauer 1985:126).

It would be easy for us to judge peasant families harshly. There are stories of bad treatment, beatings, overwork, poor food or no attention paid either to fostered or nonfostered children. On the other hand, we hear similar stories of abuse from our own society, from all social classes and conditions. Tirolean farm mothers and fathers had to adjust to a difficult environment. As Peter Petschauer notes:

> In the traditional agriculture of Continental Europe, neither teamwork, partnership, nor democratic decision-making as understood today, had as yet been invented (136). . . . Let me emphasize again that under the circumstances described, quality of life and proper parenting as understood by a small group of middle- and upper-middle class individuals today were less of an issue than having the proper number of persons on a farm. For parents and children alike, the choice was often not between growing up in one's own family and growing up elsewhere, but between growing up in a family and not growing up at all (1985:125).

American customs such as day care, family leave, baby sitters, fast food, television viewing or joint custody are our adaptations to the work that men and women must do.

Today wives in Tirol have less household help but more reasons and ways to limit births. Maids and servants disappeared rather quickly from the domestic scene when jobs were available in larger towns and cities. Disposable diapers, rubber pants and infant clothing arrived in villages during the economic transformations after the war. Women spent less time changing and washing clothes; infants smelled better and were more cuddly. They were fun to play with and to carry around. With medical care they were more likely to live. Smaller numbers of children meant more attention to each child. Swaddling, wooden walkers and baby gruel or premasticated foods were practical in the past; when the economic system changed, these kinds of customs disappeared. No longer needed, they exist now only in memory.

## From This Day Forward

Getting married serves two fundamental purposes in human societies. First, it is the best way to have babies and raise them to adulthood. Anthropologists call this the "social production of children." Secondly, it is a system to channel resources and get work done. In both ways the society continues. In traditional Tirol being married was the only way to be an adult. Single people were socially unreliable and flawed. The choice was marry, migrate or remain marginal.

Even the self-sufficient estates of the Tirol could not grow or manufacture brides for their sons. They needed wives who had been prepared and trained for the exacting duties of a mountain farm. Only a wife provided the babies that completed the hard work of the present, the sacrifices of the past and the future of the estate. Marriage to a hard-working and prosperous estate manager was the best job a woman would ever have in Tirol.

Couples did not just marry each other; they married into the village. They married people similar to themselves who had undergone an approval process with each other's families. They married someone to share the work. Ideally they married someone with good prospects or who was known to be a good provider. The bride and the groom each expected the other to bring competence and resources into the marriage. Those who fall in love with an unsuitable person, those who are unable or unwilling to take a mate or who otherwise fall short had no real future in the village.

You may think this system sounds hopelessly unromantic. You may be right. But Tirolean practicality sounds similar to what anthropologists and other observers, including novelists, tell us about the character of peasant societies wherever they are.

## Going Courting

Practices of courting and getting married also change with time and economic life. Tiroleans look to the past when they discuss marriage customs. I found no better accounts of courtship and weddings than the long and detailed ones written by the nineteenth century informant, W.A. Grohman. Today these customs are rather standardized and homogenized in most parts of the world, including Tirol. The bride wears a white gown and veil; there are presents, attendants and a party or reception afterward. We can predict everything that happens; we have been to many such events before. In the past, however, village weddings were extraordinary rituals and we are fortunate to have such a witness.

In this funny and observant account of a courtship, Grohman tells how he hiked with a Tirolean friend up to the high summer pastures. The friend was courting an alpine maiden, Kati, whom you met in chapter 3 tending her cows. Ever the proper hostess, Kati hurried to her underground dairy to fetch milk, butter and bread. Returning, she stepped daintily over large stones that enabled one to reach the hut dry-shod. The cows had left a smelly quagmire around the dwelling.

In a field of wild flowers Kati served her visitors lunch. When all had eaten, she drew a bottle of Kirschwasser from her woven basket. Shyly she offered her suitor a drink. This was a portentous moment, marked in Tirolean poetry and song. Accounts of this custom date back to the ninth century A.D. and in the fifteenth century, poet Oswald von Wolkenstein wrote about the "shared glass of adoration." An unmarried girl's offering of wine or other alcohol when a suitor came to call was the symbolic permission to begin a courtship.

As the custom is often described, a man may have brought with him a bottle of wine. If she accepted a drink, he had permission to court. If a woman had doubts or better offers, she had to make up clever excuses. "The wine looks sour." "The priest forbids me to drink." Or "I don't like that kind of wine." When a drink was offered and accepted they were engaged to be engaged; if either one severed the tie, the other was considered a jilted lover. If wine were spilt or the glass broken, this was a bad omen. In fact, people said of an unhappy marriage, "They have spilt the wine between them."

Grohman tries to convey the flavor of their courtship and the meaning of the shared liquor. He is clearly torn between reporting and judging. Did he understand the deeper meanings of his narrative?

> It is the first token by which the charmer evinces her preference, and the saying, "He has drunk of her liquor," is tantamount to—well, never mind to what; certainly to more than is good for the young people. Once that magic drink has wetted the manly lips,

> the house of the fair one, be it the lonely Alp-hut or the more substantial peasant's house in the village, is open to him (Grohman 1878:215).

For many chapters in his book about Tirolean peasant customs Grohman worries about the sex life of villagers. He is convinced that Tiroleans are having a great deal of sex, more even than members of his own class. "I have hinted at the low scale of morality of the Tyrolese; and without entering into any unpleasant details, it must be remarked that among the lower classes of the population the intercourse between the sexes is decidedly freer than in most other countries of Europe" (Grohman 1878:99).

What evidence can we find to support the claim of "easy and immoral intercourse between the sexes?" Peasant societies are normally not noted for wild sexual abandon—even by strict Victorian standards. Grohman cites counts he made in valleys in which about half of the women had children before their wedding day. Pregnancies often preceded nuptials. He also hints that blushing maidens offered marital services in advance of marriage and refers us to *Fensterln* and *Gasselgehen*. These terms refer to customs in which a lover climbed through his beloved's bedroom window late at night when it is presumed the rest of the household slumbers in exhaustion. Only matrimony and the power of priests redeemed the promiscuity Grohman suspected at every turn.

> Free as the intercourse between the sexes is, we have nevertheless to note one redeeming quality, the sacred light in which the marriage vows are held. Unrestrained as a woman's career may have been before her marriage, she becomes a dutiful, hard-working wife, when once the holy knot is tied . . . Although it is quite true that the lover very rarely forsakes the mother of his illegitimate offspring, and ultimately marries her, we must not ascribe this final act of justice solely to the good feelings of the male culprit, but rather to the power of the priest over the mind of the sinner confessing his guilt. Were it not for his lively pictures of everlasting tortures in a certain subterranean abode of sinners, the percentage of girls abandoned by their lovers would be far greater than it is (Grohman 1878:100).

Modern Tiroleans attribute the customs of climbing through midnight windows as a practical matter; some have told me that young men in the past could be assured that their girlfriends were ready to marry. If she were already pregnant, he could count on heirs to help on the estate. Or the unplanned pregnancy forced the hand of a young woman's family; they had to permit her marriage at first opportunity.

Inheritance patterns dictated long courtships and late marriage. Grohman laconically sympathized with friends who had fought gallantly for the hand of a maiden only to find themselves linked forever to a wife. These men had "lead to the altar what was once upon a time young and buxom, but now is middle-aged, a person, in fact of whose qualities of character they have assured themselves by long experience, who in the heyday of her youth rewarded her future husband, the bold champion of many a sanguinary contest for her favors, with the free love of impulsive youth" (1878:209).

For all his Victorian judgments and Freudian projections Grohman also has a warm sympathy for his characters. In chapter 3 we saw Kati's long work schedule and the texture of her daily life. As she worked, she prayed to St. Kilian, the patron saint of turnips and clandestine lovers. She asked for a visit from her suitor and for the means to consummate and consecrate their love. Here Grohman questions her actions,

> Can we grudge her, the victim of so many lonesome hours, the happy moments spent at the side of her stalwart lover? Or can we, considering all we have said, blame her, when, forgotten and apparently forsaken by the rest of the world, the friendless maiden goes one step—a short step in her eyes—farther than the codes of civilization and the laws of society permit? I say no, decidedly no (1878:217).

Getting engaged sounds simpler than it was. Courtship was not about the feelings of young lovers or the stolen opportunities for making love. Nor did their ability to communicate with each other over a glass of spirits symbolize the course of their love. The truth is that their relative and absolute economic statuses would have determined whether he had a chance to offer the glass, how long the engagement would last and how their families responded. Until he was able to support her, they were not free to marry—in fact, he was not free to ask.

## At Long Last, A Wedding

Weddings are signal events in village societies. The festivities offer beautiful costumes, dancing, drinking and opportunities for social control. The ceremonies and all the special customs affirm the basic values of the community. What follows is a composite account of the main features of a Tirolean wedding in the last half of the nineteenth century. This is for those who want a proper and romantic conclusion to the chapter.

Some of the customs noted below are specifically Germanic and

Tirolean (Forcher 1983). Other descriptions come from talented observers who attended many weddings and left elaborate accounts of these occasions. Many of the traditions described here will feel familiar, even right or ordinary, to those of us who inherited wedding customs from European ancestors. The dancing and competitions at weddings lead us easily into chapter 5 where we discuss folklore, religion and the nature of spirituality for men and for women.

Although Busk and Grohman attended many weddings at the same time in the same valleys, they came to very different conclusions. Austrian-born Grohman jauntily skipped anything that smacked of priests and pieties. "There is nothing very striking to us in the marriage ceremony of the Catholic Church, so we will accompany the whole festive party back to the inn for drinks" (1878:237). For English-born Busk, by contrast, everything was symbolic of Catholic values. She notes that the bride wore in her hair "a wreath of rosemary—a plant greatly prized here and considered typical of the Blessed Virgin's purity" (1874:103).

The bride and groom have waited. Now they are financially stable and have gathered family approvals. They have set a nuptial date in midwinter. The cattle are home in the barns and the workloads allow celebrations. The groom has appointed a *Hochzeitlader*, "a best man," whose first duty is to make the rounds of the community and formally invite relatives and acquaintances. Before the wedding the couple make a pilgrimage to a sacred shrine and cleanse their souls of whatever sins weigh upon engaged men and women in Tirol.

Typically the wedding lasted all day and into the night. Indeed, the night before the ceremony was celebrated with a barn-party. The first wedding Rachel Busk attended was in the Zillertal for what she calls "a better class of peasants." There was feasting, fighting and dancing.

> The barn was so crowded that the dancers could but make their way with difficulty, and were continually tumbling over one another; but it was a merry night, for all were in their local costume, and the pine-wood torches shed a strange and festive glare over them. The next morning all were assembled betimes. It was a bitterly cold day, but the snow-storm was eagerly hailed, as it is reckoned a token that the newly-wedded pair will be rich (Busk 1874:102).

At dawn of the wedding day the best man called for the bride at her father's house. The household has prepared a morning meal, the *Morgensuppe*. Household members teased each other or clowned around. As the other guests gathered at the bride's house for the first meal, young girls of the village gathered to dress the bride. The groom was nowhere in sight. The best man organized and led the procession to the church. Everyone dressed in traditional costumes; there was always music, a band, rifle shots, cannon shots, trumpets or whatever noisy accompaniment was available. The wedding morning procession met the groom's party on the way. He was closely accompanied by two priests and the host of the village inn.

On her way to the chapel, the bride detoured through the kitchen where women were busy cooking and preparing the numberless dishes for the day's festivities. A huge iron pot filled with sauerkraut was presented to the bride with the song which opens this chapter. This telling ritual is called "salting the sauerkraut" and affirms the community's expectations for a wife (were she still in doubt). In a few keen words, the women tell her to listen to them, cook well and treat her husband mildly. Cabbage, the chief ingredient of sauerkraut, is the symbol of married life in Tirol.

Other ceremonies such as a mass for recently deceased relatives may precede the church service. Before entering the chapel, fleet-footed guests may compete and run a bride's race, a traditional contest before the nuptials. After the church ceremony, everyone adjourned to a nearby inn for feasting, games and dancing. Sometimes the celebrants made a procession to a number of inns in the area before settling down to the banquet. Throughout the day guests could come and go. By evening the festivities expanded to include a major segment of the valley. Outside, sporting events, shooting matches, wrestling contests or other activities for men were in full swing.

Inside, the women continued to cook and to bring out the heaping platters of food. Despite his usual gastronomic reservations, Grohman's account sounds like the Tirolean version of a gourmet feast.

> Huge long tables with benches on both sides were fixed wherever there was room; and the dishes, consisting of *Knödel*, huge balls of cooked dough with small pieces of fat bacon, and *Geselchtes*, a sort of smoked pork boiled in fat rather than water, were placed in huge bowls as large as a moderate foot-pan on each table. . . . Meats cooked in various manners, in all of which, however, fat and grease predominated, were the chief features of that early dinner; and even considering that these frugal people rarely touch meat more than twice or three times a year, their appetites for this delicacy were amazing. The last dish consisted of huge cuts of bacon swimming in a sea of molten butter (1878:238, 240).

The guests had wines to drink and hard buns in the shape unique to their valley or village. There were often several kinds of soups and a dozen or more side dishes. Busk makes even a cooked calf's head into a symbolic event.

> I think fresh dishes were being brought in one after another for three or four hours more. Even in this there was a memory of the Gospel narrative, for in token of their joy they keep for the occasion a fatted calf, the whole of which is served up joint by joint, not omitting the head; this was preceded by soup, and followed by a second course of sweet dumplings, with fruit and the inevitable pickled cabbage, which on this day is dignified with the title of *Ehrenkraut*. After this came a great number more dishes of edibles, but this time of a lighter kind; among them liver and poultry, but chiefly fruits and sweets; and among these many confections of curious devices, mostly with some symbolic meaning. When these were nearly dispatched, wine and brandy were brought out by the host, the master of the inn (1874:105–6).

For hours the merrymakers danced in an adjacent parlor, on the threshing floor or wherever space was available. The musicians took breaks to eat more than a passing snack. As the music resumed the celebrants sorted into age groups. The band played yet livelier strains so the younger members might give themselves away to the spectacular dancing that characterizes Tirolean folk life.

The dances were intricate configurations in which men, resplendent in short leather breeches held up with embroidered belts or suspenders, beat their time heartily, first on their thighs and then on their feet, the *Schuhplattler*. Their partners, in satin bodices, velvet skirts, lace vests and other beautiful vestments similarly followed the intricate steps. They flirted in the ways of wise young women everywhere. Young unmarrieds seized the opportunity to show off their brilliant costumes and skill at traditional dances. Perhaps the next wedding would be theirs.

A large dish covered by a white cloth was placed on a cleared table. Behind the large dish sat the bride's godmother (or older female relatives other than her mother) and her uncle or brother. Each guest filed by and gave a coin or bill as a present to the bride and groom and a second (and third) as payment for eating and drinking. The bride's kinswoman received the money under a cloth napkin as the kinsman wrote down the donor and the contribution. The bride and groom only watched.

The *Ehrengang*, the presentation of money to the newly married couple by each person at the wedding, is an ancient tradition. The givers expected to receive the same amount of money at their marriages or were, in fact, returning the same gift from an earlier occasion. Relatives who gave furniture, tools or other practical objects expected a delayed reciprocity.

As the last guest paid, the band began the dance of honor or *Ehrentanz*. This solemn dance hailed the bride and groom, her relatives and other noted guests. The festivities officially ended with the best man's toasts to the new couple. Given the economic system of Tirol you can predict their toasts and prayers: a good harvest, healthy cattle and many children. Dancing may, however, have continued till the first church bell at dawn if guests were willing to pay the musicians.

In many valleys the Ehrentanz signaled the beginning of tricks that peers of the groom played on him. His new bride may be kidnapped and carried off to another inn where she must remain until ransomed. Or the bridegroom was challenged to drinking games or he found his horses turned loose. Or the young men played their tricks after the couple retired for the night. They played old kettles, washboards, cowbells or other noisy instruments outside the bridal bower. There are hundreds of examples in which the bridegroom was harassed, teased or tricked. Every description of a Tirolean wedding we have emphasizes these rituals of male bonding. Even at weddings, or maybe particularly at weddings, we see dancing, fighting, competitive sports, taunting and other verbal displays that characterize men's public relationships to each other. At large weddings these games often continued for several days.

By contrast and by all accounts, the bride was handled with remarkable seriousness. She changed her name and her demeanor. She received the instruction and the equipment for her somber new roles. The rituals surrounding her transition into adulthood and wifedom were firmly scripted, the outcome was known and everyone had a part to play. These ordeals for bride and groom, at the very least, confirm the communities' stake in their future.

Many customs hint at sexual matters. The clothing of the bride was supposed to indicate her virginal status or lack of it. Protecting her "maidenhood" was part of the showy rituals. She was closely watched; she could be fined or taunted if she saw or kissed the groom on the wedding eve. Her trousseau and gifts always prominently featured a bed and elaborate bedding. Many subtle customs celebrated the change in her sexual and social status, how a girl turned into a woman. Salting the sauerkraut was a small domestic chore; feeding a husband properly was not.

Since the end of World War II and the economic changes that followed, the stark picture I have painted in this chapter has softened. The Malthusian match between population and ecology is less harsh. Marriages involve more personal choices and emotional negotiation for the couple. There are other sources of money and more alternatives for the younger generation than migration, as we shall see in chapters 6 and 7. However, as long as there are land, babies and finite resources, there will be inheritance, households and weddings. The hidden patterns remain.

### An Erotic Poem

*Oswald von Wolkenstein*

[ca. 1377–1445]

Joyfully, peacefully, endearingly, tenderly,
Pleasing ever so gently and slowly, soft, sweet, fresh, pure.
Awaken thou beautiful and lovely lady.
Stretch and extend and show your delicate, proud body.

Open your luminous bright eyes.
Behold in your morning rapture how the course of the stars
Grows dim in the bright, brilliant, clear sun.
Up, up and dance.

Weave a pretty wreath of blue and violet, red and yellow,
The white shining radiance of blossoms;
Nuzzling, caressing, kissing and licking
Are words for many voluptuous and beautiful things.

May your round red mouth be engaged only by these things.
It has set my heart aflame with love,
Has delighted me truly a thousand times,
Has excited my desire in sleep and dream—

Where I say the well-formed, soft opening made for smiling
In which lay the splendor of the teeth,
Rosy, kissable, lickable, lipable,
Formed with a delicate stroke of the brush.

If she would only come
And take the painful yearning from my heart,
With her white breasts pressed against me,
My pain would be gone, I would be transported with rapture.

What other maiden so tender and so fine
Could make my heart so happy?
She takes away the pain and wakens pure, rich, ripe desires,
The mouth kissing mouth, tongue against tongue.

# 5

# The Devil in Tirol

## Things Spiritual, Sensual and Intellectual

> *In that year, 1617, the honorable and sage Hanns Jacob Schwalher, Justice of the Peace in Rattenberg, was attacked by a fearsome pain in the inside of his body, whereat he thought he must burst. While suffering thus terribly he vowed, should he recover, to make a pilgrimage with his wife to the Chapel of Maria Stein. Upon making this vow he was better. On the 17th day of October he and his wife fulfilled the pilgrims' obligation.*
>
> —Inscription from a Votive Tablet in the Inn Valley

In Tirol there are saints everywhere one looks. A man on horseback stretching out his left hand as the rays of the sun strike him about his head is Saint Paul. Saint Peter has the keys to the kingdom. Blood flows from Saint Sebastian's many arrow wounds. Saint Catherine of Sienna carries a book and presides over women's literacy. Another Saint Catherine lies broken across a wagon wheel. Saint Isidore, the patron of farmers, is portrayed with a pair of oxen and two angels who draw a plow in his place.

Crucifixes adorn bars. Contorted masks appear in midwinter ceremonies. A tour guide tells his charges about fertility rites, warding off demons, primitive rituals or magical beliefs. Souvenir shops brim with countless objects which evoke the creeds and customs of the region. How do such things make sense? What is the appropriate context for these objects and rituals in Tirol?

This chapter concerns the things anthropologists usually include under the categories of religion, folklore, ceremonialism and worldview. Most of us believe that these categories are inextricably tied to the ways people make a living, contrive their history and organize their kinship system. We think that the life of the mind and the growth of the spirit follow from our prior understanding of what daily life and the weather is like or why people want babies and fear unseen forces. So this chapter is about feelings converted into ritual and beliefs converted into objects. These beliefs and rituals bind people on a level they cannot speak directly about. They can only act out their core mythologies, write poetry under pressure, feel passion as death and dance as birds do. So rich and deep is this sensual and spiritual life in the culture area of Tirol that I am able to include only some highlights, only a sampling of the inner life of the region.

My experiences with what we might call religion and folklore in Tirol are fragmented and frustrating. Like many others I want to hear, taste and smell the richness I know exists. Tiroleans today when asked about these issues talk about events largely staged for tourists, bits and pieces from the past or ceremonies removed from their cultural context. They no longer pray in the same old way for fertility or an end to it; they go to the doctor. The masks are separated from the fears that motivated their manufacture. Avalanches have more to do with engineering and scheduled maintenance than with the wrath of an unseen spirit world. Events tied to the Christian calendar sound like what I know and have frankly tired of in my own American culture. I am dismayed by row upon row of Christmas artifacts for sale.

Many of the customs we associate with religion have been homogenized and staged for tourists; in chapters 6 and 8 we discuss some of these sound and sight bites marketed for the tourist culture. These are presented as quaint customs without anthropological context. To tap into deeper levels we have to dig into the past, listen to colleagues who grew up on peasant farms or go back to the bedrock of folktales. In this chapter, I want to show three major themes about the spiritual life in Tirol. There are probably many others.

The first theme is about telling tales. We might say that "Stories 'R' Us." Any place, person, thing or event in Tirol may provoke a story about itself: a steep mountain, Andreas Hofer, a rainbow, a needle, Jesus, Advent or a scary noise in the night. Verbal traditions, only a few of which I have the space to recount, tell us who we are, what moral qualities shape our communities and what life or death is like. This is true for Tirol as for anywhere else. My students apparently remember the stories when they may have forgotten everything else. They ask, "Can I have a copy of all those stories you told us?" "Are you going to put in that story about the industrious girl who spun herself a lover?" "That scary story kept me awake all night." "What's the story on this place?"

The second theme is about control. People want to have dominion over what is otherwise uncontrollable. Hence we conjure up magic and ritual. People have feelings: fear, anger, sorrow, joy, gratitude and others less noble. We invent ways to express these feelings, even if indirectly. Not only do humans like us demand explanations; we want cures. We want the bad things to stop; we want the hurting to cease. Many of the beliefs, customs, ceremonies and events in this chapter are about achieving those goals.

And thirdly, people make play in public settings. Every functioning culture celebrates its communal life. Public ceremonies are set apart from everyday work activities. There is food for the body and for the senses, music, dancing, costumes, art, drink. All of them affirm—whether we can articulate it well or not—some values or truths about who we believe we are. Many of these ceremonies mark off the calendar year, the achievements and survival of summer, winter, spring and fall. Other ceremonies mark the life span—birth, death, marriage and coming of age. Communal feasting is not just about food; cooking and eating serve to cement the bonds within a human group, reinforce and acknowledge them.

In Tirol seasonal Christian events attract the most attention. Starting with Advent, the season leading up to Christmas, the holidays build to Epiphany which is the twelfth day of Christmas. That opens the Carnival season and leads to Shrovetide, the three days preceding Ash Wednesday, or Mardi Gras as this celebratory period is sometimes known. The Wednesday penitence begins the forty days of religious observances which culminate in Easter. The Passion plays in the spring and summer, Palm Sunday and Good Friday processions, the decoration of holy graves, the Lenten observances and Pentecost along with assorted other holidays are the center of the liturgical calendar. Mime, theatre, visual arts and other displays spring from these themes. In fact, most of what we think of as religious pageantry in Tirol centers on the birth, life and death of Jesus.

## Controlling the Uncontrollable

The understandable desire to control the uncontrollable is a good context in which to put a thousand little daily acts and thoughts. This makes sense of what we might otherwise just list as visible, quaint or colorful. Holy water or consecrated ashes bless the fields before sowing or the cow as she calves. The willow twigs consecrated on Palm Sunday are placed in fields or in kitchens; they may protect from disasters. Storm bells, the Wetterglocke, charm the dreaded lightning away. Even when lightning strikes, villagers reason that the bells protected them from an even greater catastrophe. Crosses marked in chalk keep the Devil away. Priests perform rites to assuage needs and fears which predate their doctrines.

At unpredictable intervals disasters befall communities. Today we have many kinds of aid, assistance, insurance, legal remedies, scientific explanations and technological achievements. In the past, however, peasant communities such as those in Tirol had few external resources. There were hailstorms, avalanches, diseases of cattle, unexplainable accidents, drought, horses mysteriously lamed and babies who cried ceaselessly in their cradles or sickened without reason. Milk soured or cream refused to churn into a butter. This can be very frustrating.

Acts of nature seem capricious. Families would like to have babies when they want them, no babies at other times and a boy baby or a girl baby for the asking. Tiroleans, like the rest of us, would like to exercise some control over impersonal forces. Sometimes we personalize our fears; hence the character of the Devil. Sometimes we turn to a friend, someone who understands without judging; this impulse may explain the ever-present saints.

For example, wax figures of men, women, children, saints, and every imaginable limb or organ of the human body still decorate many churches in Tirol. The museums offer even more of these objects of devotion. Tiroleans say that wax replicas are offerings to the Virgin Mary or other saints in acknowledgment of blessings bestowed.

> The poor woodcutter, who has injured his leg desperately with his ax, on being cured, forthwith purchases a wax leg, and hangs it up at the shrine of the saint whose blessed services he besought at the hour of despair and sickness . . . The mother whose babe recovered from a serious illness, by the help of the Virgin and of her patron saint, spends a part of her savings in the purchase of a wax representation of a baby in swaddling clothes, and tying a bright blue ribbon round its neck, hangs it up at the altar of her patron saint . . . With eyes, ears, and all other distinct organs or members of the human body, it is the same way, and many a chapel's interior is more like an anatomical museum than a place of worship. Hearts, we need hardly tell our fair readers, preponderate (Grohman 1878:141).

When a miracle saved the cow with a broken leg or wasting disease, the grateful cowherder tied a waxen effigy to the altar of a nearby chapel. When a girl wanted a lover to look her way, she left a white heart on a cross.

Here is a nineteenth century example of the desire to master the unpredictable. Hiking in the mountains Grohman encountered a family making a long pilgrimage. The wife was very pregnant and he questioned why she walked so far in such a condition. Her husband replied,

> "Ah, sir, you must know that she's had five girls running, and now that her time is approaching, we are going to visit the renowned shrine of the Holy Virgin in the next village. They say there is none like it in the whole country, and maybe in the whole world, for working miracles in this particular line; you see, sons are so much more useful than girls; and now we have spent the greater part of the day in prayer at the Virgin's shrine and offered two large pound candles and a waxen boy" (Grohman 1878:49).

Sometimes ardent young couples failed to conceive. This was a serious concern in peasant communities. Did someone bear them a grudge? Had someone secured a spell or charm against them? Was a waxen replica of an ugly toad left in the barn, under the steps or where fences cross in the field? What could they do? Make a pilgrimage and ask for forgiveness, a blessing or a lifting of the curse.

And when the wish was fulfilled, they made another journey to leave an offering—a wax baby, a wax toad and other gifts. Today visitors cherish votive candles, devotional objects of wax, wood or paper and signs of the saints as wonderful folk art. I love to find these examples. One of my favorites is a votive tablet in the Inn valley just outside of Innsbruck. It shows a painted picture of a woman lying on a bed surrounded by praying relatives. Above her head is a floating baby, in swaddling clothes, and above the infant is a Madonna and child seated upon a throne of clouds. The verse beneath expresses the happiness of being in the family way and gratitude for a successful pilgrimage.

> Thanks be to you, O Heavenly Mary
> For hearing our prayers, and joining two hearts
> That now are one, but had been twain,
> By giving us a son.

Notice the hint of past problems that are now solved. Perhaps pilgrimage and prayer were a kind of peasant psychotherapy. I also interpret this verse as an example of birth control and family planning. I sense their intense feelings and deeply personal solutions.

## Deep Play: The Poetry of Movement and Competition

Imagine this scene. A Tirolean man walks into the village inn. His loden green Sunday hat is adorned with the tail feathers of the blackcock bird. The feathers which curl at the ends have been turned in a way that will signal to every native-born male in the room that the wearer seeks to quarrel. Another man picks up the challenge. He asks, "How much does that feather cost?" The wearer answers, "Five fingers and a grip."

With this exchange the two men have reached an agreement. They sit at a table facing each other. They entwine the middle fingers of their right hands. At a signal given by willing friends, they struggle to pull their rival across the table using only their fingers as leverage. As a result, "one very frequently sees in Tyrol men with a finger bent nearly double on the right hand" (Grohman 1878:52). This custom, rightly called finger fighting or *Fingerhackeln*, has in the last seventy years gradually ceased to exist.

Many things that happen in Tirol are about men playing, about rituals which bond males to each other. Some anthropologists have called this deep play, because it is difficult to assign practical functions to what are really games. Such play may answer a profound need and provide a kind of spirituality we may not often credit. Some observers think that competition, fighting and stylized hostilities serve as safety valves, channeling and releasing feelings which might otherwise be dangerous to individuals or to the public. The example of finger fighting shows an underlying structure, a subtle communication and an intense physical and emotional involvement.

Recent interpretations call this male bonding and point out the utility of training and rewarding men for physical strength and the rewards of risk-taking. Still others think that a chance for men to touch each other, look deeply into each other's eyes and act out profound emotions heals and invigorates.

Dancing is another form of deep play which reflects the most profound, although inexpressible, meanings Tiroleans give to their lives. Often males and females dance separately from each other. The dances may begin slowly. Men in heavy ironshod boots begin to caper and jump with the agility and energy of gymnasts. The dancer throws himself on his knees, folds both arms over his chest and bends backward until he can rap his head several times on the hard boards behind him. Then with one powerful motion, he leaps erect without using his arms and hands. In a variation, the dancer jumps high in the air and lands with bare knees on the floor. There his knees drum a musical measure; then with an agile bound he regains his feet.

Sometimes the dancer stomps his ironclad shoes ferociously and slaps them or his leather-clad thighs with the palm of his hand. "Shoe-slapping" or Schuhplattler adds a strenuous vitality to the strains of a waltz or polka. Needless to say, the dances are noisy and the audience must look out to keep from getting stepped on. Sometimes unusually talented dancers do special exhibitions—a woman hoists her partner on her shoulders until he balances upside down there and walks his feet on the ceiling!

In dancing, men competed with each other for women, prestige or feelings they could not name. They used to fight with knives, bottles, fists, teeth, even musical instruments. In Tirol in the past, a man put his hat on the head of his chosen lady and woe be to the fellow who transgressed this boundary, intentionally or unintentionally. In birds this habit is called "marking his territory." In humans it is called courting. Note the comparison in this quote.

> These capers, jumps, and strange twisting of the body are accompanied by shrill whistles, slapping of the thighs and of the boot-soles with their horny hands, and peculiar smacking of the lips and tongue in imitation of the gyrations and strange sounds emitted by the love-sick blackcock and capercaillie on the surrounding mountains. In the mating season these birds pirouette and flap their wings and go through other funny antics to attract the attention of the hen birds (Grohman 1908:45).

Fancy clothes, strong muscles, strength, agility and courage must be very appealing to a woman whose survival will depend on her husband's physical skills.

These rituals of play have an economic aspect in preparing and training men for the environment. Or, one may claim that the environment produced the abilities so well displayed in dance and competition. They fit the image of male suffering so inescapable in Tirol. We see life-size crucifixes with painted blood dripping off them, carvings of a peasant permanently bent to his plow and carrying yoke, the memorials to men dead on mountain trails, saints executed grotesquely and folktales which depict men evicted from their native land, depressed and suicidal. Most writers about Tirol do not associate knife fights and shooting matches with alcohol, sensuality, poetic creativity or male bonding. Nonetheless, this interpretation explains much.

Men in Tirol and other Alpine areas staged elaborate sporting competitions. Wrestling bouts, for example, typically started at the local inn on a fixed day. Each contestant picked an opponent from a different valley and traded drinks with him. Then they fought with fingers and later in the contest went outside for full body sport. The object was to grab the heavy waistband on the opponent's trousers, toss him on his back twice and take his blackcock feathers as a token of victory. When the victor felt like another fight he turned the feathers down, walked into an inn and ordered a drink.

Most of the spectacular male games occurred in late winter. Today local communities stage these competitions and spectacles largely as tourist events. The connections to courting and subsistence are less obvious than in the past. At the *Wampeler*, a celebration and competition in the town of Axams, men wear padded jackets and masks and carry short sticks. At a given point in the festival they hit each other with the sticks until the last one is left standing. In other parts of the Inn valley, men stage what we might translate as a "timber tug-of-war." If there has been no wedding, and hence no opportunity to stage games of strength and competition, men cut and decorate a larch log and the whole village turns out for a tug-of-war. The *Gauderfest* in Zillertal is famous for ram fighting, drink betting and shooting Schnaps. Other games to prove manhood and strength in Tirol include: stone lifting, bowling, tug-of-wars, arm wrestling, wrestling, as well as racing through alleys on horse-drawn sleighs (Forcher 1983).

The most important traditional sport for Tirolean men was marksmanship or sharpshooting. A Tirolean marksman was not allowed to support any part of his body or his rifle. He had to stand upright holding the heavy instrument in his outstretched arms. Sponsored by the government in traditional times, the skill of deadly shooting provided sport, entertainment, companionship and military training all in one. Actually, I marvel most at the abilities of Tirolean competitors who can achieve such feats and drink at the same time. From all accounts, they consumed prodigious quantities of Schnaps, beer and wine. The anthropological couple, Raoul and Frada Naroll, worked in a north Tirolean village in the Kaunertal and observed how very old traditions of men's groups formed the basis for modern cooperation.

> Tyroleans have a long tradition as fighting men. Tyrolean youths still get cheerfully drunk to celebrate when they pass their army physical examinations and proudly wear the lapel badge reading "fit" (*Tauglich*). Kaunertal, like other Tyrolean peasant villages, has its rifle company, organized with that of other villages of its district into a regiment. While centuries ago these companies were important military organizations (analogous ones still form the basis of the Swiss army), today they are purely ceremonial (Naroll and Naroll 1962:106).

Today throughout Tirol the Schützenkompanies march in uniform for festivals and unite all classes of men. Although the need for sharpshooting has passed, these traditions form the basis for many contemporary economic successes as we shall see in chapter 6.

*A marching band and* Schützenkompanie *parading through a village.*

## More Poetry and Deep Play

Imagine yet another scene. It is a country wedding such as we described in the last chapter. Men are dancing. But during the toasts to the bride and groom, tempers flare. Two young men sense slights and insults. Perhaps the first man was jilted by the girl he fancied or she refused his amorous advances. Perhaps his rival chooses the occasion of a wedding to taunt him and remind him of his failures. One of the dancers starts with a verse insulting the other, often in subtle ways. Rapidly the object of the affront composes and delivers his rejoinder. They take turns in verbal blows and insults.

On social occasions such as weddings, festivals or cattle markets, men may challenge each other to a song duel, a *Schnaddahüpfler*. The two rivals below exchange their poetic derision or defiance. The challenger speaks first. Alternate verses are his rival's response:

I've come up from the plain,
No path is too long for me
I've a rucksack with me
With a load of courage.

Now it rains, rains in torrents
Now fine snow falls,
Your singing goes in fits and starts.
I'm beginning to have enough of it.

Boxwood and maple leaf,
Turkish paper,
If today I only had
My iron rake with me.

Stop singing like that
And cracking jokes.
Or we'll be having a fight
Or a finger wrestling bout.

Stop singing like that,
You big bean pole,
If you broke,
You'd be too short
To be put together again.

Up there on the hill
There are three beech trees.
Let's not squabble much longer
But try out our courage.

I'm a lively lad,
I've a feather in my hat
In a roughhouse
No one has yet frightened me.

Laddie, when you hit,
Don't hit me in the eyes,
And stop me from seeing well enough
To pick up your pieces.

Henneler, Henneler,
It's time to pack up
Your boastful rhyming,
It's gone on too long for me.

(Von Hörmann 1877.)

It must take extraordinary skill to improvise poetry and impromptu slander while dancing and drinking in the Tirolean fashion.These two seem to be thirsting for a fight. As the words suggest, the song may have been only a prelude to a finger-wrestling match or other battles. Or, wiser heads might have intervened with songs to promote peace. Some song duels were composed on the spot while dancing. Others were favorite standards or old troubadour love songs; then everyone could join the singing.

Customs like this exist in many cultures throughout the world. Men dueling verbally and exchanging insults (and other information about each other) are documented from African-American teenagers in New Orleans to middle-Eastern villagers in Israel, Turkey and other countries. In Tirol men knew the rules, however covert or subtle. They played hard, insulted one another, and then forgave so the games could continue. Grohman participated in and witnessed hundreds of such competitions or sporting events and wrote several books about them. Here is my favorite image of the "real men" of Tirol.

> I was struck with the cool and off-hand manner in which the victim of the first-named injury replaced his eye into the socket, to which it remained attached by some fibers . . . The man rejoined his companions sitting round the table, all the best friends in the world now that the quarrel was settled (1878:16).

It is unlikely we could walk into an inn today and find a finger fight or a song duel. Traditions like these serve little purpose now. But at the same time, feelings and need for deep play never die.

## Passion and Miracles

People in the Catholic regions of Europe have long staged lively religious theatre. The dramas based primarily on the death of Jesus are called Passion plays. A similar kind, called miracle plays, also have a deep history. They act out common biblical stories to draw moral conclusions. Some say these presentations grow out of Catholic religious fervor, the isolation of long winters or the lack of other media for entertainment. Giving plays may also be the most dramatic way of telling beloved stories, affirming collective values and having a good time.

In 1868 traveler Ludwig Steub read in the newspaper about a Passion play to be staged for the Feast of the Assumption of the Blessed Virgin Mary on August 15 in Brixlegg. So he and many other playgoers bought tickets and climbed on the little train which had just connected Innsbruck to the village.

> It is now seven o'clock on a beautiful morning. Above the friendly little village, with its bushes and trees, rise the wild mountain peaks, each bearing its own name. But quite near us, just on the other side of the stream, one can see the long, tall building in which the Passion Play is going to be acted. A few

> flags and the red Tyrolean Eagle adorn the gable. The ticket-sellers have already taken up their seats of office, for, apparently, prudent people are already arriving in order to be sure of finding a good place. The travelling saleswomen too are setting up their tables, filling their fruit baskets or laying out sausages, doughnuts, grapes and other such popular articles. Gradually various groups, of both sexes, dressed in their Sunday best, are gathering by the gurgling stream in order to view the "theatre," the scenery and each other. Many coaches from the Zillertal and the rest of the neighborhood arrive noisily, bringing crowds of people of all age groups. The special train from Bozen and Innsbruck also rolls into the station. By now it is nine o'clock and small cannon guns announce the start of the play (Myss 1973:46).

About three thousand people watched as the events of the Passion unfolded. First there were living tableaus or pantomimes from the Old Testament which prophesied the coming of Christ. Young girls in costumes paraded before the closed curtain to explain the story line of each emergent tableau. With many starts and stops the actors eventually reached the story of the Passion of Christ, farewells, betrayals, sentencing and crucifixion.

The first act bothered observer Steub. A band and chorus played a frivolous, secular song "although the connection between this and Agony and Death of Our Dear Savior defies all rational explanation!" To make matters worse, they followed with a romantic song "better suited to a pastoral play than to the Crucifixion on Golgotha!" His personal feelings as well as his religious beliefs come through strongly as he describes the long intervals between acts.

> The whole orchestra and all the singers then leave their seats, as do many of the audience who find it too hot inside and are glad to take the opportunity of going out to get some fresh air. At the same time beer and wine bottles, bread, sausages, and other refreshments are handed round in the "theatre". And so all of a sudden the "theatre" becomes a tavern, and however respectably this may be done, it still seems a long way from the Passion of Our Lord. Whereas the rustic audience in Ammergau follows the play with pious contemplation, often with tears in their eyes, the atmosphere in Brixlegg is critical and jovial. People seem to prefer to laugh than to cry; at any rate the minor deficiencies in acting are received with cheerful sniggering. But at the moment when Judas, the traitor, dangles from his branch, quite a distinct wave of laughter runs through the packed house. But then of course this seems to be in keeping with the character of the people, for the people of the Lower Inn Valley are regarded by some as being Germany's merriest folk (Steub in Myss 1973:47).

When similar plays are staged today, thousands and thousands attend. Tickets are sold out months in advance and the same commercial atmosphere prevails. Believers and nonbelievers alike love to witness the enactments of these famous stories and see what new interpretations emerge. Tiroleans who worry about selling their traditions to travelers can take note of these nineteenth century descriptions.

Like the Passion play described above, a miracle play lasts for hours. It may take weeks to cast and organize. These dramas are always about the struggle between good and evil. The settings are traditionally the legends of the Book of Genesis and the acts of creating the earth. The sides are clear. God the Father and a host of helpful cherubs are arrayed against the Evil One. Adam and Eve appear and once again act out the parable of gender relations.

In the past, villagers staged their plays in a barn or the local inn's large room. They brought farm animals and equipment onto a makeshift stage for dramatic effect. Their friends and relatives played the roles, creating gossip for years to come. I have here summarized a miracle play that Grohman witnessed. Unmoved by pieties, he appreciated the ribald undercurrents.

As the curtain (or its local equivalent) opens, God the Father is away from the valley working at creating the world. Little cherubs (played by village children) enter first. They conspire with each other to skip their chores and be idle. At the side of the stage the Archangel Lucifer (the devil as interpreted by a senior man of the village) offers counterpoint. He tempts the earthly mortals both in the audience and on the stage with hedonist enjoyment of life. Every day, he claims, they may have chicken to eat, wine to drink and figs or dates for dessert. They have only to serve him instead of their stuffy and pious master, God the Father. The cherubs are swayed. "Forget the fasting, praying and chanting," several cherubs exhort their fellows. "Let's have fun with Lucifer."

But God the Father has the last word of the first act. At the sound of a tolling bell, he returns and lectures his audience from his throne, a high stove. An offstage threshing machine provides appropriate celestial noises and thunder to accompany his admonitions. The second act begins with Lucifer, the Evil One. The setting is his home in Hell.

> The center of the stage is occupied by a portable forge, upon which a bright coal-fire is burning, a large butcher's block stands to the right, while huge knives, gigantic tongs, and brightly-polished axes litter the foreground. To the left of the forge we see a couple of huge boilers filled with steaming water. The stage is lit up by means of the red screens, and loud howling and

> gnashing of teeth and the most piercing shrieks increase the horrors of the picture (Grohman 1878:41).

A trumpet flare announces Lucifer. He is dressed in the red costume of the marker at rifle-matches, his face blackened, a pair of horns fastened to his head, and long claws made of stiff leather, glued with cobbler's wax to his fingers. He carries a pitchfork and wears a chain of human teeth, wax fingers, witches' hair and dried toads.

Lucifer and his followers begin to tempt Eve with a snake and an apple. The script permits a number of digressions about the weaker sex and her flaws of disobedience and curiosity. In the play described, the actors playing the parts of Adam and Eve were fully clothed even before their expulsion from the Garden of Eden. As one elder chides the observer, "Yes, of course, you wouldn't have them come out in the naked state in which men and women, I am told, are not ashamed to appear on stages in your large towns and cities!"

The third scene shows Paradise. God, Adam and Eve reenact the Garden of Eden story; at this point in the staging, villagers have some flexibility in the script. They may include songs, skits with local color or novel interpretations of the age-old stories in the Bible. Adam and Eve may even tantalize their audience with suggestive dialogue and a few embraces. Other actors may perform skits dressed as animals. The play traditionally ends with a triumphant affirmation of the victory of God the Father over Lucifer, the Evil One. This is the miracle. However, the actors warn, unless everyone is properly pious, the Evil One will return. Grohman loved the play and the players but remained unconvinced that miracles actually happen.

> The peasant population of the country entertains a firm belief in legends of miracles worked by supernatural powers in bygone times; and it would prove highly unsatisfactory to endeavor to make a peasant realize the stupidity and incongruity of most of these miracles (1878:110).

## Stories in the Third Dimension

If feelings and values can be expressed in dance, poetry, songs or plays, then Tiroleans can put them into wood. No one could spend an hour in Tirol without being aware of the importance of woodcarving. Given the vast hardwood forests, the art of woodcarving makes perfect sense. What may require explanation are styles, subjects and the significance attached to the carvings.

A folktale explains how the tradition started in Tirol. It is an

example of those classic stories in which magical beings help us or give us permission to be creative or destructive beyond our ordinary powers.

> A young shepherd lad was searching for his lost lamb when he stumbled upon a cave. Curious, he entered and saw a group of dwarfs seated at their work benches. A fire illuminated the fallen chips and the tiny figures they were carving. The boy was so fascinated that he gave his presence away. The dwarfs took him

> before their king to explain the intrusion. The shepherd boy wanted only to learn the magic of producing such objects. The king told him, "Patience, diligence and skill are the only magic we use. I will teach you myself." When the shepherd boy learned to carve wood from the king of the mountain dwarfs, he returned home and taught others. They, in turn, taught their children. So the knowledge was passed from generation to generation (Plaut 1984:5).

Museums have examples of Tirolean woodcarving from a thousand years ago. Wood does not last indefinitely as stone does, so older examples are lost. The earliest written documents from the region refer to the already established trade in wooden toys, tools and devotional objects.

One carving specialist, the *Herrgottmacher* or "Lord God Maker," carved the sacred statues of Jesus, crucifixes from a few inches high to greater than life size. As a carver of sacred objects of veneration, these men had high status and were obviously powerful forces in controlling the images of Jesus in the popular mind. Purchased or commissioned for the corner of the Stube, many of the crucifixes have painted blood gushing from assorted punctures. Grohman hated them and thought them grotesque, "The same ghastly expression is stamped upon all the faces: the same weird, emaciated body, the same deformed position of arms and legs, calling forth an involuntary shudder" (1878:278). Of course, Grohman came out of a romantic artistic tradition in which Jesus is represented piously, sugary, even smilingly, and usually fully clothed. No blood, tears, sweat or muscles are in evidence. These contrasting styles, the nineteenth century sweetness and the earlier gore and suffering, are still evident throughout Tirol. This is the same folk tradition which produced the magnificent Pacher altars, the Pietàs portraying a grieving Mary with her dead son, and other wooden statuary of the region.

Probably the best examples of stories told in wood are the *Krippen*, the manger scenes or crèches depicting the legends of Jesus' birth. You may think that the nativity scenes are only about Christmas (which we will consider in chapter 8); but these scenes are as basic to Tirol as snow and transcend organized religion, religious holidays and the depths of winter.

Baby cribs with realistic infants and statues of the holy family were displayed in churches in Innsbruck and Hall about 400 years ago (1608 and 1609). A hundred years later Emperor Joseph II issued a proclamation banishing the sometimes life-size scenes from the churches. Tiroleans defied this secularization and displayed the scenes in worldly settings such as their homes, public squares and museums. In 1825 when state authorities lifted the ban, a new fashion called the "Nazareth look" replaced the older and more formal baroque crèches (Grieshofer 1987). In this style Mary and Joseph looked like peasants, not burghers, and the inn was an *Alpenhutte* complete with wooden tools and farm animals. A lively international trade developed and soon Tiroleans were selling the manger scenes internationally. Devoted admirers started clubs to collect, honor and preserve the objects. Museums added them to their exhibits and scholars wrote books about them.

However, the phenomenon of Krippen is far older. Roman tombstones had carved models by the third century B.C. Nativity scenes in some Italian churches date to the seventh century and show the infant Jesus resting in a cave. No scholar of this art mentions one compelling reason for its origin and persistence. In these centuries past, infant mortality claimed as many as half of all newborns; babies within the first few years of life were fragile and only loosely connected to life. In many Catholic countries nativity scenes, in public and private settings, are a year-round focus for mourning dead babies and giving thanks for living ones.

Originally the characters of the nativity were children's toys carved on cold winter nights; they served as story aids for religious instruction and devotions. Mountain children know cattle, sheep and hay stalls intimately. An innkeeper with no room at the inn is a familiar feature of village life to kids. Many Krippen look like Tirolean farmsteads complete with appropriate costumes and tools. The Jesuits who promoted the tradition used the crèches to assist religious education, bridging the continuum from folk beliefs to formal religious instruction.

My favorite Krippen mimic the class structure of Tirol. The Holy Family are villagers with cows, sheep and donkeys. The three Wise Men ride fine-blooded horses or camels. They dress in the style of Habsburg or Italian nobles and carry exotic gifts that any wife with a newborn child might yearn for.

Many families keep their manger scene on display all year round and add to it when they can afford to. First a stall, a crib, a Mary, a Joseph, assorted animals, a few shepherds, then Wise Men and angels. Some of the sets are collector's items, signed and numbered in limited editions. Some villages are famous for the life-size scenes they mount annually. Needless to say, the custom of Krippen makes good business. Tourists flock to the souvenir shops, art shops and bus tours of villages during the holidays. The biblical accounts in Luke 2:1–20 and Matthew 2:2–23 have become two of the most widely depicted and profitable stories in the world.

## Thrice-Told Tales

In the beginning was the word. Verbal traditions are the first art form. Legends, folktales, proverbs, sayings, myths, epics, songs and stories in Tirol, as in all other human societies, are the wellspring of the life of the mind and spirit.

Many of the folktales Tiroleans tell endow places with special qualities. They give souls or spirits to various inanimate objects, geographical features, high places, caves, forests, rivers or lakes. Some say this habit of endowing places with reverence and giving souls or spirits to things in nature reveals Tirol's pre-Christian past. Pilgrimage sites feel like the intersection of worship with environment. Others with a more practical bent point out the obvious: how could a sentient person ignore the extraordinary beauty of Tirol.

Good tour guides or historians always mention places with an associated story. "That ruined castle belonged to Oswald von Wolkenstein." "Here is Rattenberg where St. Notaburga was born." "Look at St. Martinswand where Max the Knight almost died."

Even bizarre configurations of the natural world remind the viewer of the urgency of having proper values. Outside of Innsbruck is a curious rock formation called Frau Hütt. Many believe it resembles a woman holding a child. According to the story, Frau Hütt was queen of giants that lived in those days. One day her young son fell in the mud. His mother ordered his nursemaid to wipe off the mud with pieces of fine white bread. But using bread, a holy gift from God, for such profane purposes, incurred Heaven's wrath. An angry, fearsome storm swallowed up her palaces and left a barren hillside. Frau Hütt and her son were turned to stone. The moral of this story is willful waste makes woeful want; waste not, want not. Or, spare your bread for the poor and escape a dreadful fate.

Many stories end with a moral. This is a good way to instruct children in proper manners and values. Take this cautionary tale as an example. Once upon a time a farmer plowed a furrow a little further onto his neighbor's land year by year. By his death the farmer had appropriated a good strip of land not his own. Condemned as penance to drag a red-hot ploughshare up and down the stolen soil forever, he wailed:

> O woe! The plough like fire glows,
> And no one how to help me knows.

At last an honorable heir moved the boundary stone to its original place. No sooner had he done this than the specter cried:

> Released am I now, God be praised.
> And the bound-stone rightly placed.
>
> (from Busk's translations 1874:116.)

Another peasant was returning home from a merry evening in the inn with boon companions. He was very drunk and at the stroke of midnight fell down at a roadside resting spot. Suddenly a strange women in tattered clothing appeared carrying a broken plowshare and leading a train of tiny creatures, the souls of unbaptized children. The last lost soul in line kept tripping over its long shirt, skinning its little bare feet. The peasant felt compassion and removing his own garter bound it for a girdle around the infant. When the witch saw this good deed, she rewarded him. The nature of the reward varies but the moral is clear.

Folktales from Tirol regularly include some version of this classic story. A peddler with his pack spends the night in a ruined castle. Now the peddler is naturally a bold wrestler, a courageous sportsman who knows no fear. When the clock of a distant village church strikes midnight, twelve figures in ancient armor stalk in with skulls to use as balls in a bowling game. So the peddler who loves to bowl plays with them and wins. The apparitions shout with joy and thank him for releasing them from a terrible curse. Then ten more spirits enter, each with a key to a unique door. The peddler shrewdly matches keys to doors and these ten spirits leave rejoicing at their release. The third visitation is the Evil One who is extremely put out at the loss of his captives and demands the peddler's life in exchange. So the clever peddler bargains and stakes his freedom on another game. The peddler wins; the Arch-Impiety withdraws in ignominy. The released spirits load the peddler down with gold and jewels.

Tales of sepulchral bowling, games of chance with the Devil, and the sudden acquisition of wealth are common in this region. Sometimes dwarfs in a magical mountain or a pot at the end of the rainbow provide the riches. These stories end with the homesick man returning to his native valley with his fortune and settling down on a farm. Rachel Busk collected a large number of these stories both from texts of the period and from interviewing contemporaries. She appears miffed that spirits in stories like the one above were not redeemed by acts of faith or Christian virtue. She suspected smuggling was at the root of these folktales.

> I could not help asking my old friend if he did not think this very active clever peddlar might have been one of those who according to his own version had indulged in free-booting, and . . . had invented the tale to account for his accession of fortune, and the nature of his possessions (Busk 1874:97).

Tales of sudden riches overtaking people are also common. Once upon a time (as one story goes) a peasant found a heap of fine white wheat on the road. Shocked that God's precious gift should be trodden underfoot, he stopped his team, gathered up the grains and filled his pockets. When he arrived at his destination [usually cited as a church or a shrine], he was amazed to find his pockets filled with glittering coins! Thus is piety rewarded.

Stories about the antics of dwarf miners abound. The stories are used to explain happenings that are otherwise difficult to account for. The little men are often said to rescue country people in trouble. It is believed that they come out of hidden caves and magical openings in the mountains to place gigantic foundation stones, rescue children in trouble or leave gifts for the pure of heart. A peasant girl tending her cows comes across the little men. She treats the dwarfs with kindness and is rewarded with gold. Or she chances upon a mining shaft lined with gold. Later she cannot find the door. The mini-miners are also credited with mischief, tripping people on stony paths and then hiding behind a tree to laugh. Or they mix together the potatoes, carrots, grain and flour which housewives have painstakingly sorted and stored. Milkmaids find their efforts wasted when dwarfs overturn their pails. Who else can be blamed for the myriad traps and tricks of daily life?

These classic stories appear in several versions in a number of folktale collections (Busk 1871, 1874; Wolf 1958). The beauty of these stories is the number of interpretations and associations one can make from them while enjoying the telling and retelling. Many of the stories about pots of gold at the end of the rainbow or dwarfs who work at mining have found avid followings in cultures far from Tirol.

## Special Stories with a Twist of History

The following stories mix up history with mythology, pagan with Christian, spirit with flesh. They are deeply associated with places and times in Tirolean life which still convey deep meaning. I have included legends about the national poet, the patron saint and the favorite emperor of Tirol. There are a great many stories to choose from; these are among my favorites. In these tales fairies dance, pigs moan and angels intervene in human affairs; there are many layers of truth in the best of tales.

A set of very old legends, told both in German and Ladin, tells of a singer with a magical voice or instrument who appears at a propitious or promised time. This story starts at Seiser Alm in the Grödental.

> Oswald von Wolkenstein was yet a child when his mother learned of a prediction that her son would be a gifted singer if he learned to play the harp. However, fame and talent would

never bring him happiness and peace of mind. Only if he kept away from music could he enjoy the fulfillment and richness of a life in the beautiful valley. So his mother took him to the end of the Grödental, a gloomy place where witches lived in those days. The witches put a spell on his hands: he could handle a rake, an ax or a sword; but he was fated never to touch a musical instrument without shattering it. He was called "Iron-Hand."

As he grew to manhood he felt a passionate desire whenever he heard music. He asked strolling players to teach him but always he broke their harps or lyres or fiddles. So he became a rough fellow of the forests, a hunter, a farmer, a soldier.

One noonday in a remote mountain valley a hedge of flowers burst into song as Oswald approached. Looking closely he saw a fairy dressed in shining silver clothes and singing a song which took his breath away. He listened as long as he could but as the sunshine moved from the valley the flowers, the fairy and the song disappeared. On the next day and the next, however, they reappeared.

Now Oswald knew no peace. Again and again he climbed to listen to the fairy. After seven days she spoke to him. "A dreadful spell lies upon your hands. It can be broken and you can play and sing. But the breaking of the spell would bring such great sorrow that you and I will wish you had never learned to play."

But Oswald was in love with the fairy. He wanted to know everything about her. He wanted to marry her. To this she said, "You must never learn my name or I shall be obliged to leave you. You may only know that I come from the vanished Rosengarten" [a mountain range in the Dolomites which reveals many hues of rose, red and rosy pink in the sunlight]. Oswald went to see his mother who was chatelaine of Trostburg castle. She was extremely dismayed to hear that her son was engaged to a mountain spirit.

One evening Oswald was hunting in a wild and dark country when he spied the fires of the Cristannes, creatures who lived in the most inaccessible and desolate mountains and were said to know about many mysteries. He sneaked up to listen and heard a Cristanna say, "The old Wolkenstein lady had her son's hands bewitched. She thought she was clever. But now, he wants to marry Antermoya and the spell will be broken." Oswald had heard too much!

He tried to forget. But one day as he was overcome by the beauty of his beloved he spoke her name. Then the fairy spirit wept, she called his name as she spoke a final farewell and handed her harp to him. From the center of the flower hedge she sang once more that song which had first entranced him. As she sang

> the ground opened up and great waves swallowed the flowers, the sprite and the music.
>
> For three days Oswald wandered the dark lake in unspeakable grief. On the third day, he caressed the harp, all he had left of his beloved and, behold, a powerful and haunting lament poured out. The spell that bound his hands was broken. But he was doomed to leave the magnificent mountains and wander the earth forever. Although it is said no one has ever played the harp in such splendor, he could nowhere find joy or peace of mind.

This story is adapted from Karl Wolff's collection of legends about the Dolomites. The village at the upper end of the Grödental is called Wolkenstein; the lake is still dark, deep and silent. The ruins of Trostburg Castle grace the lower end of the valley and the Rosengarten is a perpetual marvel of color and texture. The story also reminds us of many other nameless Tirolean men forced forever from their homeland, whose true happiness was left in the high mountain valleys.

A more historic story of the poet continues the legend. Oswald von Wolkenstein, born approximately 1367, was a second son. So he left home early to seek both fortune and knightly romance. He won his spurs as a mercenary in Prussia, was shipwrecked in the Black Sea, served as ship's cook on boats going to Asia and narrowly escaped death in Turkey and several other places. On his return home he had come into his inheritance, the castles Castelruth and Hauenstein and the political intrigues of Frederick of the Empty Purse, Count of Tirol. Oswald took the side of the emperor and incurred Frederick's deadly wrath. The archduke imprisoned Oswald and threatened to behead him but finally granted him a pardon, partly on the strength of his poetry. Wonderful stories about Oswald's love life, of a certain Sabina with whom he fell madly in love, are gleaned from veiled references in his poetry. She must not have returned his affection because she married an elderly but prosperous businessman while her suitor was in the Holy Land. Upon her widowhood she sued Oswald for part of his estate and plotted to turn him over to Archduke Frederick, called "Empty-Pockets or Purse" [that is another story]. Oswald outlived her and two wives.

Wolkenstein wrote approximately 120 songs, half are erotic poetry, others celebrate the beauty of the seasons and the mountains of Tirol. I included one of his more ardent examples in the previous chapter. Others seem to center on his petty courtly intrigues. Regarded as a major medieval German poet, the last of the *Minnesingers*, a statue to him stands in Merano and ruins of castles associated with his name line the Grödental. Those who wish a sharp line between fact and fiction, between legend and history, will not find it in these stories. Those possessed by imagination and romance may. Take, for example, a traveler's reaction to the legends as he stumbles across von Wolkenstein's ruined home.

> I resolved to explore the lines of debris near the wild gorge, cutting deeply in between the noble pinnacles already noticed. The return path led me past the ruins of an old castle—the Castle of Hauenstein—that formerly occupied a huge block of dolomite which had fallen from the mountain. Within its walls once lived a man renowned in his day as knight and Minnesinger. Entering its broken towers was like putting on the spectacles of history, and peering into the remote past of the Middle Ages. I never thought to experience a personal interest in any of the Minnesingers, yet here I found myself upon ground trodden by one of them year after year, and looking down on the same dark green pine woods and smiling hamlets that formed his prospect from these castle walls (Gilbert and Churchill 1864:58).

## Saints Preserve Us!

The patron saint of Tirol is named Notaburga. There are many parts to the legend and various spellings of her name. The core of the story tells how this poor but pious maiden earned the lasting veneration of her people through humility and hard work. You may judge for yourself what kind of model she presents us.

At the age of seventeen Notaburga started work for the lord of the Castle of Rattenburg. The honored knight heard of her virtue and obedience and sent for her to work for him. Raised up by her parents in Christian duty, she sent them her wages. At the castle she earned a reputation for prudence and general uprightness.

But the plot thickened. The knight's son wedded a woman named Ottilia who took over the management of the castle and inflicted a thousand mortifications upon the gentle Notaburga. Notaburga is said to have regarded this as a test sent by God and refused to shirk her duties even in the face of mistreatment. The crucial test of fidelity, however, was Ottilia's refusal to allow Notaburga to help the poor. It had been Notaburga's custom to give leftover food to unfortunates. Ottilia demanded that her servant girl feed the scraps to the pigs instead. But Notaburga's heart bled to see the needy and so she denied herself food, eating only bread and water, and each evening when her work was done, she walked down the mountainside and distributed the food which miraculously multiplied so that all who came to beg were filled.

Ottilia grew very angry and banished the now-orphaned, servant maiden from the castle forever. It is said that angels guided her path that night and sprinkled it with flower seeds; even to this day the hillside where her holy feet supposedly trod is marked with rare blooms. She applied for work as a field laborer where once again her perseverance, determination and the blessings of God earned gratitude and recognition from all who met her.

But one Saturday evening an approaching storm threatened the peasant's hay and he ordered all hands to return to the fields. The normally dutiful Notaburga disobeyed him to follow the commandments of her religion. She refused to labor in the field on Sabbath eve. God manifested his pleasure and suspended her sickle in the air where it floats to this day. This impressed the peasant farmer and others who heard the story.

Meanwhile, the odious Ottilia was stricken with a mysterious malady. In one version of the story, Ottilia was consumed by terrible visions of hollow-faced hungry people and in despair she sent for Notaburga to make amends. Notaburga melted with compassion and sympathy as the reformed and forgiven Ottilia died in her arms. In another version of the story, Ottilia, overtaken with remorse, rushed into the enclosure of the pigs and there was devoured. It is said that on stormy nights pigs of this area remember their strange repast, and as they grunt over their evening meal, the wails of Ottilia resound through the valley.

The knight of the castle restored Notaburga to her former position and gave his daughters into her tender care. Moreover the loyal servant girl also felt duty-bound to work for the peasant farmer. But Notaburga's health suffered in these tribulations and she died. They say that two beautiful young oxen wandered the valley with her funeral bier until they came to the village of Eben, near the peasant farmer's estate. Canonized, her grave is still a pilgrimage site. Notaburga with floating sickle is the patron saint of serving girls and pious defiance. My students claim that modern interpretations of the story should emphasize anorexia, the psychology of martyrdom, child abuse and reasons to avoid eating bacon.

## Death Comes to the Emperor

On the Monday after Easter of 1490 Kaiser Max went on one of his usual hunting expeditions in the Innsbruck area he loved so much. But a frightening accident happened. In one common account the chamois he was following led him suddenly down the Martinswand, a sheer wall of rock near Zirl. There he was trapped. The iron spikes on his shoes had wrenched loose. To proceed was impossible; to retreat equally so. As a popular ballad of the period attests:

> His fame and daring, that of chamois and eagle,
> Avails him naught.
> For straight beneath sinks Martin's Wall,
> The steepest cliff in all the land.
>
> He gazes down that grave of clouds.
> He stares over that airy ocean.
> He glances round and his gaze recoils.
> Like thunder, voices roll below.
>
> The Kaiser Majesty is raised aloft,
> He stands not in homage
> But in sorrow on a throne of air.
> The great Maximillian is alone and small.
> [Adapted from Busk's translation 1874:317].

Meanwhile it was very hot on the cliff. No one knew his location. He could not be seen from the top and those at the bottom had not thought to look up. Exhausted by his Easter fast and the anxiety of his position, he feared to faint. In desperation he threw notes below. Finally the searchers realized his location but were powerless to assist. Hour by hour he clung. His last feeble note thanked the people of Tirol for their steadfastness. Prepared to die he repented of his pleasure-seeking ways and requested the last rites.

Trapped for fifty-two hours on the cliff, Max was delivered at last. In some traditions an angel answered his penitential prayers and lifted him from the rock. Others claim that a bold poacher, a reckless outlaw or a reclusive gamekeeper made that daring rescue.

Emperor Max ordered the miners of Schwaz to cut a better path and set up a crucifix to mark the spot. His adventure prompted one European traveler in 1707 to remark pointedly in his letters home:

> I looked up at it with interest; it is hard to believe that any man, however great his enthusiasm for hunting, would ever dare to slide down part of this precipice without shrinking back in terror at the chasm opening up below him. With all due respect for His Royal Highness, this adventure really does make him appear inordinately stupid before the eyes of the sensible world; if he had tried this again, he would have earned the title of Archfool rather than Archduke let alone Emperor (duBlainville in Myss 1973:19).

The incident prompted many stories, some with supernatural endings. Followers of Kaiser Max "could not bring themselves to believe that so signal a danger could have befallen their hero by mere accident. They must discover for it an origin to connect it with his political importance" (Busk 1874:317). Max the Knight was the flower of late medieval chivalry, the hope of the house of Habsburg. Perhaps, people said, conspirators misled him as to the direction the chamois had indeed taken. They wanted to believe that so great a peril was a consequence of his devotion to duty rather than the pursuit of pleasure. So this tale, like the others, is told and retold with many reinterpretations and embellishments.

## The Devil in Tirol

The villain in the legends, miracle plays and the nightmares of children is the Devil. Portrayed in wood or masked in frightening costumes The One with Many Names portrays what we most fear and dread. Those who grew up or spent considerable time in Tirol have met Lucifer in some form. His presence is still conspicuous in art and story. He is the person to blame.

Grohman was visiting a homestead in which the Devil suddenly took over the body (and presumably the soul) of a man. The frightened family summoned the priest to exorcise it. After a heroic struggle of several days' duration and an escape of the Devil into the body of a dog, a heroic priest managed to vanquish the Evil One. The grateful family distributed pictures of the heart of Jesus to prevent a recurrence.

> These holy amulets against a second visit of the Devil were nailed to the house-door, stable-door, and barn-door of every house in that village; and since then the population have enjoyed a blissful security from his Satanic Majesty. For the truth of this event in all its details, save those of course that occurred in the sickroom, I can vouch, as I was present and saw the proceedings myself. The exact date, June 23, 1873. Not so bad for the nineteenth century, my readers will exclaim (1878:104).

Convinced that similar beliefs do not exist in more civilized climes like Germany or in England, Grohman thinks of these customs as relics of the past to cope with a spirit world personified by the Devil.

> A Tyrolean peasant never mentions the word *Teufel*, to him any word is better than 'Devil.' We therefore find him called the Evil One, the Black One, the Bad Spirit, or the Damned One . . . Not once, but a hundred times, have I been struck by the uneasy glance around and behind him, when, in joke, I have mentioned the word 'devil' to a rustic inhabitant of some remote little village. The sign of the cross and hasty ejaculatory prayer are on such occasions supposed to be the only preservatives against an immediate appearance of the Evil One himself! (1878:105).

Attending church was an opportunity to dress up and escape the drudgery of fields and farm. People tithed heavily to build chapels

*A procession in the village of Nassereith which features masked dancers ringing bells.*

and churches. They supported priests as they allowed increasing clerical control over their lives, especially after the Counter-Reformation. But piety and the Catholic canon of beliefs came late in historic time and did not always fill the void. The mix of Catholicism and a folk piety from a pagan period far earlier than organized religion informed customs and beliefs. Daily life brought sudden noises in the night, unexplainable deaths, beggars, a plague of murrain for cows, a plague of fevers for people or a willing worker felled by frothing fits. So what we might call pagan survived.

Mary de Rachewiltz remembers from her childhood in the Pustertal that ghost stories circulated in response to unusual events. The dying sent out messages; souls of dead people lingered for weeks. Strange noises or unusual manifestations were evidence enough of the phenomenon. The frightening climax and the tangible proof of the Evil One came on the eve of St. Nikolas. The cast of characters is large; there is Death, the Devil, devilish imps,

Everyman, buffoons, an angel, a bishop, St. Nickolas, and *Bajazzers* who are a type of clown. They are noisy and dramatic.

> On the seventh of December about twenty masked young men race through every house they find open. In certain houses the neighbors gather and there they perform the Nigglas play, in the center of the Stube. A Bajazz somersaults into the room and with great jingling greets the assembly and tells them to clear away the spinning wheels, to get behind the table, and to remain close to the wall—for the Devil is coming to pay them a visit. Then a second jingling buffoon joins him and announces the order of the play. Sometimes a few more Bajazzer tumble into the room and they all somersault until the spectators are virtually nailed to the wall. Then the jingling suddenly stops and, in deep silence, enters an Angel, dressed in a long white tunic, with drawn red sword and huge cardboard wings. He speaks of the battle between good and evil and exhorts everyone to be *fromm*—pious. Then he calls Saint Nikolaus: "*Heiliger Nikolaus, komm herein.*" Enters the bishop, solemn with miter and crosier, followed by two small angels: one carries a basket filled with apples and nuts, the other a whip . . . He asks the children questions about God and the Commandments. If they reply correctly they get an apple or a few nuts, otherwise, the whip. The bishop then retires to a corner and . . . in bursts Lucifer, in black fur, a frightening mask, horns, hoofs and tail! Two small devils hold him back with a chain, but he threatens everyone with his pitchfork and seeks out Saint Nikolaus, spouting at him the most foul insults. When the little devils can no longer cope with the satanic fury, the angel intervenes with his sword: "*Vade retro*!" It is not easy for him to banish the devils from the room; sometimes there is a veritable fight and his cardboard wings are in danger. Then enters Death: tall, thin, wrapped in white linen with a skull on top of his head and scythe. Stooping he dogs, clockwise, the steps of a little Everyman who begs to be spared (1975:88).

In the village of Afers, residents also told ghost stories to each other. We think these terrifying tales have the effect of keeping youngsters in line, defining the unknown or the unthinkable in a world where death was ordinary. It is possible that ghost stories help people cope with traumas, grief and fear without naming them directly. Scaring children with stories and ceremonies is common in cultures throughout the world. Peter Petschauer's story of St. Nicholas parallels Mary de Rachewiltz's. She has poetic memories; his sound frightening.

> Until thirty years ago, St. Nicholas and the devil still came to the various houses of the village on the evening of December 6th; the bishop rewarded the good children and the devil

> punished the bad . . . The devil was alive and well indeed (Petschauer 1990:721).

> Never will I forget one terrible December evening on which Sankt Nikolaus and the most realistic devil imaginable for a seven-year old, came to the Egarter Hof [his adopted family's farmstead]; little did I know then that the devil was the mother of our neighbor, a woman I had never liked to begin with. The hairy monster chased me under the living room table, chains clanking, hoofs stomping, appearing it wanted to drag me off in its carrying basket . . . The devil, illustrated so realistically in tales and near-events and portrayed so hauntingly in numerous images, remained a constant in my life until long after I emigrated to the United States (Petschauer 1985:138).

Peter Petschauer has analyzed these spooky stories from the viewpoints of a frightened child and a grownup historian. He suggests they are a type of projection, a transferral of feelings people have which are too difficult to talk about openly. So we have a substitute form. The stories, the plays, the rituals of Christmas, the masks of ancient ceremonies are, on one level, about the devil; but they go far beyond.

> Since many of them deal with the devil, the shadow-side of God, they must be connected with God. I suspect that they were a way of expressing hostility toward the all-controlling being no one understood. Life, weather, fertility, fortune, health, death, all of them under his jurisdiction; and the dead weight of his power spawned hostility. But how could a peasant express this discomfort without being implicated, even condemned? In part it was done in the subversive hostility that permeated all too many relationships in the community, and to an extent it was released by adults in the transferral of hostilities from God to an almost physical presence of the devil. Although in the end it made little difference to children whether their mistreatment originated with projection or transferral: adult behavior toward them originated in transferral as they tried to cope not with the devil in themselves, but to find a being other than God against whom to vent their inexplicable powerlessness (Petschauer 1985:138).

According to these witnesses, the masks of the Devil, carved in wood and painted in potent colors, are frozen fears or trapped angers. The grimaces portray the face of a spirit world where the Evil One rules. Perhaps pilgrimages, piety, hard work, dancing or tokens blessed with holy water will keep the death and disaster he brings at bay. Perhaps reason and science or social change and economic development will vanquish the need for him forever.

# 6

# We Sold the Cows

## Tourism, Change and Economic Development

*Over the Rhine did three fellows cross,*
*There they took rooms from an inn's lady-boss.*
—A classic couplet

In the depths of winter on the top of Berg Isel where Andreas Hofer and his Tirolean troops fought the army of Napoleon, Austrian heroes once again sought victory. A revolution, a post-war boom built on snow and travelers, had swept Tirol. It was raining tourists and the Olympic Committee had selected Innsbruck as the site for the 1964 Winter Olympics. The new ski jump hurled competitors down the precipitous slope and up over the curling edge. They seemed to hang, suspended in the air, above the cathedral spires of Wilton and its adjoining cemetery.

This is the crystalline moment and propitious place to look at the culture area of Tirol in the last half of the twentieth century. Although a traveler care system functioned from the Roman occupation, tourism has dominated Tirol in our times. The burgeoning hospitality industry supplanted dairy farming many times over and rescued the depressed agrarian economy. It prompted the construction of excellent road networks linking remote valleys, and halted, even reversed, the flow of emigration from them.

The last half of the nineteenth century and the first half of this century were seriously depressed times for Tiroleans. The agricultural-pastoral economy did not produce enough surplus to sell; it was good but not bountiful subsistence. Young people had to migrate, permanently or seasonally; many had no hopes for ever marrying and raising a family. There were simply not enough jobs or other sources of income apart from the farms. The cottage

industries could not compete with the goods flowing from the factories outside Tirol. The higher the farms and villages, the harder hit they were. This mountain blight led to an exodus of young men and women. As the hillsides stagnated, the valleys bloomed.

Today Austria, Italy and Switzerland top all the countries in the world for hosting tourists. At the intersection of the three countries is the culture area of Tirol. As Austrian tourist agencies point out, the number of beds for travelers quadrupled since the 1950s and now there is one bed for visitors per every six Austrians. Tirol is only 15 percent of Austria's land area and only 8 percent of its population, but it is its premier tourist destination. The major share of Austria's tourist income comes from Tirol. The Italian Tirol is a small fraction of Italy's land area and population but tourist spending there has made it part of northern Italy's prosperity too. In fact, the reasons for Austria's success in the hospitality industry are duplicated in Italy.

Today Tirolean tourism is regarded as one of the most successful examples in the modern world and Tirol one of the best places to study such development. This chapter gives you a basis to look at some inevitable questions tourists and students have. What is the natural history of tourism in the region? What are the advantages and disadvantages? How is Tirolean tourism connected to environment, ethnicity, history and world affairs? Will it destroy or forever alter village life?

To illuminate some of these questions, I have included two samples of economic development and tourism, one from Bundesland Tirol (Obergurgl) and one from Südtirol (Grödental). Understanding how the industry has evolved leads us into chapter 8 and the experiences of travelers themselves in Tirol.

## The Grand Tour

Aristocratic parents in the seventeenth and eighteenth centuries often sent their offspring to spend a year or two abroad. The usual route was London to Paris, a slow progress through France and Italy capped by months in Rome and a return through Germany and Holland with intermediate stops. They studied languages, riding, fencing, dancing, good manners and dabbled in art and literature. They met their peers in other countries. This travel experience was thought to broaden their perspectives; afterward they returned home and settled down. Many of these elite travelers wrote diaries or journals of their trips.

Thus the term "tourism" dates to the custom of a grand tour for European elites, the first tourists in the modern sense. These young people also painted, drew or wrote about what they saw, so there is a considerable body of art, poetry and music inspired by Tirol, as well as the rest of Europe, in these privileged periods. Today, student groups do study-tours in somewhat the same spirit.

But "aping one's betters" or following "the lifestyles of the rich and famous" has a long history too. The grand tour was slow and leisurely, a form of postgraduate training for developing the manners and social networks the ruling classes needed. Soon, however, the aristocracy had to run to keep ahead of the emerging bourgeoisie. They had to move fast to stay ahead of the masses who went on vacation. As the elites tried to escape their common imitators, they invented new reasons to travel and new places to be seen. They created a boom in bathing spas and health resorts. Then seaside resorts surged in popularity, hence the association of the Mediterranean coast with royalty and wealth. Culture, pleasure and health were one set of motives. Another attraction for the privileged classes became the pursuit of nature and of physical challenges, hence winter sports, hiking and outdoor activities in the mountains.

The masses were in hot pursuit. Famous businesses like Thomas Cook, Lloyds, Hapag, Michelin, Baedeker and Alpenverein democratized travel for ordinary people. Travelers came from a broad cross section of social classes. Ordinary workers began to expect holidays away from work, trips to someplace different even on a limited budget. With time and entrepreneurship, this touring became a packaged holiday vacation. As Ludwig Steub notes in 1875:

> Now that the railway has been opened, the whole world rushes to see the Pustertal, but the inhabitants of this valley are cunning enough not only to withstand the onslaught bravely but also to make it both pleasant and profitable. It does not often happen that a region is lifted with such speed and with such energy from darkest obscurity into the Central European spotlight, as has been the case with the long, green and magnificent Pustertal. But its natural beauty and its large, white radiant villages are complemented by another circumstance. Good people love good hostelries, and in this respect the people of the Pustertal, although they have long kept themselves to themselves, can claim the greatest distinction. It is true that the large three or four hundred year old guest houses in Tyrol often disconcert one by their naively impracticable architecture, but a broadminded person can find a certain charm and can easily accommodate himself to the inconveniences which they have brought about. The rooms are always furnished with good beds and can often even be called luxurious. The innkeeper's wife rules over the house with consideration and kindness with the help of her friendly daughters and shapely serving-girls. The whole typifies that old, upright, German, Tyrolean spirit which one may hope that God will long see fit to preserve (Myss 1973:99).

## Solid Ground: The Disciplines of Village Life

But how could Tirol have economic development in the face of the whole house practices? Traditionally, peasants fear change and modernization. What the estate manager calls security, the economist calls stagnation. Their rural worldview frames everyday life in religious terms: Tirol is a holy land and the farmer is its faithful servant. These are not assumptions we normally associate with business mentalities or planned social change.

The structures of village life, however, that promoted survival in the past were already in place and proved adaptive for a new era. For reasons we have discussed, villages have a remarkable social homogeneity. Villagers throughout Tirol practice a form of government based on a council; the village is the primary unit. The Gemeinde or village commune elected men who were residents as well as citizens—that means born or married into the village. Commoners or *Burghers* as citizen-residents managed their own local political life. The council, the *Gemeinderat*, deals with problems of administration: taxes, public works, local projects to benefit the village, (irrigation, transportation, building permits) and sets holidays and school schedules.

The village council supervises a number of tasks that affect everyone but cannot be handled from a farmstead. This includes right-of-ways, access roads, stray animals and public works projects. The council hires an auctioneer, someone to keep vital statistics and land records and people to care for village property such as machines, tools or forests. Someone must fill out the forms to satisfy the government. In the past, council members had to certify products like milk, inspect the animals for disease and manage the village's breeding bull. Burghers are expected to train for the militia, be available for emergencies and supply food, wine or Schnaps on occasion. Some of these bureaucratic requirements date to the twelfth century.

Buttressing and cross-cutting the governance structures are a number of voluntary associations which have serious economic, social and political power. These include political parties (which do not operate as they do in America), the volunteer fire companies (in villages made of wood fire is a constant danger, especially in the winter), the rifle company (Schützenkompanie), the village band (*Musikkapelle*), the age and gender graded groups in the parish church and the Alpine organizations for sports, rescue, guide certification and other duties of mountain life.

The political boundaries rather naturally follow the peak lines. A valley is a natural work unit, a parish, a school district or a place to court and find a mate. When issues arise which cross communal boundaries, councils representing the entire valley have authority. This is the same model as the villages have, only larger. This is why valleys have reputations, characters or corporate personalities. It is also why they are equalitarian and independent.

Two points are important. This system is very old and, unlike many other European and world experiences in self-governance, is extremely effective. This system is largely responsible for the extraordinary success of the modern development in tourism.

## Hit the Slopes

Tiroleans should probably have ceremonies for honoring snow. Winter sports are now their bread and butter. One geographer notes that if all of the Austrian Tirol ski lifts were strung together, you could be lifted from New Orleans to Nashville. If all the ski trails of the Austrian Tirol were put end to end, you could ski from New Orleans to Chicago! (Frantz 1983:21).

Seventy percent of Austria is mountainous. Unlike any other Alpine country, Austria has cities and urban amenities deep inside the mountain ranges. In Innsbruck and Bregenz, young Austrians can ski on their lunch hour and Viennese enthusiasts are never more than an hour from the powder. This means that skiing is not just for the rich and privileged as it is in France and Italy. Kids from poor families have as much access as anyone; in fact, the valleys and farmsteads are the source of Austria's greatest athletes.

Austrians promote their champions through highly organized ski associations which grew out of the men's sports organizations in the villages. These traditions date back hundreds of years. Today, scouts locate, encourage and pay for the equipment of promising young people. Government subsidies go to the most promising. For example, the ski associations helped Egon Zimmermann, victor of the men's Olympic grand slalom (downhill race over a zigzag course marked by poles).

Zimmermann's parents were peasant farmers horrified by their son's passion for skiing. But the years after World War II had transformed their village of Lech into a winter sports resort. The three sons helped their father build an addition onto their 300-year-old farmhouse to host tourists. The Zimmermann home became the Haus Bergfrieden with carved wooden balconies and green shutters. Prosperity brought changes; as the family said, "We sold the cows." Young Egon started to ski.

> The ski lift was only a minute away from school and the house and every day at noon during the long winter we used to gulp down a sandwich and head for the lift. Up and down we went until it was time to return to class. In those days skiing was pure fun and no discipline. It was an escape from everything. I remember how we raced madly over the slopes, jumping over rocks and trunks, slaloming between trees. Once late in the

*A ski region of the Alps.*

> afternoon when the snow was hard, I took a bump badly and instead of landing below, I found myself hanging from the branches of a tree, like a parachutist who had made a bad landing! . . .

Egon's mother was hostile to the idea of skiing. She was particularly upset when all of her sons had broken legs or other ski injuries at the same time. Eventually his parents' peasant practicality prevailed and they required him to learn what they considered a real trade. He reasoned that a resort village could always use a gourmet cook; so at the age of fifteen he went to Paris for training. When he returned home at eighteen he was barely able to ski. Despite his young successes he had never had lessons. As he said,

> My childhood coincided with postwar Austria's period of poverty. Our trousers looked like bloomers, our skis, which were shaped like a ski jump, were not secondhand, but fourth or fifth hand. Some of our racers at the 1948 Olympics had ski poles of unequal length. For myself, I never took a skiing lesson. I just watched the champions and tried to imitate them (*Sports Illustrated* 20. 1964).

Egon's village of Lech, just outside the modern boundaries of Tirol, is near the world-famous ski school of St. Anton. Here, in the 1920s just inside the borders of Tirol, a skier named Hannes Schneider developed the forms and standards for the modern sport of skiing. His Arlberg method remained the standard until the 1950s when Stefan Kruckenhauser of Tirol evolved refinements at St. Christoph. These developments coincided with the infusion of capital and world attention after World War II. At least 20 million dollars of Marshall Plan funds for rehabilitating Austria after World War II went into the country's ski resorts.

In the 1950s, the feats of Austrian skiers and the glamorous new infrastructure of sport drew thousands to Austria. To learn and practice the Austrian method of skiing, they reserved rooms at Tirolean inns in places like St. Anton, Zürs or Kitzbühel. Once there they bought Austrian sweaters, boots, after-ski clothes and shopped avidly in what was then a delight for those who traded dollars for schillings. Austrian-based ski firms like Kneissl, Kästle and Fischer boomed both at home and in the export trades. The career of ski instructor opened up to thousands of young men on rural estates and in small villages. Other careers, including prestigious competitions, resembled the life Tirolean men had always led. It is no wonder Austrians were ecstatic when the Winter Olympics Committee chose Innsbruck in 1964 and again in 1976.

## Local Village Makes Good

What happens when the ageless struggles of farmers against scarcity meet what we call progress and modernization? Max Preglau's case study of the Austrian village of Obergurgl is a good example of the evolution of winter sports and tourism throughout Tirol. One of the highest villages anywhere in the Alps, Obergurgl "is a poor little community, with eight months of winter and no month free of snow. It lies at an altitude of nearly 6,300 feet. Here one has to appeal to the hospitality of the village priest for such simple accommodation as one can expect in so isolated a spot" (Grohman 1908:101). There were certainly no inns or tourist facilities.

Young men and women could not stay in Obergurgl to raise families. Those who remained grew poorer and poorer relative to the rest of their country. Ever-longer workdays and intelligent decision making did not alter their limited resources. They could not compete with or even join a society in which agriculture was backed by machinery, capital and international markets. In fact, like much of rural America at the same time, outdoor toilets were the norm.

But Obergurgl, at the foot of glaciers, had scenery, accessibility and cultural attractions. A few pioneers started to add an infrastructure: lifts, paths, roads, rooms. Then travel writers and sports enthusiasts discovered Obergurgl in 1964, the Year of the Olympics.

> Obergurgl has more to recommend it than isolation or even the name, which alone is good enough. Located just 55 miles from Innsbruck by a road that usually requires chains or four-wheel drive, Obergurgl is tucked into the highest extremity of the Öst Valley and at 6,266 feet takes pride in calling itself the highest *Kirchdorf* (village with a church) in all Europe. Obergurgl not only has a church, it has 22 glaciers surrounding it, and it is so cold that hardly anyone bothers to venture up there until the first of March. After that and into the summer, the skiing is marvelous, the six lifts never crowded, the powder snow is deep and untracked, and the prices remain low. Obergurgl is, in fact, like the rest of Austria: it gets better the farther you go (Roy Terrell in *Sports Illustrated* 20. 1964).

Today 85 percent of the households live in part or whole by income from tourists. At the time of his research, Max Preglau calculated that for every bed a resident of Obergurgl slept in, there were eight beds for tourists to sleep in (Preglau 1983:49). The number of houses and families have almost tripled. The exodus has stopped; indeed, the village provides work for hundreds of commuters during peak season. Farming is now the smallest occupational category. Family and work are separate spheres and work is for wages.

As the villagers changed their patterns of earning a living, their values began to shift. The ethic of "making do and pitching in" became the twentieth century belief in the endless possibilities of growth, dynamism and expansion. Preglau was concerned with the question of how modernization had altered older values. So he used the criteria of social prestige. How are fellow villagers judged? He compared Obergurgl to Vent.

> In contrast to Vent, a nearby village that has yet hardly been touched by tourism, social prestige in Obergurgl is founded on commitment to village affairs, performance and economic success, property and wealth—which are all modern prestige criteria. In Vent, on the other hand, traditional criteria like popularity, morals, and diligence are the most important prestige criteria (Preglau 1983:50).

In a modernized village, people judge each other and confer prominence or position on the basis of material successes. In the village of Vent, traditional values of character and hard work remain.

Modernization brought a succession of problems. The village of Obergurgl and the Tirolean hospitality industry are habitually in a dangerous cycle we might call "the tourist trap." Under the impetus of economic opportunity the population grows. The demand for tourist services swells beyond predictions. But local resources are finite. There is only so much land available, safe from avalanches or not already in use. If the quality of the environment declines from the impact of tourists, then demand may fall. If too many hotels are built or too many families are dependent on only one source of income, then few, if any, in the village will fare well. This cycle has happened before; mining is a good example.

Tourism devours the landscape. It requires extensive building: airports, roads, railways, lifts, hotels, guest homes and holiday centers; it pollutes the air, water and social environment. Its very growth kills the thing of most value, an experience of untouched nature.

As the elders of Obergurgl realized the implications of a downward spiral, they grew alarmed. Their very success carried the seeds of destruction. So they made plans to reduce growth and prevent fragmentation of open land areas. Better management techniques led to quality rather than quantity: some hotels reduced the number of beds. They started to send summer tourists on circular tours and separate day visitors from long term guests. Trained local guides shepherd the visitors and emphasize natural history and conservation. A sewerage plant reduces water pollution; quiet zones reduce noise pollution. Traffic in the village is restricted; places and plants are openly and consciously protected. Lifts and cable railways are excluded from the avalanche-prone west side of the valley. Ground-holding vegetation anchors the ski-runs. Fragile wild flowers are safe.

Farmers who were estate managers now manage the landscape. They receive premiums for the agricultural and pastoral work which stabilize and preserve the terrain. Ironically, these farmers earn too little to support themselves by producing or selling milk and cheese; they earn far more by using cows to manage and save a delicate ecology.

But Obergurgl was an early development of tourism and matured through the trap before other areas. The villagers developed a successful compromise between ecology and economy. This explains why the busses park below or the lifts cost so much or why the guides require their charges to stay on the path and enforce customs that may feel restrictive.

Obergurgl is an example of the good and bad. Yes, it survived because of tourism; people and houses increased in number. But at a price. The village cooperation that fueled the first initiatives has given way to class conflict. Some want to take the money and run; others want controlled development through time. Tradition is no longer the ground of being, the breath of life, the warm peasant smock. It is a commodity to be marketed and sold. A choral group, an old village custom, reflects the agony of choice. What happens if they organize it now: is it relaxation and group solidarity or an attraction for tourists? Obergurgl's success creates elite seclusion; they must control the influx of day trippers and overnight stays by charging high prices. They must cooperate with each other in new ways and coordinate all the services to avoid bottlenecks. Above all, they must protect the environmental pot of gold at the end of the rainbow.

## Wooden Soldiers and Gilded Angels

The Grödental, home of Oswald von Wolkenstein, the largest meadow in Europe and some extraordinary Dolomitic panoramas, is also home to an extensive manufacture and marketing of nostalgic and religious objects. This curious trade has a long history and is a wonderful example of on-site success and the development of peasant cottage industries into modern businesses. It also fits seamlessly into the late twentieth century tourist boom.

In the past the Grödental of Südtirol was isolated; most of the population spoke Ladin as their first language. People raised cattle, sheep and goats, carved toys and puppets or wove fabric unique to the region, loden cloth and Gröden shag. Because few travelers came to this remote valley, the local people had to take their handiwork to the rest of the world. Hundreds of Grödener men loaded their wooden backpacks in the spring. Through the summer they sold or bartered their wares for goods unavailable back home. Other family members cut the hay, tended the herds in the high pastures, gardened, cut firewood and prepared for winter. Reunited for the cold winter they spun thread, wove or tatted lace.

Despite its geographic isolation, residents had ties with European artisans from the fourteenth century on. A number of famous woodworkers from the Grödental received formal training in sculpture studios in Italy and Germany. Churches and museums in Brixen, Innsbruck, Vienna and the valley itself have the works of the masters from 1650 to 1750. Many of these carvings are gilded or painted so vividly that one forgets the artistry which underlies them. One of the artists during this period hired other carvers to copy from his master models. The early practice of reproducing master copies is one of the foundations of contemporary economic life.

By 1788, however, woodcarvers had depleted the primary forest zone. Their voracious industry stripped the best trees. Alarmed, the imperial government in Vienna issued a decree reducing the number of woodcarvers in the valley from 300 to 150. The protest was loud and immediate. The government revoked the order only when the citizens agreed to adopt strict conservation methods and a form of sustained yield timbering. The woodlands' preservation measure allowed a contemporary livelihood and represented one of the first government mandates in Europe to protect the environment. Although the ancestors of valley families were angry and rebellious about the conservation decrees, their descendants are grateful and proud.

The restrictions effectively concentrated and enhanced the local industry. Within twenty years two-thirds of the population earned a living from woodcarving. By 1864 Grödeners had expanded to establish over a hundred branch companies. In 1856 a road leading into the valley was constructed. In 1867 the railway over the Brenner Pass connected that road with the rest of Europe. The new European railway network made it possible to supply customers without the traveling peddlers. The products of the valley entered the outside world in ever more enterprising ways. Toys, crosses and nativity figurines reached the bazaars of Paris. Wooden soldiers were gifts for rich children and collector's items in the capitals of North America. Roman Catholic missions all over the world treasured their carved wooden crucifixes from Grödental. You will

*A Tirolean woodcarver in the village of Thaur.*

also note for purposes of chapter 8 that kitsch found a foothold in the region at the same time.

The adventuresome English tourist, Amelia Edwards, was roaming the Dolomites on muleback during the peak of the nineteenth century prosperity. Her vivid observations show the economic and personal power of nostalgia. She was astonished to ride into St. Ulrich and find pieces of her childhood.

> Now the capital of Toyland comes in sight—an extensive, substantial-looking hamlet scattered far and wide along the slopes. The houses are real German Tyrolean homesteads, with broad eaves and bright green shutters, and front gardens full of flowers. There are two churches. And there are at least half a dozen inns, all of which look clean and promising. The whole place, in short, has a bright, prosperous, commercial air about it. . . . We had never even heard of St. Ulrich till a few weeks ago, and now we find that we have, so to say, been on intimate terms with the place from earliest infancy (1873:338).

In her nursery back home she had played with toys made in the valley. There were animals on little wheeled platforms; jointed dolls of all sizes, from babies half an inch in length to mothers of families two feet high, whose complexions always rubbed off with washing; monkeys that toppled over a stick; painted rocking horses; and wooden soldiers with unnaturally thin waists and triangular noses. "All these—all the cheap, familiar, absurd treasures of your earliest childhood and mine—they all came, Reader, from St. Ulrich! And they are coming from St. Ulrich to this day—they will keep coming, when you and I are forgotten" (1873:339).

Entranced to find that the magic of her childhood had such an origin, Edwards and her companion, Miss L., arranged tours of the workrooms and warehouses in the village. They questioned the owners who politely showed them through the village businesses. They recorded statistics from the last census of the valley. The business of craftsmanship and distribution of work fascinated them.

In her journals, Edwards struggled with the differences between artist and artisan and the disturbing effects of mass production. She learned quickly that labor is divided by gender and by task. "Some of these carvers and painters are artists, in the genuine sense of the word; others are mere machines who make toys, as other human machines make match-boxes and matches" (Edwards 1873:341). The census showed 3493 souls living in Grödental; 2000 of them were woodcarvers and many others were painters and gilders. Carvers had regular work. Their products were simply stored to wait for the big orders, sometimes 30,000 pieces of a doll at one time. Only when the big orders had to be filled did painters and gilders work to fill the order. Carvers, particularly the individual artists, had better pay and higher status.

Here she describes an artist carving a statue of Christ ordered for a cathedral altar. He faced a solid block of wood fixed upon a spit between two upright posts.

> It was yet all in the rough, half tree trunk, half Deity, with a strange, pathetic beauty already dawning out of the undeveloped features. It is a sight to see Herr Senoner at work. He has no model. His block is not even pointed, as it would be if he cut in marble. He has nothing to guide him, save his consummate knowledge; but dashes at his work in a wonderful way, scooping out the wood in long flakes at every rapid stroke, and sending the fragments flying in every direction. But then Alois Senoner is an artist. It takes him ten days to cut a figure of three-quarters life-size, and fifteen to execute one as large as life (Edwards 1873:344).

On another day they toured workshops and were amazed to find a type of mass production in which each person turned out the same item day after day. Women did the routine carving and the painting on toys or small pieces.

> In one house we found an old, old woman at work, Magdalena Paldauf by name. She carved cats, dogs, wolves, sheep, goats, and elephants. She has made these six animals her whole life long, and has no idea of how to cut anything else. She makes them in two sizes; and she turns out, as nearly as possible, a thousand of them each year. She has no model or drawing of any kind to work by; but goes on steadily, unerringly, using gouges of different sizes, and shaping out her cats, dogs, wolves, sheep, goats and elephants with an ease and an amount of truth to nature that would be clever if it were not so utterly mechanical. Magdalena Paldauf learned from her mother how to carve these six animals, and her mother had learned, in like manner, from the grandmother. Magdalena has now taught the art to her own grand-daughter; and so it will go on being transmitted for generations (Edwards 1873:343).

There were other specialists like the Paldauf family; one household only painted red horses with white points, another grey horses with black points and a third did the saddles and head gear. One family carved only the skulls and crossbones for the base of crucifixes. "Not a cheerful branch of the profession," comments Edwards.

As the products of assembly line productivity piled up, they were stored. One warehouse they visited held more than thirty large storerooms, twelve of which were filled with dolls for export. A room contained only horses, another only the wagon to be pulled and yet another had only unpainted doll's heads. An export warehouse stored collectors' items like elaborately carved horses and saints gilded in gold. The specialty of that warehouse was:

> Christs of all sizes and for all purposes . . . Some of these are perfect as works of art, faultlessly modelled, and in many

> instances only too well painted. One life-size recumbent Figure for a Pietà was rendered with an elaborate truth, not to life, but death, that was positively startling. I should be afraid to say how many rooms full of smaller Christs we passed through, in going over the upper storeys of Herr Purger's enormous house. They were there, at all events, by hundreds of thousands, of all sizes, of all prices, of all degrees of finish. In the attics we saw bins after bins of crowns of thorns only (Edwards 1873:342).

But houses bursting with toy soldiers and wooden crosses were really an omen of doom, yet another boom-bust cycle for a Tirolean valley. With prosperity came burgeoning population growth, more mouths to feed and lower family incomes. The increased productivity at the expense of quality drove prices down for everyone. Carvers began to use softer, uncured woods and shoddy paints and varnishes. The carvings cracked and peeled. The woodcarvers' reputation for quality went downhill. By the last decades of the nineteenth century the methods of mass production described here had effectively ruined the market.

## New Industries From Old

In 1914, a young man named Anton Riffeser from an old Grödentaler family joined the Tirolean Guard. Sent to the Russian front to fight for imperial Austria, he and a group of other soldiers from the valley were captured and held in Siberia.

In harsh and uncomfortable captivity, Anton and his friends managed to survive. They carved figurines using Russian peasants as models while they laid plans for the future. Anton Riffeser decided to start a company which would use traditional methods coupled with innovative ideas. Hoping to bring the valley out of its economic doldrums, he planned to bring together the best woodcarvers, train apprentices, establish designs and develop select external markets. It is said that he learned to speak English because it is the international language of business. Finally released, the men of the valley returned by freighter from China to Venice. They learned that under the Treaty of St. Germain they had become new citizens of Italy, one of the nations they had fought against!

The repatriated Anton Riffeser decided to name his business, ANRI, after the first two initials of each of his names. The new company would avoid the mistakes of the past. Woodcutters harvested only alpine maple trees, handpicked and at least eighty years old; trees were cut only during winter when the sap runs. Workers trimmed the logs, drained the sap and stored the timber outside to cure for two to three years before a final drying in factory kilns.

Instead of using cottage industries, Riffeser centralized the operation for better supervision. He consolidated the operations under one roof instead of jobbing out the carving to homestead workers for the winter months. The great stacks of drying wood, the workshops and offices in Tirolean style edifices and the well-equipped, well-lighted factory floors are today a different kind of work space from the mountain estates of their past. Workers, artisans and master craftsmen have specialized tasks. A few artisans precontour the figures so that carvers have a prepared block. Artists from around the world prepare the prototypes, drawings and the master model from which the line of products will be drawn. The company hires and trains not only carvers but joiners, assemblers, lacquerers, decorators, and painters.

However, the company does not train more people in these crafts than can be employed. The crafts still tend to be gender and age specific; young women do the painstaking gilding and painting. This is probably a time-honored practice: young women in Tirol have traditionally worked for wages for a few years before marriage.

In the art series each piece is signed, numbered and registered. ANRI practices what they think of as careful quality control; they place limits on their production lines and retire the sculpture when the edition reaches its designated number. In this way, a number of lines or pieces become collectors' items. ANRI has agents and distributors in the United States and in European and other countries. There are serious collectors' clubs and networks internationally.

The king of the mountain dwarfs bequeathed the knowledge of woodcarving to humans. Modern companies are supposed to follow his tenets of patience, diligence and skill. What do they produce from this ancient legacy? The products of the Grödental today fall largely into categories we might call religious, nostalgia or kitsch.

First and foremost are the cast of characters for the Krippen, the Christmas tableaus. Virgins, babies, sheep, shepherds and the fanciful Wise Men or Magi come in graded heights depending on the size of the crèche buyers already own or have always wanted. One hundred angels in various stages of completion are lined up neatly next to one hundred Josephs. Some heavenly creatures hang from the manger roofs; other kneel in worshipful poses. It takes two people to push carts with shelf upon shelf of suspiciously Tirolean-looking cows without which no scene is complete. Entire rooms contain nothing but sized and stacked stables believed to resemble those of Jesus' birth.

Other product lines center on themes Tirol made household images. There are carousel horses and endless versions of St. Nikolas. The most successful lines feature happy, highly idealized children evoking a warm rural past. Needless to say, these figurines are extremely popular. The youths are dressed in clothes reminiscent of the nineteenth century and are engaged in a variety of naive and charming ventures. One boy stands beside a loyal dog or bravely carries a candle to bed. A young lass gathers eggs or goes caroling with a lantern in hand. The boys wear suspenders or knee pants and girls wear bows and aprons. The woven baskets they carry, their smiling faces, the very slant of their hats evoke filial piety, a lost age of innocence and a romanticized image of childhoods that never were.

Few argue that this is high art. It is true that the figures tug at buyers' sentimentality, nostalgia and the collector's urge. Many will argue this is an excellent example of technologies of scale and the astute utilization of a unique environment. The ANRI woodcarving cooperative and production company illustrates both the perseverance of the craft, the appeal that such objects have and, most of all, the possibilities for local and creative economic development. It continues a very long tradition, supports a number of people in the valley and buttresses a tourist trade which has exploded in the last half of this century.

In the past Grödeners were mostly farmers, mountain guides, fabric makers, musicians or woodcarvers. Today they basically do these same things, certainly in the same place; but now they are linked to the world tourist and consumer societies. Today young people who want to advance speak German, Italian, Ladin and English, often with French or Spanish thrown in. They may be engaged in producing specialized parts of the fabled Italian fashion industry—winter resort clothes and ski paraphernalia. The remote valley of romantic adventures is now a sophisticated winter sports resort, a tourist destination only a few hours from Munich.

I wish I could say that I discovered this fascinating valley and its indigenous industry on muleback like Amelia Edwards. But the truth is, my parents made me go. They have lovingly collected Nativity characters and the carved figures of horses for years. Still unable to pronounce the name of the valley, they picked it as the only place in Europe they wanted to see. Their pressures mounted and finally on a trip to Austria, we drove into the valley. Delighted, I returned again and again. Now I take students there on field trips. Sometimes parents are right. I am also grateful to the staff of ANRI who guided us through their history, factories and workrooms. More than a century later, I have had the opportunity to witness and experience the events Amelia recounted in her journals.

## Participatory Hospitality or Why Does Tirolean Tourism Work?

Many observers believe that the development of tourist industries in Tirol is the most, or one of the most, successful stories of its kind in the world (Herbin 1986). The Austrian sector began first and is best known. But Italian Tirol is fast catching up. What makes them so successful? Can this model be imitated or exported?

Tiroleans start with built-in advantages like the mountains. They work double seasons, summer and winter. They combine sports, outdoor recreation, music, food, nostalgia, history and hospitality. Tirolean tourism is based in old population centers, self-governing villages whose roots go back for six hundred years or more. No new or sudden "villages" spring up. Fake tourist environments, manufactured or homogenized, are absent.

Tirolean tourism is a "family host system." The hospitality is famous. When we stay in a village we are usually staying in someone's home. Tourists are like bread from heaven. There is as much mutual regard between host and guests as the practice of tourism ever allows. Hosts and hostesses play multiple roles and have multiple activities. They do not carry suitcases or change sheets for a multinational corporation whose offices and profits are in New York or Tokyo and whose administrators have not a clue about what makes Tirolean life tick. This local initiative has been called "practically perfect auto-development" (Herbin 1986).

The pace of development has been slow and progressive; it has been entirely in the control of the commune or Gemeinde. The laws of Austria define residency and citizenship and exclude elites or foreigners. This means that outsiders cannot take over a village for building vacation chalets or second homes for themselves. External promoters have no land base for schemes outside of communal control. Hotel chains cannot build yet another cookie-cutter complex that bears no relationship to historical patterns and local inhabitants.

The infrastructure of tourism has not overwhelmed either the people or the landscape. The population (in large measure) favors tourism and believes it is their economic future. They intend it to last a very long time. Some refer to the mining boom and busts of the past and want to avoid those kinds of destructive cycles. Tourism is diffused through the countryside rather than concentrated; this is a conscious decision to protect both the environment and the patrimony or cultural inheritance. Appropriate land use maintains the mountains. There is a symbiosis between tourism, agriculture and artisanship. Nature is protected; history is preserved.

For the hosts, tourism offers survival and preservation. Tiroleans can remain in the ancestral valleys and still earn their daily bread. Buildings and customs remain alive. The disparity between poor mountain villages and well-to-do towns has vanished. Even high mountain regions are having a net population growth, a reversal of the decline and depression. There are varieties of both permanent and seasonal jobs. For centuries the limited carrying capacity of the land meant that kids could not remain in ancestral villages. Now they can.

Local families run their own small businesses. The money stays in the community; the community, in some measure, controls its tourist policy. This means that people can afford gracious homes because renting out rooms pays the costs and profits. Of all the tourist accommodations in Austrian Tirol, more than a third are rooms to rent in private homes. This means that families from abroad with low incomes and children can still have holidays. In fact, you will see advertisements: "Spend your vacation on the farm." Ironically, rooms to let makes the life of a farmer affordable.

The hospitality industry is successful because it has extended and reinforced jobs that already existed in traditional village life. The peasant farmer and his wife are now innkeepers in the same modernized estate that supported their ancestors. They must hire cooks, waitresses, chambermaids and baby sitters. Labor needs still contract and expand as in the past. Women, be they the owner's wife, the owner or the hired help, wait on customers. There is less need now than in the past for herdsmen, goatherds, shepherds, alpine dairymen and milkmaids. Analogous jobs like mountain guide, ski instructor, lift operator and others are open. Any one person probably has income from several sources.

In 1977 the federal province of Tirol granted subsidies to farmers for maintaining mountain pastures; Italian Tirol did the same in 1981. The managers get a fixed amount of money for each animal grazing on alpine pastures. The intent of this land and resource management policy is to prevent a tourism that disrupts or destroys the agricultural base. There is a long tradition of such measures from Habsburg times. The subsidies have proved beneficial because they increase the number of cattle on high pastures and decrease the amount of fodder the farmer must collect or buy. Valuable land at the lower elevations is freed for growing food for family tables rather than cows' stomachs. The greater variety of foods has improved local menus and the profits from exports.

Tourism is a big, big business. It generates foreign exchange, provides jobs, employment, investment and complements other productive activities. With the infrastructure in place many new developments can come alive. This often translates into systematic financing for public and private investments and reinvestments in the hospitality industry. The offices of tourism are exceptionally strong and efficient and represent Tirol well in international markets.

Recreation, escape, adventure, sports and cultural encounters of a different kind are increasingly symbols of social mobility, a significant "lifestyle activity" for many people in the world. The tourist masses still chase the traveling elites.

## Does Tourism Kill Tourism?

First and foremost, the carrying capacity of the land has expanded dramatically, but in the long run it is finite. What happens when that boundary is reached? Can tourism as economic growth go on indefinitely? Can the rest of us learn anything? Is there a worm in the mountain apple?

Some areas are at the edge. For example, despite laws and good management, parts of the environment are already damaged or destroyed. This is particularly evident at the edges of urban areas where factories, dumps and development disorder proliferate. In small villages designed for hay wagons, modern trucks and busses pass close enough to score the sides of houses and churches. Salt used on winter roads and in glacial skiing areas of Tirol to improve the quality of the snow washes down the fragile slopes and penetrates the ecosystem.

Some people bear the brunt without the benefits. For example, truck, tourist bus and transit traffic through the narrow neck of the Inn Valley between Munich and the Brenner Pass is shaking villages and towns to pieces, filling the night air with noise and fumes and leaving destruction and pollution without compensation. Local regulations now restrict part of this heavy international traffic.

Although local control has many advantages, it also means that there is no central zoning or development plan for the province. For example, some of the ski services, buildings and equipment are not logically placed given the terrain. Their operation and location reflect communal designs. Villages may have more beds than guests; they have high debts and a low return on their investments.

Tourism is a monolith. It takes over. In subtle ways community life starts to slant. Young people learn different sets of values and rewards. Urban life beckons and agriculture is no longer valued. Apprenticeships for life on the land are no longer filled. This is not just a loss of Tirolean culture but a danger to the industry itself. The participation in village life is the main draw; what happens if village integration is forever compromised? Ancestral organizations in agriculture, music, sports, men's activities and other folk customs hold village life together and attract tourists. These are not just quaint holdovers of the past. The loss of such charms will hurt. Like the environment, they must be protected. But can they be meaningful or even observed systematically outside the cultural context?

As a monolith, tourism overshadows all other kinds of economic initiatives such as hydroelectric power, technical industries and mining. Ultimately there are questions of class. Will elites who can afford high prices be privileged? Should there be restrictions on mass tourism? In Austria a real estate law generally slowed or impeded outsiders from purchasing land. This did not stop Austrians from buying land and building second homes. So despite regulations both Tirols are having a building boom. More than 50 percent of the houses have been built since 1960. So fast is this construction that the previous boundaries of the villages are largely lost and a kind of "rural sprawl" grows more obvious.

Remember that the actual population density is very high. The mountains may look vast, but only about 7 percent is suitable for settlement. The population seems small, but add tourists to the locals and the culture area of Tirol has the highest density of people sharing space in Europe. That's very crowded.

Meanwhile, people do not agree about the goals of development. There are inevitable creative tensions, even conflicts, as new possibilities and adjustments unfold. Many argue for an unlimited growth. As Klaus Frantz notes in his study of Tirolean tourism, "One of their arguments is that this is the only way to remain competitive. On the other hand, more and more voices are raised against such groups. The latter demand a moderation or even a standstill of this growth. Emphasis, they say, should be on quality rather than on quantity" (1983:22).

An example of this is the pressure building in recent years to allow summer skiing on glaciers. The environment watchers worry about the degradation of delicate ecological zones when tourists surge in. The economic optimists look gleefully at the money such development brings into the community.

Ski lifts and trails take up about the same space as the road system, but they lie above the timber line. The summer pastures at this altitude are very fragile. It takes about two hundred years for specialized vegetation at this height to regenerate if disturbed. The governments of the Alpine countries have developed assorted laws and policies for plantings and soil protection. In Austria, cable car companies are required to restore and protect the original ecological system as much as possible. That is why the lifts seem so expensive to Americans; about 20 percent of the ticket is mandated environmental protection. Cable car companies must pay farmers to pasture their cows under the lift.

Mass tourism is often called a "landscape guzzler" and a destroyer of traditional cultures. On the other hand, one must ask the question: What alternatives are there?

> As the native population constantly rubs shoulders with the way of life of the urban dweller on holiday, the traditional values change too. Can you really blame a young mountain-farmer's son from a winter ski resort if he leaves the hard work in the stable and the fields which gives him no free time for himself and becomes a ski instructor, a job full of prestige? Or is it not understandable if mountain farmers no longer milk the few cows they have in the stable but, as "tourist farmers" or even hotel proprietors, make an easier and more profitable living? (Frantz 1983:9).

But subtle effects of capitalism replace the rural, whole house patterns. Class structures harden. Now there is a gulf between rich and poor, self-employed and salaried. Families are separated, split by work and competition. Detractors worry that tourism creates a colonial atmosphere. There is a danger that much of the money will leave the community, even the country, creating dependency rather than internal autonomy. Some areas are rich and some remain poor; the same is true for individuals. Tiroleans generally favor tourism but "on the negative side, tourism introduced competition into a previously cooperative folk society and seasonally disrupted the family life of those involved in the business" (Jordan 1988:390).

Tourist industries absorb a lot of unskilled labor; the hours are long and the pay is low. This is particularly true for women whose work is largely invisible. Someone is changing all those tourist beds and washing those sheets every day. In fact, some people are beginning to believe that life was better in the past.

Demand is unpredictable. Like estate managers, tourist officials are at the mercy of everything from off-seasons and bad weather to wars and shifts in international currencies. Fuel crises, the Chernobyl explosion in Russia, terrorists in the Arab world; anything may affect demand. So there are cycles of overbuilding and underusing or underbuilding and overcrowding.

Today folk piety and economic interests are linked. The tourist industry supports and encourages a shallow nostalgia, a promise of timelessness or permanence it cannot deliver. Advertizing qualities like "ancient," "authentic" or "original" imply that these customs did not grow and change. Festivals and ceremonies are forms of cultural capital, folkloric assets and good business. Tiroleans have very strong feelings about the exploitation of their culture.

> Tourist managers throughout the world have long been adept at exploiting customs, folk music, dancing and local costumes for their own purpose. Folklore events, as well as those of a social or sporting nature, are part of an attractive tourist resort. "Genuinely authentic customs" are a draw in the same way as reasonable accommodation; folk dancing and folk music groups have become the normal accessories on promotional tours and at tourist fairs. The "folklore evenings" which have become the stock-in-trade of Alpine resorts constitute a particularly crass form of such utilization (Caramelle 1987:160).

Nor is this a new phenomenon in Tirol. For several hundred years Tirolean groups in "national costume" with songs and dances altered to popular tastes have toured the world. Tiroleans in the past marketed their culture and traditions. They have been both praised and criticized for this. In 1828, the German writer Heinrich Heine wrote about his anger at the exploitation of Tirolean customs.

> When I visited the glittering concert rooms of London's fashionable world last Summer and saw these Tyrolean singers, clothed in their local costume, taking the stage, singing those songs which are yodeled in the Tyrolean Alps in such a sincere and unaffected way and which sound so incomparably beautiful even to a North German heart—everything was so distorted that I felt thoroughly embittered; the complaisant sniggering on genteel lips stung me like snakes; I seemed to be seeing the chastity of the German word being most coarsely insulted and the sweetest mysteries of German inner life being profaned in front of foreign rabble. I found it impossible to join in the clapping at this disgraceful bartering away of virgin purity, and a gentleman from Switzerland who left the room with the same feelings as myself remarked quite rightly, "We Swiss give away a lot for money too, our best cheese and our best blood, but we can hardly bear to hear the Alpine Horn being blown anywhere away from home, let alone blow it ourselves for money (translated in Myss 1973:44).

This dialogue goes on continuously. Tiroleans and tourists alike fear that the richness of village culture will be reduced to museum pieces. Tourism may turn customs into trivial clichés or only a commodity to be bought and sold. Multistoried hotel architecture imitates the style of one or two storied farm houses of the past. All tourist resorts follow a standardized and pretentious form sociologist Max Preglau calls "yodel architecture." He concludes that "the loss of cultural identity is at stake" (1983:57).

For the majority of tourists, the privileges of elite travelers will always be elusive. As travel is democratized, the lines for lifts, the traffic jams, souvenir shops, and the control of agencies and packages prevent the experiences with nature or indigenous culture that motivated our travel.

Tourists are temperamental. We need (or think we need) a "culture of travel," the same experiences, encounters and comforts we are accustomed to at home. We take our habits with us wherever we go. Soon all tourists and the places we see tend to look alike. Tourism promotes the easy cliché, the sound bite of travel or pigeonholes for superficial experiences. We take our images of "the other" with us. Klaus Frantz compares today's Alpine area with the American west.

> There are also certain similarities concerning the images that the urban society outside had or still has of the way of life and customs of the native population in the American West or in today's Alpine area. These images, which were certainly partly impressed on us by such people as "Buffalo Bill" Cody or by some advertising strategies of the recreational industry in "Wild West Shows" or commercialized tradition shown in Tyrolean evenings have several things in common: they convey a picture of the local people which is only mildly true to reality (1983:7).

Then there is the "Porcupine Principle," the psychological burden on hosts of always being on display. Just as the prickly animals use their quills to protect themselves and keep intruders at a distance, so do those in the hospitality industry. One more question, one more demand, one more seemingly small miscommunication: at this point tourists become tormentors. The hosts bristle, they snap back, they retreat.

Most traveling is over-determined. The hidden hand of the tourism industry hinders rather than helps authentic contact with hosts. Guests and hosts meet each other only on calculated and superficial levels. In fact, this produces a third culture: the tourist culture, the intersection of the indigenous culture with the tourists' own culture to produce yet a third subculture. We will take up this culture of travelers in chapter 8 as we continue the anthropology of tourism.

The transit trade in Tirol is ancient; economic development comes and goes. It is my theory that much of what we embrace or lament as change is just another phase of cultural, physical and economic adaptation to the special environment and history that is Tirol. For a thousand years travelers have slept in high valleys with the smell of newly mown hay and the sounds of cows entering their shuttered windows. For thousands of years Tiroleans shifted cattle, wood and other loads up and down the mountainsides as a way of earning their daily bread. Now they carry tourists and skiers over those same paths to survive.

packages prevent the experience [illegible]
[illegible] known [illegible] travel.

Tourists are [illegible]. We [illegible] we need [illegible] [illegible] the same experience [illegible] at home. [illegible] [illegible] the second [illegible] of travel [illegible] [illegible] American [illegible].

There are [illegible] [illegible] [illegible] [illegible] [illegible] [illegible] [illegible]

[illegible] [illegible] [illegible] [illegible] [illegible] [illegible] [illegible]

Most traveling [illegible] [illegible] [illegible] [illegible] [illegible] [illegible] [illegible] [illegible] [illegible] [illegible] [illegible] [illegible] [illegible]

The [illegible] [illegible] economic development [illegible] [illegible] [illegible] [illegible] [illegible] [illegible] [illegible] [illegible] [illegible] [illegible] [illegible] [illegible] [illegible] [illegible] [illegible] [illegible] same paths [illegible].

7

# The Unredeemed and the Disinherited

## Ethnic and Familial Conflicts; Social and Economic Resolutions

> *German and Ladin speakers were on their death march. Had the fascist policy of denationalization continued, only remnants of our German-speaking agricultural population could now be found and only in remote mountain areas . . . According to the Italian census of 1951 more than twenty percent of our men over forty had not yet gotten married. This fact alone reveals serious problems in the economic and social lives of German and Ladin speakers in the South Tirol.*
>
> —Silvius Magnago
> Südtirolean People's Party, 1974

The sounds of bullets and bombs, not alpenhorns, resonated through Südtirol from the late 1950s to the late 1960s. Tirolean extremists called for a general uprising against Italy, and nationalists bombed power stations, railways and industrial plants. At the bar of the *Gasthof* in Sarentino, a farmer with a blue apron over his Tirolean jacket told a journalist from *Newsweek* in 1961, "We will turn the mountains into another Cyprus until we get free of these Italians."

The Italian government sent troops. Officials resurrected old portraits of *Il Duce* (Mussolini), the dead Fascist leader, and tacked them on public buildings in old town squares as a reminder and a threat. Italian courts sentenced captured terrorists as well as moderate political leaders to long jail terms.

A perilous ethnic conflict was building. There were three languages and two nationalities. There are two nations: Austria,

# The Conflict
## A Chronology

**1919** Peace Treaty of St. Germain. Südtirol and Trentino ceded to Italy.

**1920** Mussolini takes power in Italy. Mass settlement of ethnic Italians in Südtirol. Denationalization of the Austrian population.

**1939** Hitler-Mussolini Pact and the "Option." Südtiroleans are forced to choose between declaring themselves Italians or emigrating to Germany.

**1946** The Paris Agreement signed: Italy and Austria agree to special measures to preserve the ethnic identity of German speakers in Südtirol.

**1948** First Statute of Autonomy. Provinces of Bozen and Trentino are merged into one region, giving it a majority of ethnic Italians. Important measures to protect Tiroleans are delayed.

**1957** Südtirolean Peoples Party (SVP) under Silvius Magnago demands separation from Trentino Province.

**1960** Austrian Foreign Minister, Bruno Kreisky, takes Südtirol's case to the United Nations which urges all parties to resolve their differences and implement the Paris Agreement.

**1961** Bombing attacks in Südtirol attributed to terrorists.

**1964** Geneva Conference of the United Nations; a joint committee of experts addresses the problem.

**1969** Both Italy and Austria approve the Paket and a calendar of operations for implementation.

**1972** Second Statute of Autonomy passed. Proposed implementation, two years; actual implementation, twenty years.

**1992** All sides agree that the Paket and the last steps of the calendar of operations have been successfully implemented. The United Nations declares an end to the dispute in Südtirol.

inheritor of Teutonic nationalism, one of the major legacies of German-speaking peoples to the world, and Italy, a nation-state still struggling for its national consciousness. Factions in Germany, Austria and Italy yearned for the reunification of Tirol, for some form of self-determination and independence. As violence persisted, the United Nations and other world agencies entered the quarrel. They feared that ethnic warfare and strife would ignite and spread to other parts of Europe.

By the mid-1970s all parties had compromised. They defused their bombs and their bitterness. Today Südtirol is often cited as a model for the resolution of ethnic tensions. The people of Südtirol achieved a new blend of regional harmony in a world characterized by irreconcilable ethnicity and revivals of ethnic politics in places such as Yugoslavia and the former Soviet Union.

What happened? How were these threatening tensions resolved? What do we learn about the social and economic life of Tirol as a result of this process? Can we generalize or export this ethnic success story?

## Kinfolk and Kittens

The Südtiroleans had reason to worry through most of this century. The Treaty of St. Germain outlined the moral obligations of the Italian government to respect the cultural and linguistic heritage of its German-speaking minority. But the treaty had no teeth. Italians dragged their feet; they generated no policies to insure recognition or autonomy for Südtirol. Indeed, Mussolini's public policies threatened the survival of the population base and fundamental cultural traditions in Italian Tirol. As he said in a newspaper article in 1926:

> The Italian language is now obligatory throughout the country. All postal and railway officials are Italian; Italian families are everywhere being settled in—we mean to send one thousand families of former soldiers in the land as colonists. In Merano we have settled four hundred families and a further hundred are occupied in the neighborhood.

Again in 1946 the Italian government promised to give autonomy to the region. Instead they fused the Bolzano region with the heavily Italian Trent Province into an Italian-dominated Trentino "autonomous region." In fact, Italians believed that they themselves had suffered from centuries of ethnic discrimination under Habsburg rule when Trentino was administratively part of Austrian-held Tirol. They merely wanted to redress a prior grievance (Levy 1988).

Italy looked like a mother cat trying in frustration to corral all her little kittens into eating, sleeping and being washed while the kittens wanted to run and play. The Italian government was reluctant to allow its regions to assert any kind of autonomy or historic individuality. Bureaucrats enacted policies which centralized control in Rome and favored a single definition of Italian citizenship. These preoccupations resulted in a patronage system which discriminated against German speakers.

> Political clientelism in Italy is distinguished by the granting of special favors: jobs in the state bureaucracy and financial retributions. The exclusion of German speakers in South Tyrol from bureaucratic jobs has been a long-standing and well-documented grievance (Katzenstein 1976:281).

In addition, the provincial government in Bolzano had little or no resources to initiate or assist in economic development. This was in sharp contrast to Austrian Tirol where business had begun to boom.

Political scientists use the word *irredentist* or *unredeemed* to refer to a region under the political jurisdiction of one nation but which is related to another through culture, language, history or other claims of ethnicity. Italians popularized the term in the late 1800s as they worked to unite the regions of Italy and establish a national identity. They wanted to "redeem" regions which they felt history had linked to the new nation-state of Italy. People who felt strongly enough about the acquisition of a region to vote on that basis are called "irredentists."

The focus of German nationalism historically was a commitment or longing to gather up German-speaking groups throughout Europe. This cultural or emotional imperialism formed what we call "kin-states." A kin-state is a government which has policies devoted to the defense or liberation of one's own ethnic group rendered a minority in another state. By this definition Germany and Austria were kin-states. The region in question is like a lost relative and the political issue is reuniting severed families. Regardless of the reasoning behind their claims, both nations wanted the same piece of territory.

Südtirol, as one of Europe's border ethnic groups, was the political prize for two competing nationalist ideologies: the pan-Germanic ingathering of lost cultural parts and the Italian Risorgimento, the liberation and unification of its geographic regions. Both sides believed their claims should have priority. Excellent discussions of the roots and the resolutions of this conflict are found in Alcock (1970), Jacob (1981) and Katzenstein (1976).

Austria, of course, had long-standing historic interests. But with the end of the Habsburg dynasty, two world wars and the defeat of Nazism, Austria developed a new national awareness. This centered on a doctrine of neutrality and to some extent, an acceptance of its marginal status within Europe. For some Austrians the grief of losing Südtirol served as a symbol and as a point of mobilization. A lobbying organization in the Austrian province of Tirol named after Berg Isel, the site of Andreas Hofer's battles, worked for self-determination and independence and brought together Tiroleans from both sides of the border.

At the time of the terrorism, the population of Südtirol was two-thirds German-speaking and about one-third Italian-speaking. Ladins, while socially active and symbolically important, were only about 3 percent of the population. Ladins are the third minority, perhaps the only true one in Tirol. The Ladins identify with and are culturally indistinguishable from the agricultural Germanic folk. However, Italians believe that Ladin is a Romance language, therefore a dialect of Italian. Hence, for Italian irredentist policies Ladins were yet another group to be redeemed for the motherland.

In the election years from 1958 to 1968, the voting public was polarized; ethnic conflict became electoral conflict. A new and potent political party grew. In German-speaking areas a political party is less a set of opinions and allegiances than a whole way of life. So people voted the language they learned in their cradles. And the South Tirolean People's Party, *Südtiroler Volkspartei* or SVP for short, spoke German.

## The Package Deal

Eventually cooler heads in Italy and Austria brought the issue to the United Nations. The two sides began to meet and each gave a little. Beginning in 1969, policy makers hammered out an accord called the *Paket*. Italians acknowledged the presence of German-speakers within their borders, offered public education in the language and legitimated a form of autonomy for the region. In their hearts most Austrians, especially in Bundesland Tirol, may have favored self-determination for Südtirol. But political realism led political leaders, especially in Vienna, to demand and then accept assurances from Italy that autonomy would be respected (Katzenstein 1976:278). By the mid-1970s the two national parliaments had approved and implemented the Paket and its 137 detailed measures of ethnic and cultural survival. The agreement, known as the Statutes of Autonomy, effectively ended the conflict.

> In the Tyrol, the conflict was managed precisely because the primary antagonist of the German cultural group, the Italian state, was made a partner in the preservation of a German cultural and linguistic reality it had long sought to assimilate (Jacob 1981:277).

The real meaning of the Autonomy Statutes is to ensure that essential cultural, social and economic affairs are conducted in proportion to the ethnic populations of the province, not in proportion to the entire country of Italy.

Italians recognized Südtirol as a special region within Trentino-Alto Adige and gave the new region authority in areas such as agriculture, industry, commerce, natural resources, transportation and employment. Other provisions granted them political representation in Rome as well as more control concentrated in the provincial capital of Bolzano. The success of the Paket was in direct proportion to the formal guarantees given to German and Ladin speakers about participating in the Italian brand of client-centered politics. Under the new regime, jobs and contracts in administrative positions, courts and other public offices were filled in numerical proportion to the population of the three ethnic groups. A central Raiffeisen Bank to assist local businesses was formed.

Silvius Magnago, one of the leaders of the People's Party during this period went from a separatist ideology to pragmatic accommodation. He believed that the successful resolution was a first for modern Europe. For his statesmanship he was nominated for the Nobel Peace Prize. In speeches he articulated Tiroleans' awareness of victory, compromise and hope. He feared only that Tirol would lose its next generation to assimilation or migration.

> It is easier to cheer up against every physical danger, against outward oppression, against economic and social discrimination, than against spiritual infiltration. And infiltration is today the greatest danger for us (1974:163).

In a small but symbolic provision, the Castle of Tirol was restored to the now autonomous region for whom it held historic pride of place. The most important symbol was the return of the name. Today the highway signs say Südtirol.

To be sure, not all Italians were happy about this. However, increasingly, a moderate line from the People's Party allayed their fears.

> The continued political vitality of the SVP, having forsaken the legitimacy of any further claims of self-determination, would henceforth be played out within the baroque fabric of domestic, Italian politics (Jacobs 1981:271).

*A high mountain chapel at Brenner.*

The People's Party was transformed from ideological isolation and sympathy with the instigators of terrorist acts to ethnic independence and political success. As an anti-Communist and conservative Catholic group, it has become a successful player in the wider fields of Italian politics.

## A Multicultural Marriage Is Consummated

How and why did the Paket work? What has happened since? What can we conclude about the success of ethnic regionalism in Europe?

First, language is the bedrock for ethnic differences. Anthropologists generally say that our perceptions, values, worldview and concepts of self result from and are rooted in our primary language. At the very least, language was the defining earmark of ethnicity for Südtirol; people who spoke German also ate dark bread, raised cows, lived on hillsides, farmed for a living, told each other stories with Teutonic themes, passed down their lands intact to one heir, sent surplus children off to work and had hierarchical family structures.

One third of the population lived in the valleys, ate white bread, identified with urban living and industrial jobs, divided inheritance as well as family responsibilities among all their children. They voted Italian and spoke Italian. Governments cannot legislate away language and its associated meanings for groups such as these. The honest course rested in recognition and acceptance.

Second, religion counts. In the political culture of Südtirol, religion and ethnicity reinforced each other. As in Poland, the Catholic church was a potent force for community and solidarity. The clergy and ecclesiastical organizations were strongly anti-communist and pro-Tirolean. But they were also catholic, in the global sense of that word, and tied to the leadership in Rome. Whenever possible, church leaders cornered the influence of television, radio and schools to work for ethnic accommodation and a solution to the conflicts. They played such a central moral and social role that the People's Party became a political extension of the church. During the explosive stages of the conflict Catholic churches held mass meetings. These were better attended than the political meetings.

Third, numbers add up. Population statistics are always a contested arena in ethnic battles. No side trusts the figures collected by the other. In fact, the two sides did not agree about the actual geographic borders of the region. The Italians called the region, Trentino-Alto Adige, a definition which fits the old borders of Tirol but includes the established Italian population of Trentino. Claims of German-speaking Tiroleans were correspondingly diluted. Although German speakers were a minority within Italy, they were the majority within the region if narrowly defined. But only Italians collected the statistics and defined the region.

Although the two sides argued about statistics, all of the figures showed beyond doubt that Italians had moved into the valleys in ever larger numbers since 1910. Südtirol was progressively Italianized through the Second World War, especially in the urban areas of the valley floors. Towns and cities became bicultural islands in the midst of a monolithic and monolingual countryside. When the Italian government halted assistance and incentives, Italians no longer moved into the region. Their occupation of the countryside was a failure.

Everything but urban areas in the valleys was in the hands of German speakers whose birthrates remained high. The plan for resettlement that Hitler and Mussolini devised for German speakers from 1939 to 1945 had not radically altered the population base in South Tirol. Most of those who left for good were young urbanites, people who did not own land. More than ever, the undiluted countryside held German-speaking farmers.

So major elements of culture were assured: language, land, schools, jobs, church, history. Although the Schützenkompanie do not carry arms when they march in Italian territory and Italian priests are still not happily welcomed in upland villages, the union is judged a success. There are hundreds of daily adjustments, but an expanding economy makes them possible. The growth of industries and a revived transit trade strengthened the countryside and buttressed rural life. The politics of ethnicity heated up and cooled down in Tirol.

In June of 1992, Austria and Italy formally resolved their dispute about autonomy for Südtirol before the United Nations. Representatives of the two nations jointly approached the Secretary General of the U.N. and declared their complete satisfaction with the implementation of the Paket. With this act they formally ended the dispute. A chronology of the conflict is included in this chapter.

## Everyday Adjustments

When Italian authorities forbade German instruction in the schools, communities organized what were called "catacomb schools," recalling the persecution of early Christians at the hands of other Roman authorities. These clandestine schools are fondly remembered as an adventure in defiance. They clearly kept not only the German language alive but Tirolean spirits up. During the years of anger and terrorism, it was obvious that any detente with the Italians would have to include educational reform and concessions to acknowledge linguistic realities.

First and foremost in the package deal was the status given to German and Ladin languages. "The economic and social protection is really of no use, if we cannot also ensure the linguistic and cultural survival of these groups'' (Magnago 1974:157). German and Italian are created equal in the Statutes. In practice this means public signs and documents are in both languages and private documents can be in either. Public agencies such as courts and bureaucracies must speak and write in the customary local language. This puts a pressure on Tiroleans to learn both German and Italian. Ladin speakers must also know other languages since outsiders do not learn Ladin. But their language is supported through radio, television and newspapers.

Schools are key places where the cultural life of minorities is writ large. Under the conditions of the Statutes, Südtirol has two separate school systems. Each linguistic group has its own kindergartens and schools. Instruction in nursery, elementary and secondary schools is in the pupils' mother tongue by teachers whose first language is the same as the students. Hence, there are German-speaking schools, Italian-speaking schools and Ladin-speaking schools. Gradually the second language is added to the curriculum.

In practice, parents have some flexibility depending on their feelings and local conditions. Sometimes there are not enough Italian speakers in one area to fill or staff a school. One hears about Italian families who send their children to German schools because the standards are firmer. A second language gives anyone who wants to live fully in Südtirol an added advantage. Because the Statutes give German speakers preference in hiring for administrative jobs, they are less subject to unemployment than are Italian youth. Moreover, German speakers largely control the tourist industry and the infrastructure of local government. Italians sometimes feel like a disadvantaged minority and find that learning German advances them. Ironically, the official minority of German speakers are the majority in the province.

## Ethnicity In Private

What about getting along in ways the government does not rule on? Do people from different ethnic groups marry each other? If they do, what happens to ethnic boundaries? How do couples adjust?

Once again the best study of the consequences of identity and ethnicity comes from Cole's and Wolf's comparison of St. Felix, a German-speaking village, and Tret, its neighboring Romance-speaking village. Their rather poignant and pointed conclusion is that marriage is a serious business and gender is a more basic category than ethnicity. The advantages of being male or female weigh more heavily than group identity does.

> Quite apart from considerations of ethnic or political identity, marriages of St. Felix men with Romance-speaking women are discouraged by the demands placed upon such marriages by the structures of family and authority in the Tyrolese village. It would be difficult for a Romance-speaking girl, accustomed to more distributive decision-making and to active social relations with collaterals and affines, to adapt herself to the patterns of unitary and exclusive authority characteristic of St. Felix . . . Tret men, in turn welcome marriages with German-speaking women. They value the fact that their wives have been raised in more rigid households: they say that they work harder than Nones women, and add jokingly that because their hands are larger, they can fashion more sizable dumplings (Cole and Wolf 1974:259).

In short, if you are a German-speaking woman in Tirol, you might consider marrying an Italian man. You will work less hard and for shorter hours in a looser family system accustomed to getting together often with others both inside and outside your village. You will be allowed to participate in discussions about the problems that families need to solve. Your husband will appreciate you and will not take for granted all your good training and domestic skills. When you go out to work, you may be able to control your wages and spend money on fashions, consumer goods and travel.

On the other hand, if you are an Italian-speaking woman, you should think hard before marrying a German-speaking man, particularly one who is or will be an estate manager. He needs a hard-working partner who already has serious management skills appropriate for an agricultural kingdom. As we learned in chapters 3 and 4, the needs of the farmstead come first, dawn to dusk, seven days a week. Traditional ways of parceling power and affection will seem very strict, rigid or constraining. Social ties and contacts outside the family may not involve the easy reciprocity or casual exchanges you are used to.

When the distinction between brown bread and white bread is not the working symbol of the way people make a living, when they can buy bread instead of baking it themselves, then ethnic distinctions fade. In other words, when economics favor individual work and the workplaces are separate, then ethnicity is on the same level as class, religion and age as a consideration for marriage. Nonetheless, marriages across ethnic lines involve a minority of couples. Most people marry within a social sphere or circle of those with backgrounds similar to their own.

As anthropologists regularly observe, the way people get married is constantly changing. (The fact that we universally and regularly marry each other never changes!) Generally what we have seen in peasant societies is a move away from "tradition" into more individualistic styles where couples negotiate, even innovate, around gender roles instead of following the inscribed paths. They may live together before marriage, get a divorce if it doesn't work out, or believe that domestic work should be shared equally. Couples who live in cities are channeled into very different social lives than those from family farms.

What appears to be happening is that more and more Südtiroleans are learning to live in a multilingual, multicultural world; for some of them as for some of us this means new forms of marriage and other adjustments.

## Ethnicity in Public

Whether people speak Italian or German matters at all levels of village life. Villages in Tirol typically elect estate managers and other heads of households to the communal council. These men regulate concerns between households, manage corporate lands or responsibilities and enforce government rules—from whatever country is in charge. Within each Tirolean village are associations for young men. Their marching bands, fire-fighting groups and shooting companies retain the flavor of Tirolean militarism. The political party is also hierarchically organized and, despite time and shifting tactics, has at its core a canon of loyalty to the folk culture. The fourth element in village structure is the church. In Tirol religious life is formed around a hierarchy which serves both the nation and the clergy. This is not the separation of church and state Americans are used to.

In fact, this entire cultural scene contrasts rather sharply with the Italian worldview which values the intense networks of kinship more highly and the dubious joys of rural life less. Eric Wolf says that Italians in Südtirol are

> disenchanted with politics and utterly unmilitary, they rely only upon themselves and their kind to maintain what equilibrium they are capable of maintaining . . . While the church is granted competence in matters of personal or interpersonal morals, its affiliation with the state is regarded with considerable cynicism. From the state, they expect neither help nor mercy (Wolf 1962:11).

I have heard it said that Italian Tirol is the most conservative part of Austria and Germany. Ironically, the people there have distilled, like Schnaps, the essence of being Tiroleans. The loss of a part of an emotional homeland can become the focus of nostalgia for the past or a fear of current and future changes. This cultural concentrate would account for the German and Austrian tourists who make up the bulk of visitors to Südtirol each year or the homesickness which Austrians remark on from time to time.

## The Disinherited

The hidden story behind the ethnic battle lines is about shifts in how people earn a living. As the ethnic conflicts peaked, so did rapid demographic changes and a distinctly Tirolean process of rural modernization. Economics eventually took precedence over ethnic issues. Politics came down to money, not meanings.

One out of every five men in Tirol after the Second World War was not married. Men could not marry until they had stable financial prospects and could support a family. Lack of work and economic opportunities also caused many young people to leave their natal villages permanently. As the introductory quote in this chapter shows, this fact pained Tirolean leaders.

In the quarter century after World War II, the Tirolean countryside was transformed economically. The number of farm hands dropped dramatically. The number of wage workers and employees not on farms increased dramatically also. In other words, family farm hands took new and better paid positions outside of agriculture. At the same time, agriculture and pastoralism remained the backbone of the local economies. As one political scientist commented

> The key factor in this distinctive process of adjustment lies in South Tyrol's inheritance laws . . . that system has proven to have an astonishing capacity to withstand and assimilate great social and economic changes (Katzenstein 1976:228).

Although the Fascists had suspended the traditional system of impartible inheritance and only permitted it again after 1954, some estate managers had contrived to save their farmsteads and pass on many of them intact. Few of them had migrated in the period of the Option. Despite the continuing exodus of young people from the hillsides, the families, the farms and the system they practiced adjusted. They integrated the German-speaking areas into a modern economy.

Most people moved back and forth from part-time farming or helping relatives in the high season to new industrial or service jobs created by Italian national policies and the rise of tourism in remote valleys. They could commute to work on the new highways and autobahns. Within this rural modernization there were many creative ways to keep one's ties to the land and still earn a living as we saw in the last chapter.

## Ethnicity and the Second Son

Side by side, the German village of St. Felix and the Italian village of Tret have the same setting and the same environment; they both have cows, crops and a lot of work. But the Italian families practice, as much as circumstances permit, divisible inheritance; the German families, as circumstances permit, maintain primogeniture and a system of closed holdings. The consequences reach deep into their collective lives.

Inheritance patterns determine how power and authority flow within the family. St. Felix and Tret share the same constraints of ecology and in many ways look alike because of this. But, on closer observation, the families within each group are different, shaped by how the means of production, their land, is passed on. Americans rarely think that people's feelings, the privacy of their marriage beds or their daily schedules are determined by a factor such as land tenure. It is also important to remember that even people who are not sharing in the whole house patterns or divisible inheritance may be nonetheless shaped by them.

But Cole and Wolf make a very sophisticated case that both groups must solve the common human problems of structuring their kin groups, including some and excluding others, while channeling resources toward some goal. The pivot is the person with the power. Here is what the soap operas and power struggles we discussed in chapter 4 feel like in German-speaking St. Felix.

> The battle for authority is not only fought between father and heir apparent, it is also fought between older and younger brothers, and among all brothers and all sisters. Brothers are fierce competitors for inheritance; because only one can inherit, the others must either depart or resign themselves to serve on their brother's estate as *Knecht*, as family servant in return for maintenance . . . Brothers must also compete with sisters, for a sister will either marry and contend for family resources to obtain a dowry, or she will remain an unmarried dependent, entitled to support in times of illness and need, but subject to her brother's authority (Cole and Wolf 1974:242).

A second son or brother had to accept these conditions. One brother won in the competition for dominance on the holding and had the right to install his growing family. If something happened to him the estate would probably go to the winner's sons, not the waiting brothers. Staying in the vicinity was uncomfortable for everyone. Can the disinherited siblings make claims or cause trouble? If they leave, what will draw them back? Relations are cool. This colors the rest of social life.

> There is hardly any visiting from house to house in St. Felix. Men meet at the tavern, in church, and at council meetings. Women meet at the store and at church; but the warm friendliness of food and wine shared between friends and neighbors in the household kitchen, so characteristic of Tret, hardly exists in St. Felix. Transactions between households, such as exchanges of labor or favors, are carefully tallied and precisely reciprocated (Cole and Wolf 1974:243).

As many have observed, the estate manager in this Germanic tradition is a lord in his own castle, a structure that anthropologists who study peasant cultures call monolithic. When authority is concentrated in the hands of the father, everything and everyone else is subordinate. The inheritance determines what rights and powers a person has. This is what we have called the problem of the second son, which means not the birth order of siblings, but the loss of control over the estate to all sons but one.

When the inheritance is split and divided, as in Italian practices, then power and authority also flow outward. The Italian families resemble a corporation in which the members hold shares. In-laws, siblings or generations can well afford to visit each other continuously, share the work, and count on reciprocity in time of trouble.

> The Italian family consists of a web of equivalent, cross-cutting ties, and interpersonal contacts emphasize the principle of reciprocity. The German family, on the other hand, divides kinsmen into lineal units, and interpersonal relations are marked by the principle of balance. In sharp contrast to the German village, in the Italian one labor exchanges and social calls are frequent and involvement with the outside world is high. The social universe in the Italian village is viewed as coterminous with the relations among past kin and potential future kin. In the German village that social universe is constructed out of separate, lineal family units welded into different public associations. Core values such as hierarchy and orderliness exist therefore outside of the network of kin relations in the German village while in the Italian village values such as equality and casualness are part and parcel of the kinship system. In the Italian village political relations are personalized and political conflict is de-escalated and made private. In the German village political relations are organized and political conflict is escalated and made public. The structure of Italian political organizations emphasizes the principle of equality and the Italian political process resembles a circle composed of equivalent social and political units. German political organizations are hierarchical and the German political process approximates a wheel with different spokes converging in one center (Katzenstein 1976:289).

Wolf and Cole observed that people who came out of Italian cultural traditions invested time, energy and resources in what they call many-stranded coalitions (1974:174). These coalitions include their relatives, in-laws and neighbors in the village, in nearby towns and as far away as America. When an older sister or a favorite uncle migrated to America, they still kept in touch. Within the vicinity there are social visits back and forth. They exchange gifts, workdays and help each other with the rituals of growing up and being a good Catholic; baptisms, confirmations, weddings, funerals and other ceremonials are network events. This contrasts with what they call the single-stranded coalitions favored by German-speaking farmers. These interactions are oriented to specific tasks and limited in time.

It is interesting to note the echoes and shadows of these patterns which Europeans took to the Americas. You may be able to see what effects these genes of social heredity have produced in ethnic groups with which you are familiar.

## Success for the Second Son: The Proletarianization of the Work Force

Tiroleans have been immensely resistant to any form of inheritance other than impartible. At various times, outside groups have tried without success to modify or eliminate this custom. There had been the weight of the Habsburg empire, the Napoleonic Code under occupation forces, the nineteenth century parliaments of Vienna, the Fascist government of Italy in the twentieth century as well as other forces arrayed against the custom of the whole house. At every turn Tiroleans resisted. They passed the Homestead Law of 1900 to guarantee the rights of the eldest son. The Treaty of St. Germain and the split of the Tirols outlawed primogeniture. The reinstatement of impartible inheritance was one of the major demands of the terrorists, later embodied in the Autonomy Statutes.

In Südtirol today inheritance laws are complex. Italian law permits a category called "a closed Hof." This is a farming estate which is recognized by the local estate or Hof Commission to be able to support no more than one extended family. Once so classified or entailed, the owners must keep the estate intact. They may not sell the Hof to an unrelated person or use it for a primary purpose other than farming. Otherwise the estate would have to be reclassified. When the head of a closed Hof passes away, the headship usually passes to a designated offspring, most often a son.

This designated heir does not actually own the land outright. He succeeds to a bundle of rights and obligations related to the estate.

He must manage the estate as a farm, marrying, raising his family there and caring for any surviving, elderly parents as well as dependent siblings. Indeed, the estate commission may decide that the heir should pay his siblings an amount of money in compensation for not inheriting. Meanwhile, as in the past, surviving siblings inherit the right to live and work on the estate if they can be accommodated. They can expect to share in the distribution of assets should the closed holding ever be turned into something other than a farm. They cannot, however, expect to support a spouse or children from the estate.

What is noteworthy is how many core Tirolean customs are preserved even under Italian law. These customs are still the lineal descendants of impartible inheritance with older echoes of patriarchy and primogeniture. They are more than just symbols of the ethnic differences between German and Italian speakers. For example, if the head of an estate dies without designating a successor, then the estate Commission has the authority to appoint one. According to the present Südtirolean law, the commission should favor males over females and older sons over younger ones. I am indebted to Paul Magnarella, anthropologist and lawyer, for helping me understand how the intersection of Italian laws and Tirolean habits works. As he pointed out, should this law ever be challenged, it will probably be declared in violation of the Italian constitution's sexual equality provision.

Despite Tirolean determination, not all homesteads are entailed or closed. There is evidence that only half of the homesteads are passed on intact (Cole and Wolf 1974). Yet the pattern is defended staunchly. "We may now ask why this pattern of inheritance has proved so resistant to change" (Wolf 1970:111). He makes an argument from power and the need for a pool of cheap labor. The estate manager is like the lord of the manor. His siblings must marry out, move away, work for keep on their brother's farm or hope to find jobs in the neighborhood. Willing, inexpensive and docile workers are critical for the survival of the homestead, and relatives are the best source. In effect, social class is less between economic groups than between siblings. But disinherited family members cannot form a revolutionary class, unite and change their lives. They will remain divided, scattered and without power.

Ironically, the rise of National Socialism (the Nazi party in Germany) gave positions, jobs and ultimately, power and hope to a legion of younger sons and daughters of Südtirol and Austria. The Nazis recognized the potential of a cohort of supporters and passed laws to help them. Absorbed into the army, the arms industry and other wartime work, the disinherited found places for themselves outside the farmsteads and left the inequalities of impartible inheritance behind without abandoning families or traditions.

> If my own field experience in the South Tyrol is characteristic of wider areas, as I believe it is, it was primarily through the advent of National Socialism and through its incorporation of the disinherited siblings into a dynamic and militaristic *Reich* that this dependent population came to envisage for itself new social roles in a greater society beyond the confines of their individual homesteads (Wolf 1970:112).

This may help explain the attraction to or defense of Nazism which runs deep in the generation who reached adulthood as the Nazis rose to power in Germany and Austria. The disinherited found freedom from the old social order which had disenfranchised them. It may also help explain the very large numbers of older Germans who make pilgrimages to Tirol.

After the war, alternatives for the disinherited grew exponentially. Service trades, manufacturing, tourism and modernization of the rural sector changed the social order permanently. The economic changes in all of the culture area of Tirol since the end of the war are a familiar story. Cities grew, industries increased. Commercial possibilities expanded and entrepreneurs abounded. There were construction, processing, transport and many other opportunities. The scale of tourism, unimaginable to earlier generations, has grown at rates hard to comprehend. John Cole and Philip Katz call this social and economic transformation, the proletarianization of the work force. The former servant or Knecht becomes an employee or worker, an *Arbeiter*. The Knecht or servitor

> could rarely predict where he would be from year to year. One summer he might be employed in the lowlands as a farmhand, and the next might find him working as a herdsman for an upland village. In the winter he might find work as a woodcutter, as a teamster in a lumber operation, or he might return to his natal village to spend the winter with a landholding brother. Wherever he found himself, he was excluded from participation in the political process and his chances of ever marrying and raising a family were poor (1973:40).

In the last fifty years, however, the subservient brother has become the independent wage earner, the Arbeiter. There are many secondary occupations that stem from farming, tourism and industry—all done Tirolean-style. "One result of these economic trends has been to raise the income of landless laborers until it matches, and in many cases exceeds, the income of their estate-managing brothers" (Cole and Katz 1973:52).

Peter Petschauer notes these same patterns in the village of Afers. He speaks of changes in the twentieth century. What he affirms is that even under Italian laws, patterns of inheritance remain stable, even classically Tirolean. The primary change is the entrepreneurial success of second sons. Once again we see, the servant becomes a worker.

> The family traditions of inheriting remain basically the same to this day, with two exceptions. From the 1890s to the 1920s several farmers were temporarily able to buy up more land than they used themselves and in the last twenty years the later-born siblings have been able to find employment outside the village and thus to get married and build rowhouses in it . . . The determination of work patterns remained in the hands of landowning men until the early 1950s, a set of years when servants disappeared almost overnight (Petschauer 1990:728).

Many workers still believe that the agricultural way of life is the best, the most healthy and the most properly Tirolean. They, too, will try to mix wage labor with agriculture in some way. They will look forward to retirement or some clever maneuver which gives them enough land to farm full time. All of these trends conspire to keep the countryside alive and well.

In Tirol the rural areas have remained prosperous. This contrasts sharply with many areas of the world, including parts of the United States, where rural hinterlands have been stripped of opportunity and economic power in the rush toward urban life. In both Tirols, farmers change their strategies in order to stay farmers. They will live in their natal village and commute to town for jobs to earn money to buy more land. They will build a new farmhouse with extra rooms to rent or add a little shop or restaurant for tourists and count on an energetic wife to manage them. They will sell agricultural produce in the wider market economy of Austria or Italy. They will rent, lease or accept subsidies from the tourist interests. Yes, they have remained conservative but not tenaciously resistant to external influences. We might say that they have grown modern by finding new ways to preserve their ancient heritage.

The myth of Tirol has three sacred parts. The peasant part is about the profound links to the soil and to the countryside, rather than to urban life. The political part stems from a privileged and protected history, the right to elect officials, to practice indivisible inheritance and to bear arms. The third part is the sacred covenant with Jesus which makes them a chosen people. Each part demands heavy duties and constant vigilance from those who call themselves Tiroleans.

# 8

# Traveling Behind Tourist Lines

## Culture Shock and the Anthropology of Tourism

*Look at me and mine.*
*Look at yourself and yours.*
*And if you find yourself without fault;*
*Then go and despise me.*

—Verse carved on a threshing machine
From St. Peter in Ahrntal

This chapter is about the culture or subculture of people who travel; we call ourselves tourists. I have included accounts from the journals of students and other traveling writers as well as my own experiences. We will define and analyze the phenomenon of tourism and the three cultures that come in contact through tourism. We will talk about culture shock and what my students call "culture schlock." Some of the major themes are the search for and experience with the Other, the question of authenticity and the anxiety that tourists will alter pristine cultures forever. Once again I make note of tourism as one of the three leading industries in the world; this certainly justifies taking an anthropological approach to its cultural patterns.

Tirol provides an ideal setting to examine these matters. We discussed how fundamental the hospitality industry has been and continues to be for Tirolean identity and economy. We know the outlines of the traditional culture and the appeal it has for many generations of travelers. In addition, most of us have traveled to or lived in another culture for a period of time. We have certainly seen festivals, museums, souvenir shops and other manifestations of tourism; we have probably experienced culture shock, even if we could not immediately name it.

19C+M+B93

As tourists we are in a state of temporary separation and suspension from whatever constitutes normal life. The need to sleep, eat, interact and to find personal meaning in our experiences temporarily dominates our lives. For places like Tirol, the culture of tourism is permanent; they live with it all the time.

## Studying the Culture of Tourism

The anthropology of tourism is a fairly recent area of investigation (Smith 1977). Most of the social science research has been in the area of development and acculturation involving Western tourists and non-Western hosts. Professionals frequently center our studies on how tourists impact or change the host countries. We looked at the natural history of tourism in Tirol from this point of view in chapter 6.

Another and smaller concern for social science researchers is tourists as subjects, or the culture of tourism. Tourists are usually seen as adversely influencing their hosts; but what happens to us, the tourists, is also worthy of study. This includes what I call the tourism feedback loop, in which hosts and guests exchange ideas, artifacts and benefits, reflecting and altering each other's cultures in a reciprocal process.

There are many definitions of tourism (Nash 1981; Smith 1977). Here is the one I find most satisfying.

> Tourism, even of the recreational sort—sun, sea, sex, and sport—is a ritual expression—individual or societal—of deeply held values about health, freedom, nature, and self improvement, a re-creation ritual which parallels pilgrimages and other rituals in more traditional, pervasively religious societies (Graburn 1983:15).

Applying this definition we see that Tiroleans visited shrines in olden times for the same reasons that we visit Tirol today. The emphasis on traveling as a ritual process comes from anthropologists like Victor Turner (1969) who speak of two kinds of rituals. First are "rites of intensification," or the periodic or cyclical rites which renew the social and natural world. These are usually part of an annual cycle, such as the midwinter ceremonialism in Tirol and the United States. Second are events we call "rites of passage." These are the critical or nonrecurring rituals in any individual's life cycle. Predictably these are birth, marriage, death and other occasions for coming of age.

The modern version of tourism exhibits both of these characteristics (Graburn 1983). We say "we are getting away from it all," meaning work, homework, housework and the workplace. In this light, our idea of recreation can be rephrased as "re-creation." We can see tourism as part of social time, such as Christmas holidays or our summer vacations. We can simultaneously view tourism as a kind of personal life passage. The students who take courses while traveling are excellent examples. They are involved in "socially sanctioned rituals of life's progress . . . where modern societies may not impose enough satisfactory rites of passage for people to mark the progress and vicissitudes of their lives" (Graburn 1983:13).

This ritual has three very distinct stages: First is separation. Suddenly we are loosed from our ordinary social routines and familiar faces. In any kind of transition rite (tourist, secular or sacred), each individual leaves behind his or her structured expectations. Second, we are suspended in what we call a liminal state. In this liminality, regular certainties dissolve; we are open to a new awareness, feelings and vulnerabilities. We are forced into the company of others who are also suspended. The bonding which we find with them has many emotional layers, spontaneity and togetherness. Events, places and people take on auras of the sacred or the special. This stage is called *communitas*.

Communitas is a state of play, what I called deep play in chapter 5. Tourism—being a tourist—as a form of play is very arduous work; it is hardly what I would call leisure. Tourism as a ritual of passage calls into question our fundamental structure of beliefs about the world and arouses deep emotions in us. It is a kind of self-testing, as we prove to ourselves that we can change, grow, adjust.

So a tourist is half a pilgrim and a pilgrim is half a tourist. Even in crowds on beaches or in museums, we may experience a symbolic, even sacred, form of communitas with others. When we walk alone in what we call nature, we may feel what Turner calls flow. Student's journals are full of their recognition of these revelations or encounters:

"Air, glorious, clear, not even entertaining moisture, and green of every possible depth and hue—and mountains, hulking shadows, rising snow-capped in the distance as a picture postcard, right here a safe base for our studies, full of fruits and vineyards and marvelous patterns of carefully guided growth. These are the first overwhelming impressions and still I come back to the air . . . surrounding us, filling us, draining our smoke, bus exhaust, car smog, filling our bodies with energy in a sweet hard way so that we slumber like tired children every night."

What kind of comparative or relativistic framework explains why people travel or what happens to us as we travel? Some researchers view tourism as consumption and consumerism, the activities of a leisure class produced by industrial capitalism. Others say that when we travel we act out our basic cultural myths and project our personality characteristics onto others we perceive as different from ourselves. Other investigators point out that tourism is intricately linked to the question of finding authenticity. Restored villages or staged ceremonials appeal to us. Perhaps we travel to restore the authenticity we feel is missing in our lives (Nash and Smith 1991). This is one explanation for Christmas customs and the popularity of kitsch, which we shall examine later in this chapter.

As we know from chapter 6, the original tourist was typically a young European male from a privileged family who spent several years in pleasurable, educational journeying. The quote from Goethe which introduced chapter 1 comes from the extensive journals he kept of his grand tour of Italy. He left his German home from 1786 to 1788, going through Tirol on the way. He is the ancestor of wandering youths going abroad to Europe, separating from parental values and testing new ones.

The prototypical contemporary tourist is a lineal descendant of the tradition of the grand tour. Scouring the world in search of new experiences, we are educated and affluent relative to the rest of the world; we probably are seeking authenticity, wanting to understand the world and to bring parts of it home (Graburn 1983). We use imageries which imply conquest or making the unknown safe and knowable. We find our images of travel in space, the wilderness, foreignness and the past. This helps explain the growth of related things such as museums, photography, collecting and souvenirs. "Styles of tourism, like other rituals, may fall along a continuum between nostalgia—the satisfaction found in confirming the expected and cognitively familiar—and serendipity—the pleasure of coming across the exciting and unexpected" (Graburn 1983:20). We are travel consumers, who purchase and sample parts of the world, its sights, history, peoples and their cultures and who return, almost competitively, with stories of exoticism, traumas overcome, ordeals passed and bargains found. We carry back clothes, artifacts, cuisines, styles for home, recreation and holidays. We integrate them into our own culture and thereby change ourselves.

When any of us travel we are part of three different cultures rubbing against each other. First there are the local ones: these unique and historically specific cultures are often richly described by anthropologists. Second, there are the cultures or subcultures which represent home to the travelers, our own native culture. Third, something happens in the intersection between the first two. This is the tourist culture, defined as:

> a way of life practiced by tourists while traveling . . . though temporary in nature for individual tourists, from the host

> community's point of view, the tourist culture is quite permanent, with its own peculiarities. The tourist culture and its practitioners . . . can be identified by a combination of many markers, their phenotypes, costumes, language, place of residence (e.g., hotels), their leisure activities, and more. It is a culture which makes room for itself in many niches internationally and has the potential to interfere with the host culture and even to dominate it: a potentially conflict-prone situation (Jafari 1984:71).

These three cultures constantly rub against each other, sometimes they rub off on each other or they rub each other the wrong way. Both resident-hosts and travelers are like ethnic groups. We are multidimensional; we have our own language, our daily habits and our worldviews that we pack up along with the rest of our baggage. Guiding student groups through Tirol has given me as much anthropological experience with tourist culture as with Tirolean culture. I have been a traveler, observer, writer, teacher and tourist. I have learned to predict some of the contours of our adjustments and reactions.

## Packing Our Baggage

When we travel we carry our cultural baggage with us. Sometimes our baggage is the heavy kind which weighs us down. Sometimes it is unconscious assumptions that color everything we see and do. With our passports we carry a set of notions, beliefs, attitudes, stereotypes and judgments. Travelers inevitably or unconsciously expect certain amenities and comforts. We make rapid and rather harsh judgments about the "natives."

For example, one of my students wrote in her journal that she felt angry and confused. The people in the village (whom she assumed to be locals) were staring at her. She wanted them to stop looking. I interpreted her feelings first as a reaction of culture shock. Later I learned that she had worn a "California girl" costume in the village, a tank top and shorts. Or perhaps the locals were staring at a beautiful girl carrying an open beer bottle. Many localities have ordinances or customs banning such a practice. Tourists are allowed considerable latitude for testing local standards, but we may not be exempt from reaction. Californian customs permitted her activities; Tiroleans have different standards.

Another young women walked into the German-speaking village of Dorf Tirol wearing a T-shirt which proclaimed, "Italians Do It Better." This is a tourist item on sale in many places. Not only did German-speaking villagers remember the Treaty of St. Germain and the division of Tirol, but recognized that "It" on the T-shirt probably refers to sex. This may be interpreted as provocative. Several young Italian men followed her home. They hoped she meant it. She didn't. Several German fellows also followed her home. Ethnic or perhaps only masculine competition started to accelerate. We almost had a cross-cultural incident.

Here is a wonderful nineteenth century example of the cultural baggage we take with us. Amelia Edwards and her companion prepared for their journey into the Dolomites by stocking up on the foods and other supplies they believed they would need. In their minds they were headed into a remote and primitive area where necessities, never mind amenities, would not be available to them. It seemed reasonable to carry the minimal requirements for decent living. They shopped for several days. "We bought two convenient wicker-baskets, and wherewithal to stock them—tea, sugar, Reading biscuits in tins, chocolate in tablets, Liebig's Ramornie extract, two bottles of Cognac, four of Marsala, pepper, salt, arrowroot, a large metal flask of spirits of wine, and an Etna" (Edwards 1873:11).

Their idea of travel resembles a picnic. In the British realm biscuits are cookies, extract is for making bouillon soup and an Etna is a portable stove. Much to the amazement of their guides, the two women carried all the necessary ingredients for daily high tea, English style, including a maid to serve them. They also spent a great deal of energy to locate two side saddles since no proper English woman would be caught riding astride an animal!

The two women planned to travel by carriage or its local equivalent to central locations from which they could embark on short trips of a week or ten days by mules. To do this they had to examine all the maps they had, sort out their stores and repack. They had to:

> solve the oft-propounded problem of how to get the contents of a large portmanteau into a small black bag . . . Henceforth our ways would lie among mountain paths and unfrequented mule-tracks, and tomorrow we must start upon an expedition of at least ten days with only as much luggage as each could carry packed behind her own saddle (Edwards 1873:198).

She exaggerates the lightness of their luggage. A close reading of their journal reveals many things Victorians simply took for granted as necessities. They carried their sketching traps, the provision baskets, rain gear, umbrellas, telescopes, the portable stove as well as rugs and fold-up chairs to sit on. Meanwhile, Miss L.'s maid was in charge of their rooms and the remainder of the baggage. They traveled with their entire class structure intact.

The travelers and writers in the age of Romanticism believed ardently in a woman they called "Nature." They called Tiroleans "a race" with no sense of the biological absurdity nor of the terrible price in human lives such a designation exacts. They made "civilization" an abstraction which represented the highest order of culture. Every travel writer of the period notes that Tiroleans are not "civilized." They generally concede, given the problems of "civilization," that it may be a good thing since the "natives" would not be corrupted by outside influences.

Grohman laments, as do most of his fellow travelers, that people he met in Tirol had unfortunate habits of cleanliness. He complained of Dame Nature who has been "instilling into their minds a wholesome horror of all doctors, and, alas! of water also." In short, they don't bathe enough for his tastes. Projecting our standards of hygiene on others is a frequent, albeit ethnocentric, response to being far from home and plopped down in a foreign culture. He also commented, as do many in the twentieth century, that one could always recognize where Italians live. They hang their washing out the windows. In fact, Austrians may stigmatize American students with the same criticism and ethnocentric evaluation. They say, "Don't hang your laundry out the window. People will think you are an Italian."

## Shock, Cultural and Otherwise

When we enter other people's worlds we inevitably feel what anthropologists call culture shock. "Another direct consequence of tourist-host contact is the anxiety inherent in strangerhood" (Nash 1981:467). We respond to stranger anxiety in a variety of ways. The first signs may be a self-righteousness, even a rising anger. We tend to take little things very seriously. One response is to clump together against the enemy, the hosts; another is compulsive friendliness. Then we make demands on our hosts or organize plans to leave at the earliest possible moment. We escape into tears, alcohol, withdrawal or anything that reminds us of home. Whatever habits of adjustment we brought with us are accentuated in a new environment. I have seen tourists who believe that only by yelling can they have what they think they need. Others become quite reasonable, although their behavior or standards may not strike others as reasonable at all.

As a student recounts in her journal. "We listed a lot of things that bother us. We have linguistic shock. You can't eavesdrop; you can't communicate. The tourists, are they changing the culture? 'Interacting with the culture' may mean something very different

*The host and hostess of a guest house serve traditional Tirolean cuisine to travelers.*

to us. If that means interacting with Tiroleans or Italians the way you interact with Americans, you won't get that here. A lot of our views of farming are 'quaintified,' blurred by being tourists. I am comfortable with never being part of this culture, always being a tourist, but some people are not interested even in being comfortable with that. They complain too much." Homesickness is another part of culture shock. Students often spend a great deal of time and energy, never mind schillings or lire, searching for "real" foods, like Fruit Loops and Diet Coke. They are dismayed to find that an order to a waiter for water has gained them carbonated mineral water with no ice. Whoever heard of serving such a thing! One of my students returned from a shopping trip with what she called "the find of all times!"—Captain Crunch cereal.

Travelers have many of their best and worst moments with food, lodging and transportation. After all, these are the fabric of the daily life of tourist culture. One of the most awful moments is to have no place to stay. Gilbert, Churchill and their nameless wives arrive deep in a Dolomite valley to find that the only inn was full.

> How we had pictured to ourselves cool rooms, hot water, tubs *ad libitum*, and refreshing changes of raiment! Now, with our baggage in a heap on the ground, and the nearest village more than an hour distant, we had to discuss an imminent disarrangement of our plans." (1864:108).

Most travelers murmur indiscreetly when we do not have our cultural comforts. The nineteenth century travelers' accounts predictably mention the unavailability of what the British call "real" brandy or "good" brandy in Tirol. Today my students fill their journals and evaluations with descriptions of how difficult it is to place a phone call or launder their clothes. They miss their pets or their favorite pillow. They rush to the McDonalds on Maria-Theresien Strasse, the main street of Innsbruck, for their fast-food fix.

All travelers have, at some time or another, complained loudly of transportation problems: late planes and trains, discomfort, bad smells, no toilets, high costs and signs in foreign languages. Here is advice to women traveling in Tirol from the best guidebook of the nineteenth century. The author compares Tirol with Switzerland where trained animals are easy to rent.

> The case is different in the Eastern Alps. Animals accustomed to carry ladies are not often to be found. There are very many passes traversed by beasts of burden, where the unaccustomed load of a lady seated on a side-saddle might become a cause of real danger. A lady wishing to explore the beautiful districts of the Eastern Alps, who has been able to secure a satisfactory animal, will do well to take it with her throughout the district, and to allow it sufficient intervals of rest (Ball 1879:xv).

Amelia Edwards gives us a firsthand account of mule travel. She often had to back her mule into a corner and mount from a chair, much to the delight of local observers. Some travelers, she claimed, seemed to understand mule management. "My mule and I, on the contrary, never arrive at terms of intimacy. Perhaps he knows that I am the heavier weight, and resents me accordingly; perhaps he dislikes the society of ladies, and prefers carrying half-ton loads of hay and charcoal, which is the sort of thing he has been brought up to do. At all events, he refused from the first to make himself agreeable" (Edwards 1873:183). When train schedules are hopeless, planes are late and travel feels generally uncomfortable, I remember mules.

Here is a marvelous description of what culture shock and the encounter of two different cultures look like. Miss Edwards and Miss

L. have been on the road for some time. They miss mail from home and the creature comforts they regard as basic. They believe in their own reasonableness. Everything grates. They have what they consider only a few, very modest requirements:

> We are not, I think, unreasonable travellers; but we have been riding and walking for nearly twelve hours, and wish, not unnaturally, for water, towels, food and coffee. For all these things we have to wait interminably. That we should require a table-cloth is a serious affliction, and that we cannot sup, like the hay-makers, off polenta, is almost more than young Signora Cercena knows how to bear. A few small lumps of smoke-blackened meat, a dish of unwashed salad, and some greasy fritters are at length brought; and this young lady, while professing, I imagine, to wait at table, walks over quite coolly to a looking-glass at the farther end of the room, and there deliberately tries on L.'s hat and all my rings and bracelets (Edwards 1873:305–306).

On another evening, tired, they arrive at a roadside guest house and negotiate a night's lodging. When they have fed the mules corn and their guides bread and wine, the two women retire to their room, light up their portable stove and brew a dish of their favorite bouillon soup. The travelers grow angry with four women from the inn who watch them, examining their movements and the objects they carry.

> The women of the house—and there are four of them—pursue us to this retreat and stand, wide-eyed and open-mouthed, in a fever of curiosity, watching all we do, as a party of children might watch the movements of a couple of wild beasts in a cage. They examine our hats, our umbrellas, our cloaks, and every individual article that we laid aside. The Etna stupefies them with amazement. As for L.'s field-glass lying in the window, they eye it askance, taking it evidently for some kind of infernal machine that may be expected to go off suddenly and blow up the whole establishment. They are, in truth, mere savages—rosy, hearty, good-natured; but as ignorant and uncivilized as aboriginal Australians (Edwards 1873:320).

But Amelia and her companion have been watching the village activities with a telescope, drawing pictures of villagers and their houses and writing in diaries and notebooks about them. Note the judgment that Amelia Edwards renders: the women are savages. The British at the height of their colonial empire liked to compare others to the most exotic and "primitive" people they themselves had ever encountered, the first inhabitants of Australia. Savages are sensual, even sexy, hence immoral, friendly and innocent but basically "ignorant and uncivilized." They are like children.

Meanwhile, the four women appear to have made their own judgments about the tourists. From the conversation Amelia recorded in her journal we can imagine what the hostesses were thinking about the strange creatures who had descended on them. The women began to cross-examined the tourists.

"Where have you come from?"

"From Caprile." [a town in the southern Dolomites at what was then on the frontier of the Italian-speaking and German-speaking areas]

"No, before that. Where were you born?"

"In England."

"Madonna! Born in England! So far away and you came all this way like this?"

Amelia nodded. She assumed her hostesses referred to the two mules on which the travelers arrived. She imagined the women were concerned about how they came so far with only a small bag each. She reassured them firmly that their travel arrangements were well thought out in advance and that they were managing fine. The women had an altogether different sort of problem in mind. They all talk at once.

"God have mercy! All alone, you came all alone?"

Another woman asks, "Are you sisters? No. You are not sisters! Are you married? Where are your husbands?"

Consternation. "What! Not married! Neither of you?"

"Good God. Alone. Not married. No relatives. Poor, poor little girls." The women shake their heads.

This encounter with four residents who cross-examine them about what kind of women they are and then pass judgment is a good example of cultural understanding and misunderstanding. The local women pity two traveling souls far from home, without relatives or husbands to care for them or give them a social identity. The travelers patronize their hostesses and laugh at them. The Englishwomen feel lucky to have escaped a fate which their hostesses regard as the highest calling for women. The women cry out "with an air of such genuine concern and compassion that we are almost ashamed of the irrepressible laughter with which we cannot help receiving their condolences" (Edwards 1873:322).

A field trip to Schwaz gave Rachel Busk the kind of culture shock travelers regularly experience. She and her companions had to get up very early, miss their breakfast, walk about twenty minutes to the train station and arrive finally to find no welcome at the inn. We can just hear her indignation.

> A repeated knocking at last brought a buxom maid out of the cow-shed, who seemed not a little amazed at our apparition.

> 'Had she any coffee! Coffee, at that time of day. Of course not!' True, the unpunctuality of the train, the delivery of superfluous luggage to the care of the station-master, and our lingering by the way, had brought us to past nine o'clock—an unprecedented hour for breakfast in Schwaz. 'Couldn't we be content with wine? In a couple of hours meat would be ready, as the carters came in to dine then.' Meat and coffee at the same repast, and either at that hour, were ideas she could not at first take in. Nevertheless, when we detailed our needs, astonishment gave way to compassion, and she consented to drop her incongruous propositions and to make us happy in our own way. Accordingly, she was soon busied in lighting a fire, running to fetch coffee and rolls . . . and very soon appeared with a tray full of tumblers and queer old crockery. The black beverage she at last provided consisted of a decoction of nothing nearer coffee than roasted corn, figs or acorns; and the rolls had the strangest resemblance to leather; but the milk and eggs were fine samples of dairy produce, for which Schwaz is famous, and these and luscious fruit made up for the rest (Busk 1874:170).

Having led several field trips to Schwaz and having heard many of these same reactions from students, I feel that I know Rachel. I also suspect that she may have had a rather elitist outlook, but she kept wonderfully detailed journals. Miss Busk, who steadfastly avoided direct personal experiences, loved to translate and tell stories. As she struggles with a dawning notion of cultural relativity, she draws this moral. Unfortunately, she sounds patronizing.

> These poor country folks, whom the educated traveller often passes by as unworthy of notice in their benighted ignorance and superstition—while they would not forego their salutation of the sacred symbol by the wayside, which marks their intimate appreciation of truths of the highest order—put us to shame by their indifference to sublunary indulgences. We had come to Tirol to study their ways, and I hope we took our lesson on this occasion, well. We were not feasted with a sumptuous repast, such as might be found in any of the monster hotels; but we were presented with an experience of the struggle with want; of that hardy face-to-face meeting with the great original law of labour (Busk 1874:172).

Her century-old account points up the relevance of the journals we ourselves keep. If we find passages in her books (or any others) that make us thoughtful or amused or angry, imagine how our journals will sound to others a hundred years from now.

Sometimes the tables are turned and we see ourselves as others see us. One lovely summer day Herr Grohman climbed Gross Glockner, the highest mountain in Austrian Tirol. He plopped down in lazy enjoyment of the view. "Having passed three nights in haylofts, I was not a particularly clean-looking individual, my weather-stained leathern shorts where they were not patched were torn, and my knees were as brown and scarred as any young native's."

As he rested he saw an unmistakably British family, father, son and two pretty daughters toiling up the path loaded with knapsacks and picnic equipment. The son addressed him in "the most execrable German ever used by a young Oxford undergraduate" and heaped the bulky luggage on Grohman's back. The youth airily assured his sisters that "these fellows don't feel fifteen or twenty pounds more or less on their backs."

Going along with the joke, Grohman carried the load to the next inn where the young man pressed two coins into his hand, "Here, my good fellow, is something for your pains." Just then the innkeeper and several guests greeted the well-respected gentleman. Grohman had also attended Oxford. "Shall I ever forget the look of blank surprise on that man's delightfully ingenuous face as he stood there with outstretched hand, when an unexpected *dènouement* suddenly divulged my identity!" (Grohman 1908:157). Versions of this story, the tourists patronizing the natives, abound.

Within the tourist culture itself are inevitable conflicts and tensions. I call this group shock. The following entry from a student's journal is a good example.

> An aside, this is probably a group shock category—I am getting balance and energy from one of the buttressing walls of the castle (in the shade, of course) as I watch a student hanging her laundry out. The bees are buzzing by; there is the sound of the maniac Italian drivers on the mountain, her irritation at the lack of clothespins and her persnickety-ness (did I spell that right?) makes me laugh. She strikes me as a spoiled rich suburban only child, probably raised with servants and a lot of cash. Everyday details she may never have had to attend to before are so punishing and overwhelming that she seems to forget we are in this beautiful place.

## Eden Vanished

One of the most consistent responses of students to traveling in Tirol is their concern that outsiders like us will alter pristine cultures forever. They are genuinely anxious about this problem. They often express the feeling that they are the last generation or group to experience a place without it changing forever, presumably for the worse. Sometimes they seem to believe that the past was more stable, that there was a golden age where disruptive changes were far away and peasants were protected from foreign influences. The touring Romantics routinely bemoaned the loss of innocence and fervently believed that the very tourism they participated in was ruining the very people whose homes they visited. They feared that old customs were dying or being destroyed by visitors. They often believed they were the last witnesses to the real thing. This is an extremely common conceit.

Grohman complained that good customs like ferocious battles or finger fighting were passing away. He blamed railways and tourists.

> Regarding the changes that are overtaking not only the Dolomites, but the whole of Tyrol, the reader will perhaps pardon my letting off some steam, for I should like to confess being possessed of a strong desire to see Tyrol spared the worst features of Switzerland's fate. The exploitation of scenic attractions carried on in such a barefaced manner in that country should not be encouraged to extend into Tyrol. The eggshells and greasy sandwich-paper that befoul the greensward of the Wengern Alp, and the gramophone braying on the balcony of the Little Scheideck, shock one's eyes and ears (Grohman 1908:146).

He also bemoans the electric wires, the mountain railways, the hundreds of huts erected by Alpine Clubs, the pegs, posts, ropes and paths where Nature never intended them to be. In particular he resents "plastering prominent objects with gaudy advertisements as unsightly as they are repulsive to one's aesthetic feelings" (Grohman 1908:148) and the unsightly blotches of red, blue and green paint on wayside rocks and trees. On the other hand, what he regards as destructive modernism I regard as environmentally sensitive public policies which have stood the tests of time. I appreciate the paths marked and maintained by the Alpine Clubs and local municipalities. They publish detailed maps and guides to every face of every mountain. They keep tourists from overrunning everything!

Tourists routinely feel that the very business of tourism is ruining everything. Here Amelia Edwards worries that her fellow British tourists will impose bad manners and greed and destroy the homely, peasant charm. She comments that her hostess was wounded to tears by the suspicious conduct of an English touring party who

> secured all their possessions under lock and key every time they ventured outside the doors. The same people on going away, disputed every item of their moderate bill, as if, no matter how little they were charged, it was to be taken for granted that they were being imposed upon somehow. . . . The ultimate result of

> such conduct on the part of our dear country-people is sufficiently obvious. The old inn-keeping families will ere long close their houses against us in disgust; a class of extortionate speculators, probably Swiss, will step in and occupy the ground; newer and smarter, but far less comfortable hotels will spring up like mushrooms in these quiet valleys; all direct communication between the native townsfolk and the traveling stranger will be intercepted; and the simplicity, the poetry, the homely charm of the Dolomite district will be gone for ever (Edwards 1873:222).

But there was no time in the past when Tirolean culture (or any other) had a golden age that will remain untouched forever. Yes, tourists change things; on the other hand, Tirol has been dealing with travelers for a thousand years.

## Culture Schlock: Souvenirs and the Tacky Tourist Trade

Souvenirs are a commoditization of experience, tangible proof of having been there. This is a chicken and egg deal. What came first? Did tourists bring psychic pressure to bear on their hosts to produce objects which satisfied their guests? Or do the host cultures create the market and produce the endless objects for commercial reasons? Friends of mine who work in museums, restaurants and places related to tourism and the hospitality industry report that they have to provide carry-away objects or visitors will take "anything they can get their hands on."

When I collected journals during one course, I found a student who had kept meticulous lists of every item she purchased, a detailed description of them and the prices in local currencies and American dollars. She compared what she had paid with prices for the same items in other stores. She rated each place she visited on the attributes of the shopping available. She ranked museums, art galleries, churches or other classic tourist visitation spots by the quality of shopping it afforded her. I have never been certain whether this was some kind of career planning for her, an example of the denial embedded in culture shock or her fundamental view of the world. Some of the things she purchased had a genuine use (wool sweaters); others were gifts (bottles of alcohol); others were travel-associated or souvenirs. Some of the items she could have bought in her local shopping mall (clothes, watches, crystal). She did, however, what tourists are supposed to do. She bought things.

A depressing number of my students ask me, "We're going on a field trip to where? What can we buy there?" Or they return from a field trip and observe, "Yes, it was interesting but there was nothing to buy." One of the predictable customs of the subculture of people we call tourists is to climb off the bus, get their bearings and head for the nearest souvenir shop. One of the predictable customs of people we call hosts is to arrange the opportunities and physical space for us to buy their things.

I stage a contest in my classes on occasion. I call this the tacky tourist contest. The student contestants shop for the souvenir or tourist object that most defines kitsch, the fast food of art, high tourist camp. Each one brings their cheap object to class and justifies that it should win a prize for being the most truly tacky, that is, the best of the genre.

The ultimate kitsch is a souvenir, a tacky postcard or a reproduction of the painting of the Last Supper on a pot holder. It is the plastic Virgin on the dashboard which says Souvenir of Grand Canyon, Made in China. Kitsch is something without good taste, something which mimics or masquerades as art.

But kitsch is great business. Kitsch coincided with or originated in mass production, in machinery which can produce objects in bad taste as often and as cheaply as objects in good taste. This leads us to a notion of a "culture industry" just as we might speak of the automotive industry or the entertainment industry. The history of the ups and downs of the woodcarving businesses in Tirol is a good example.

Sometime around the 1860s or 1870s painters and art dealers in Munich began to use the German word *Kitsch* to apply to cheap or "fake-artsy" objects. From there the word and the concept entered the English language. There is no way to prove that kitsch originated in Tirol—and no point in doing so; but the association remains very close. Tirol was a heavy part of the inspiration for Romanticism; Tiroleans were already producing these clichéd cultural objects and exporting them for sale outside the region. Many of the common objects we think of as souvenirs can be traced to Tirol for their inspiration.

The mid-nineteenth century in Europe was filled with contrived "Romance." Contemporary reality was often painful so many people replaced it with clichés. They escaped into an idealism of history and geography and met their emotional needs with sentimentality. "To a large extent we can see kitsch as a hackneyed form of Romanticism and a parody of aesthetic consciousness" (Calinescu 1976:7).

Kitsch is not the same as folk culture which grows organically from ordinary people and their daily experience. Objects produced for everyday use and with an intrinsic beauty are a kind of participatory creativity. Consumers with money only have to decide

*Artist painting furniture in an Austrian factory.*

to buy or not to buy; we do not need the object or intend to use it for the purpose for which it was invented. Nor do we have cultural associations with the objects we buy. However, kitsch feeds off and finds inspiration in folk culture just as it does in popular culture.

Art, like tourism, was for the elites and those descended from privilege. But when the middle classes of Europe and America began to expand they demanded the experiences they saw in the upper classes. Many scholars think of kitsch as a flight from daily reality, an escape for people who can afford to do it or those who want to imitate them. We can escape through time—a sense of history that promises the past, even the future, is better than the present. We can escape through space, traveling through exotic lands in imagination or in fact. There are many reasons for the existence of kitsch.

> Combining the historical approach (kitsch results from Romanticism), the sociological approach (kitsch is closely linked to modern industrialism and to increasing leisure in society), and the aesthetic-moral approach (kitsch is false art, the production on a smaller or larger scale of various forms of "aesthetic lies"), we can come close to an understanding of the

> phenomenon . . . Kitsch is produced for the market and, cheaper or more expensive, it is entirely subordinated to the laws of the market. Crowd-pleasing, and often devised precisely for mass consumption, kitsch is meant to offer quick satisfaction of the most superficial aesthetic and pseudo-aesthetic needs or whims of a wide public whose ideal life-style is that of the middle class. Basically the world of kitsch is the world of *aesthetic make-believe* (Calinescu 1976:19).

When we recall that tourism is one of the three major industries in the world, kitsch becomes a very powerful social phenomenon. It is the ultimate interface between indigenous cultures and the culture of tourism. The production and sale of kitsch, a kind of ersatz fantasy, has enormously enriched the contemporary tourist industry not only of Tirol, but of the entire world.

Tiroleans sell objects that carry either the visual imagery of the traditional culture or the reminder of a visit to that particular place. So this is what we carry away from Tirol—a cowbell with flowers embroidered on it. We don't even own a cow. A loden green hat with artificial blackcock feathers on it. We can't walk into a bar and start a fight. A linen apron. Who among our family and friends wears an apron to work? Postcards, books of pictures, a crystal object or pewter plate. Christmas tree ornaments. A dried flower wreath. A woodcarving of a sweet child sweeping the path. Were these made in Tirol? Sometimes. Do such objects accurately reflect the traditional life of Tirol as we understand it? Probably not.

As we have seen, this is the manufacture of and trading on our emotions, our nostalgia. Most of our experiences as tourists are manufactured just like the souvenirs we buy. Most of these experiences are only shadows, reminders of the more genuine traditions of other cultures.

## Culture Connections: Questions about Authenticity and Otherness

History, nature, geography, ethnicity and culture become inseparable from tourism itself. Not even the local or indigenous people know what is real. We see this in Mardi Gras in New Orleans. There I am hostess, part of the host culture. I like sharing my house and time with the members of the tourist culture and enjoy telling visitors about the pageantry and social structure of my beautiful city. However, we are probably inventing some of our customs and our culture as we celebrate each year and focusing the representations of this culture in contrived and imaginary directions.

Knowing this makes it difficult for me to put the fundamental seasonal customs of Tirol into an ethnographic perspective. I have saved midwinter ceremonialism to discuss last because it seems to tie together many of the points and meanings in this book. But I have trouble sorting out tourist activities, economic activities, traditional culture and my personal response. Most available sources on Tirolean folk life contain long and detailed accounts of Christmas customs and other winter ceremonialism. Sometimes I feel overwhelmed by the attention paid to these descriptive items. I want to be objective, properly anthropological and fair to a culture I am trying to interpret. On the other hand, I am probably not objective. I frankly dislike Christmas, either in my own culture or in other peoples' cultures.

This is probably my most acute, even painful experience of culture shock in Tirol. Sometimes I feel like Amelia Edwards in the toy factory in the Grödental. She was swept by nostalgia and memory, unexpectedly reunited with her childhood. Sometimes I sympathize with Herr Grohman when he grows peeved with "Christian superstitions and peasant pieties." I am more frequently on the side of Scrooge than allied with the spirits of Christmas. Even at the height of summer in Tirol I feel the heavy weight of the "Holiday Season" still bearing down on me.

The events of the liturgical year in Tirol feel deceptively familiar and at the same time strange and threatening. I often need a context, an emotional place to put these experiences. The long winter's observance of the birth of Jesus, what we call Christmas, is a northern European culture complex raised to exquisite proportions in Tirol. Many of our own cultural practices, both secular and sacred, are borrowed from German-speaking areas. Traveling Tirolean choruses made "Silent Night" the premier song of Christmas. One of the classic seasonal greeting cards is a Tirolean winter panorama. In chapters 5 and 6, we discussed spiritual and economic value of the Krippen, the Nativity scenes. While seemingly based in religious observances, they are a year-round economic reality. Many of the souvenirs or gifts travelers return with from Tirol are related to Christmas. Many American tourists have told me that Christmas in Tirol feels more like home than the same holiday season in America does!

The question is: can we be objective or analytical about Tirolean holidays when they feel so familiar to us? What I have discovered about my awkward relationship to these customs is that the further away from me they are in cultural time, the easier it is to understand them as an anthropologist and even to accept them as a kind of participant. On the other hand, the interpretation which I assign as an anthropologist is often different from what people deeply immersed in the customs will offer by way of explanation.

It is not an accident that the holiday season in an Alpine farming culture starts when the hardest summer work is finished and ends as spring arrives anew. Tiroleans often view these vivid events during the cold season as an expression of their deep religious and mystical view of the world as well as a connection to the natural lives of their ancestors. The ceremonies where people are masked and dressed up as *Wilden* or "wild ones" are said to drive out the evil spirits as well as winter (Forcher 1983). It takes little sophistication to see why people feared and dreaded winter in Tirol. The magical reasoning they used is powerful: work hard to do everything practical and humanly possible to ensure survival. Then acknowledge and placate a world beyond ordinary control, beyond the manipulation of hard work. So they played together in public rituals and ceremonies. They played with ideas of death and the spirit world as hard as they worked to tend cows and babies. It is little wonder that the marketing of tourist culture we discussed in chapter 6 is so pronounced in winter.

Christmas seems to last a long time in Tirol. Advent, or the events leading up to Christmas, is filled with the noise of *Perchten*. These fiercely masked youngsters promenade from house to house and receive small gifts such as fruit and nuts. On November 1 or All Saints Day, in some parts of Tirol masked boys go from household to household begging and "grabbing for donuts," *Krapfenschnapper*. They carry large rattles modeled after various animal heads (including mythical beasts). Farm girls have prepared a treat of doughnuts and other small gifts and pass these out to the youngsters.

In many Catholic countries November 1 is the Day of the Dead. Relatives go to their family graves, clean them, decorate them, share food, and even leave food or gifts for the deceased. The evening before All Saints Day is what we call Halloween, where masked children also extort treats. We generally disassociate this day from Advent or even from its links to the ancient and pagan world. The association with witches, pumpkins, devils, and graveyards are still quite evident.

The custom of Christmas trees as we know them started in the latter half of the nineteenth century. But tree veneration has much older pagan roots in northern Europe, particularly Germany. Romantic Victorians brought the trees inside to honor them in a new way. Tree ornaments and the related Christmas paraphernalia are for sale in Tirol throughout the year. The first ornaments were probably made there; kitsch reigns at Christmas.

The St. Nikolas we read about in chapter 5 is, of course, the lineal ancestor of Santa Claus. It is easy to trace the evolution of our folk beliefs about "old Saint Nick" when we remember sleighs, bags of toys, magical and miniature helpers. Analytically, we also realize the historic complexity and religious syncretism in the person of the Devil.

According to seasonal legend, three kings or Magi visited the infant Jesus on the sixth day of January at his temporary stable-home; this, the twelfth day of Christmas, is called Epiphany in the liturgical calendar. Deep in the past, three youths in costumes and masks went about from homestead to homestead singing. The three impersonators sang about their long journey following the star; the star-singers or *Sternsingen* also hinted at how welcome refreshments would be. Some villages still practice the custom of blessing the stalls of their cattle at Epiphany in honor of the visit of the three Wise Men. These three kings figure prominently in Tirolean Christmas commodities and mythologies.

As part of a ceremony called *Räuchern* on the eve of Epiphany, estate managers or other heads of households write C + M + B and the date over their doors with a piece of consecrated chalk. Students who are good observers spot these signs very quickly and question their meaning. Some people believe that these letters are an abbreviation of the names of the three kings: Casper, Melchior and Balthasar. Those familiar with Latin say that the initials are short for the prayer, "Christus Mansionem Benedicat"—Christ bless this house. The origins of such a custom are only speculative. There were excellent reasons to seek blessings for a household and its inhabitants long before the appearance of Christianity. Like the sacred fires, however, the signs endure. That is why a drawing of the chalked blessing above the door graces the beginning of this chapter.

Winter has always been the time for communal activities in Tirol. For example, the habit of groups strolling around singing for other citizens is mentioned from the municipal records of Innsbruck from the early 1500s. The records indicate that singing was part of begging; singers walked long distances, not to continue a civic pleasantry, but to beg alms in times of economic hardship. In recent decades urban and rural Tiroleans gather during Advent, Christmas and Epiphany for choruses, folk music groups, choirs and poetry readings. Today, the carolers collect for charity. These are not new customs or even revivals of old ones; they are an evolution, a natural blossoming of old winter habits. They have also been exported to wherever Christmas is practiced. One of the best-selling carvings in Tirol features earnest children singing with uplifted eyes under an old-fashioned street lamp. Caroling, greeting cards and special seasonal songs (both secular and religious) are persistent, even unavoidable, features of these holidays.

Later in winter, thousands of Tiroleans don traditional costumes and parade, perform, sing, dance and even race through the streets wearing fearsome masks and making noise. Masked demons and other creatures of the Other World leap about, yelling and screaming. The *Fasching* celebrations today, like Mardi Gras or carnival, feature parades with costumed revelers, imaginatively decorated floats, mythic themes and creatures of the imagination. This celebration is ostensibly a Catholic custom centered in the time span between Epiphany and Ash Wednesday, which marks the first day of Lent and the contemplative forty days leading up to Easter.

The idea is to go out on the streets in costume and act a little crazy before somber Lenten observances start. The superficial Christian theology of the occasion, however, did not fool the Austrian government. In the early nineteenth century they prohibited these public spectacles and denounced them as heathen and immoral. The linkage of fertility with sex and public masking with orgies united church and state in opposition. Resurrected in the twentieth century, the marketing of this tradition is now big business as tourists pour in to see the parades, the gigantic witches or the fanciful headdresses and masks. Like the Mardi Gras festivities in New Orleans, locals and tourists alike go wild. Most of us who participate have no sense of religious orthodoxy or conformity. We just have an unabashedly good time.

Winter, in these high valleys and on the slopes, feels very long. Inhabitants want to be reassured that spring will return. Just as Advent and Christmas are the depths of winter, at the time when the daytime sunlight is at its shortest, so the ceremonies and celebrations from that moment on prophesy the coming of spring. It is easy to trace the origin of such customs as Mardi Gras and Easter to ceremonies which celebrate the coming of spring. It would be hard to ignore the association of these ceremonies with fertility, the increase of crops, herds and humans and indeed, the inevitable sexuality and sensuality which springtime encourages. We are not surprised that Tiroleans make Easter eggs or bake loaves and cakes in the shape of rabbits, chickens or lambs when springtime finally comes. Christian theologians placed their resurrection stories at this time of year.

These so-called festivals are part of the packaging of the Other or the Authentic, the experience of culture. Today winter in Tirol is the season which brings in the money and snow is the raw material of survival and well-being. Cold weather customs have adapted, in large part by responding to the culture of tourism. I sometimes wonder: what is Christmas really about? Do Tiroleans believe in the rituals they stage? Do Americans believe in the rituals we stage?

## Taking Leave: "It Was Worth All the Uphill"

The final stage of the ritual of travel is severing the ties with this natural high and reintegrating ourselves with our ordinary realities. We have to return home. Anthropologists compare the rituals of tourism to a vision quest which Native American seekers made. We note the physical separation, the token objects [souvenirs], the inability to fully reveal or even explain what is happening [superficial postcards], the homesickness and reentry shock. We know that seasoning, ordeals and new insights change us forever.

The stereotyped tourist experiences include writing postcards home, picking up the final souvenirs or presents and packing suitcases suddenly doubled in volume. At this point we have forgotten our shock, perhaps we have traded it for schlock. We have made a list, often not too subtle, of the comforts we have left at home and will be glad to be reunited with. A great many travelers changed their lives; they are not the same people who left home weeks ago.

Here students write of their last moments before they pack to leave. Each of them has gone somewhere to have some moments at an activity which they have learned to do and enjoy, which they have clearly done before and which takes on a new meaning for them.

"At St. Nicholas in Merano, near the walkway to Dorf Tirol. I'm weeping as I listen to an organist play—the richness, the history, my own family and religious history—such peace, deep relaxation spreads over me like a sudden covering with a down comforter. So pleasant and cozy because it cuts a draft or chill you were not conscious of until it is removed. Thank you."

"I had to come back alone to this incredible Alpine meadow. I feel amazement and thankfulness for such beauty. This is the most incredible place I've ever been. I sit here under a Wyoming-blue sky in the middle of a field full of ten kinds of wild flowers, looking at snow-capped mountains, amazing conifers, listening to rushing icy melted snow over rocks in the stream. There are even sheep with bells. I feel so FULL. I think we are better learners, better people, because we are seeing such things."

This is the last journal entry on the last day for a student who has hiked high up the mountains to say goodbye. She records her farewell memories and feelings.

*A typical Tirolean scene.*

"Waterfalls. Mountains. Valleys. Sky. Rocks. Cows and Goats. Shadows. Sun. Bridges. Laughing. Racing hearts. Clean air. Green trees. Small paths. Mountain springs. Clouds. Footsteps. Uphill. Downhill. Narrow. Chains to hold on to. Flowers. Butterflies. Both in every imaginable color. Beauty. Serenity. Peacefulness. Nature. Health. Breathtaking. Bells. Magical wonder. These are the things I will remember about today's hike. By 7:15 we returned to the castle with blisters, empty stomachs, but full of energy. I felt so alive. We went out to eat with our friends at a restaurant in Dorf Tirol. When we returned, everyone was hanging around outside with candles and a guitar. It was worth all the uphill in the world."

# Bibliography


Alcock, Antony E. 1970. *The History of the South Tyrol Question*. London: Michael Joseph, Ltd.

Ball, John. 1879. *A Guide to the Eastern Alps*. London: Longmans, Green, and Co.

Berkner, Lutz K. 1972. The stem family and the developmental cycle of the peasant household: An eighteenth-century Austrian example. *American Historical Review* 77:398–418.

Busk, Rachael Harriette. 1874. *The Valleys of Tirol: Their Traditions and Customs and How to Visit Them*. London: Longmans, Green, and Co.

______. 1871. *Household Stories from the Land of Hofer*. London: Griffith and Farran.

Calinescu, Matei. 1976. The benevolent monster: Reflections on *kitsch* as an aesthetic concept. *CLIO* 6(1): 3–21.

Caramelle, Franz, Ingo Schneider and Hella Pflanzer. 1987. *Tirol*. Innsbruck: Pinguin-Verlag.

Cole, John W. 1969. Economic alternatives in the Upper Nonsberg. *Anthropological Quarterly* 42(3): 186–213.

______. 1972. Cultural adaptation in the eastern Alps. *Anthropological Quarterly* 45(3): 158–176.

______. 1973. Social process in the Italian Alps. *American Anthropologist* 75(3): 765–786.

Cole, John W. and Phillip S. Katz. 1973. Knecht to Arbeiter: The proletarization process in South Tyrol. *Studies in European Society* 1(1): 39–66.

Cole, John W. and Eric R. Wolf. 1974. *The Hidden Frontier: Ecology and Ethnicity in an Alpine Valley*. New York: Academic Press.

Dellago, Edmund. n.d. *The Priceless Tradition of ANRI. The Legend of the Dolomite Valley: From Seclusion to World Renown*. ANRI: St. Christina. Gröden, Italy.

de Rachewiltz, Mary. 1975. *Discretions: Ezra Pound, Father and Teacher*. New York: New Directions.

de Rachewiltz, Siegfried W. 1983. *Brot im südlichen Tirol*. Arunda.

______. 1988. *Die Arche*. Arunda 22.

Doob, Leonard W. 1962. South Tyrol: An introduction to the psychological syndrome of nationalism. *Public Opinion Quarterly*. 26(2): 172–184.

Edwards, Amelia. 1873. *Untrodden Peaks and Unfrequented Valleys: A Midsummer Ramble in the Dolomites*. London: Longman, Green, and Co. Reprinted in 1987. Boston: Beacon Press.

Frantz, Klaus. 1983. The development and regional structure of Austrian tourism. In *Tourism and Culture: A Comparative Perspective*. ed. E. C. Nebel. Third Biannual Symposium of the University of New Orleans and the University of Innsbruck, 7–26.

Friedl, John. 1974. *Kippel: A Changing Village in the Alps*. New York: Holt, Rinehart and Winston.

Forcher, Michael. 1983. *Dämonen Blasmusik und Schöne Trachten. Von Brauchtum und Volkskultur in Tirol*. Innsbruck: Haymon Verlag.

Gilbert, Josiah and G. C. Churchill. 1864. *The Dolomite Mountains: Excursions through Tyrol, Carinthia, Carniola, and Fruili*. London: Longman, Green, Longman, Roberts, and Green.

Goldberg, G. 1982. Late Gothic painting from South Tirol. *Apollo: A Magazine of the Arts* 116(248): 240–245.

Goldsmith, James and Anne. 1989. *The Dolomites of Italy: A Travel Guide*. London: A & C Black.

Graburn, Nelson H. 1983. The anthropology of tourism. *Annuals of Tourism Research* 10:9–33.

Grieshofer, Franz. 1987. *Krippen*. Innsbruck: Pinguin-Verlag.

Grohman, W. A. Baillie. 1878. *Gaddings with a Primitive People: Tyrolese Life and Customs*. New York: Henry Holt and Co.

______. 1908. *Tyrol*. Illustrated by E. H. Compton. London: Adam and Charles Black.

Herbin, Jackie. 1986. A model tourist development: The case of the Austrian Tirol. *Society and Leisure* 9(1): 95–116.

Honigmann, John J. 1963. Bauer and Arbeiter in a rural Austrian community. *Southwestern Journal of Anthropology* 19:40–53.

Jacob, James E. 1981. Ethnic mobilization on the Germanic periphery: The case of the South Tyrol. *Ethnic Groups* 3:253–280.

Jafari, Jafar. 1983. Understanding the structure of tourism. In *Tourism and Culture: A Comparative Perspective*. ed. E. C. Nebel. Third Biannual Symposium of the University of New Orleans and the University of Innsbruck, 65–84.

Johnson, Lonnie. 1987. *Introducing Austria: A Short History*. Vienna: *Österreichischer Bundesverlag Gesellschaft*.

Jordan, Terry G. 1988. *The European Culture Area: A Systematic Geography*. 2nd Ed. New York: Harper and Row.

Kates, George N. 1963. Tirol: 1363–1963. *Arts News* 62:28.

Katzenstein, Peter J. 1976. Ethnic political conflict in South Tyrol. *Österreichische Zeitschrift für Aussenpolitik*, Part I: 16:221–30; Part II: 275–291.

Leidlmair, Adolf. 1985. Migration patterns in the mountain farming settlement area of the Alps as a problem in political geography: The South Tyrol as an example. In *Environment and Human Life in Highlands and High Latitude Zones*. eds. A. Leidlmair and Klaus Frantz. Universität Innsbruck, 93–97.

Levy, Miriam J. 1988. *Governance and Grievance: Habsburg Policy and Italian Tyrol in the Eighteenth Century*. W. Lafayette, Indiana: Purdue University Press.

Lutz, Berkner. 1972. The stem family and the developmental cycle of the peasant household: An eighteenth century Austrian example. *American Historical Review* 77:398–418.

Magnago, Silvius. 1974. The situation of the German and Ladin linguistic minorities in South Tyrol. Lecture to the Federalist Union of European Nationalities. *Europa Ethnica* 31(4): 146–165.

Minghi, Julian V. 1963. Boundary studies and national prejudices: The case of the South Tyrol. *Professional Geographer* 15:4–8.

Myss, Walter, ed. 1973. *Tyrol through the Ages: Travel Pictures and Diaries from Seven Centuries*. Innsbruck: Wort und Welt Verlag.

Naroll, Frada. 1960. Child-training among Tyrolese peasants. *Anthropological Quarterly* 33:106–114.

Naroll, Raoul and Frada Naroll. 1962. Social development of a Tyrolese village. *Anthropological Quarterly* 35:103–120.

Nash, Dennison. 1981. Tourism as an anthropological subject. *Current Anthropology* 22(5): 461–481.

Nash, Dennison and Valene Smith. 1991. Anthropology and tourism. *Annuals of Tourism Research* 18:12–25.

Penz, Hugo. 1985. The status of the Alpine pastures in the scope of Alpine agriculture. In *Environment and Human Life in Highlands and High Latitude Zones*. eds. A. Leidlmair and Klaus Frantz. Universität Innsbruck, 115–121.

Petschauer, Peter W. 1990. The outside and the inside: Stability and change of *mentalität* in a small village. *Journal of Social History* 23(4): 715–734.

______. 1989. The childrearing modes in flux: An historian's perspective. *Journal of Psychohistory* 17(1): 1–41.

______. 1987. Intrusive to socializing modes: Transitions in eighteenth-century Germany and twentieth-century Italy. *Journal of Psychohistory* 14(3): 257–270.

______. 1985. Children of Afers, or "Evolution of Childhood" revisited. *Journal of Psychohistory* 13(2): 121–144.

______. 1985. *Afers: Gedanken zur Geschichte*. Brixen: Verlag A. Weger.

Plaut, James S. 1984. *The House of ANRI: A Popular Account of Woodcarving in the South Tyrol*. Club ANRI: Randolph, MA.

Preglau, Max. 1983. Tourism kills tourism: Environmental, cultural and economic consequences of tourism. In *Tourism and Culture: A Comparative Perspective*. ed. E. C. Nebel. Third Biannual Symposium of the University of New Orleans and the University of Innsbruck, 35–64.

Pristinger, Flavia. 1980. Ethnic conflict and modernization in the South Tyrol. *Nations without a State: Ethnic Minorities in Western Europe*. ed. Charles R. Foster. New York: Praeger.

Potter, Jack M., May N. Diaz and George M. Foster. 1967. *Peasant Society: A Reader*. Boston: Little, Brown.

Robertshaw, Alan. 1977. *Oswald von Wolkenstein: The Man and the Myth*. Göppingen: Verlag Alfred Kummerle. Nr. 178.

Rowley, A. R. 1986. Minority schools in the South Tyrol and in the Austrian Burgenland: A comparison of two models. *Journal of Multilingual and Multicultural Development* 7(2,3): 229–251.

Smith, Valene, ed. 1977. *Hosts and Guests: The Anthropology of Tourism*. Philadelphia: University of Pennsylvania Press.

Turner, Victor. 1969. *The Ritual Process*. Chicago: Aldine.

Von Hörmann, L. 1877. *Tiroler Volkstypen*. Vienna. Translated by Eric Mosbacher.

White, Peter T. and Volkmar Wentzel. 1961. Austria's Tirol, Province in the clouds. *National Geographic* 120(1): 107–141.

Wolf, Eric R. 1962. Cultural dissonance in the Italian Alps. *Comparative Studies in Society and History*. 5:1–4.

______. 1970. The inheritance of land among Bavarian and Tyrolese peasants. *Anthropologica*, New Series 12:99–114.

______. 1982. *Europe and the People without History*. Berkeley: University of California Press.

Wolff, Karl Felix. 1958. *The Dolomites and their Legends*. Bozen: Verlagsanstalt Athesia.

## Appendix A

# Places to Know

This list of place names has been provided to help you familiarize yourself with the geography that serves as a backdrop to this book. Where two place names appear together on a line, the first is the German name and the second is the Italian name for the same location. Names that appear by themselves are either specific to the Austrial Tirol or are universally recognized.

Adige River
Adige Valley
Bavaria
Berg Isel
Bozen    Bolzano
Brenner Pass    Brennero
Brixen    Bressonone
Bruneck    Brunico
Brunnenburg
Danube River
Dorf Tirol
Eastern Alps
Eisack River
Etsch River
Etschtal (Etsch Valley)
Fassatal    Val di Fassa
Gadertal    Val Badia
Grödental (Gröden Valley)
    Val di Gardena
Inn River
Innsbruck
Inntal (Inn Valley)
Jaufen Pass
Kaunertal (Kauner Valley)
Meran    Merano
Milan
Munich
Nonsberg    Val di Non/Anaunia
Paris
Pustertal (Puster Valley)
    Pusteria
Reschen Pass
Rhine River
St. Felix
St. Ulrich    Ortesei
Schloss Tirol
Schwaz
Seiser Alm
Sella Gruppe    Gruppo di Sella
Südtirol    Alto Adige
Trent    Trentino
Tret
Trostburg Castle
Venice
Vinschgau    Val Venosta
Zillertal (Ziller Valley)

## Appendix B

# Words to Know

Here is a list of words which appear in this book. Some are German, some are English and a few are Italian. Many of them you will already know. All of them are defined within their cultural contexts in the preceding chapters. I hope that having these words available will make reading and the development of concepts more pleasurable. I include them as a reminder of how much you already know, as a tribute to how much you have learned or as a guide to learning more.

Advent
*Aldstadt*
Allies
alluvial
*Alm* (n.), *Almen* (adj.)
almanac
*Alpen*
*Alpenhutte*
*Alpenstock*
Alps
amulets
Anabaptists
Andreas Hofer
*Apfelstrudel*
*Arbeiter*
*Arbeitsgemeinschaft*
ard
autonomy

*Bajazzers*
Baroque
bathing closets
*Bauernschmaus*
Bavarians
bellcow
bilingual
Bishopric
blackcock
bourgeoisie
Bronze Age
*Burgher*/burgher

caldron
cantilevered
carabinieri
Carnival
carrying capacity
carter
cash crop
catacomb schools
Celts
chamois
chinking
Classical
cobbler
corbel
cottage industry
Counter-Reformation
cradle saw
crampons
crèche
crucifix

culture of Alpine continuity
culture area
culture shock

developmental cycle
*Dirndl*
Dolomites
dovetail
duchy

ecology
econiche
*Edelweiss*
*Ehrengang*
*Ehrenkraut*
*Ehrentanz*
Epiphany
erosion
*erste Knecht*
estate
ethnographic present
Everyman

*facchino*
*Fasching*
felt
*Fensterln*
*Ferggl*
*Fingerhackeln*
flax
fodder
frieze
*fromm*

gable
Gaismair, Michael
*Gamsbart*
*Gasselgehen*
*Gasthaus*
*Gasthof*
*Gauderfest*
*Gemeinde*
*Gemeinderat*
gentry
*Geselchtes*
Gothic
grazing
*Gröstel*

Habsburg
hanging valleys
*Herrgottmacher*
*Herrgottseck*
*Hochzeitlader*
*Hof*
hope chest

impartible inheritance
inheritance
insolation
Iron Age
irredentist

*Kindsmagd*
kin-state
*Kirchdorf*
*Kirschwasser*
*Kitsch*/kitsch
*Knecht*
*Knödel*
*Knödelsuppe*
*Kraksen*
*Krapfenschnapper*
*Krippen*

lactation
Ladin
larch
leadstrings
*Leiderhosen*
Lent
livestock
lineage
linen
loden
longitudinal valleys
Lucifer

Magi
Magnago, Silvius
Malthusian dilemma
manure
many-stranded coalitions
Maria Theresa

*maso*
mast
Maultesch, Margaret
Maximillian I
medieval
Middle Ages
miller
*Minnesingers*
monarchy
monolingual
*Morgensuppe*
murrain
*Musikkapelle*
Mussolini

National Socialism
Nativity
Nazi
Neo-classical
Neolithic

old town
oriel
oxen

Pacher, Michael
*Paket*
pan-Germanic
*Pappele*
partible inheritance
pasture
Peasant Wars
Pentecost
People's Party
*Perchten*
physic
Pietà
plane
Pleistocene
"Porcupine Principle"
poultices
primogeniture
proletarization
purlin (purline)

radical reformation
rasp
*Räuchern*
Reformation
*Reich*
Renaissance
resins
Rhaetia
Rhaeto-Romansch
*Risorgimento*
Rococo
Romance
Romanesque
Romanticism
*Rücksack*

Sacred Heart of Jesus
saddleback roof
salting the sauerkraut
*Schnaddahüpfler*
*Schnaps*/schnapps
*Schuhplattler*
*Schützenkompanie*
*Schwärzers*
scree
scutch
scythe
self-determination
sibling set
sickle
slalom
slope
soot
*Speck*
St. Isidore
St. Nikolas (St. Nicholas)
St. Notaburga
staggered system
*Stampfe*
star-singing
stem family
*Sternsingen*
*Stube, Stuben, Stübchen*
stucco
stye
*Südtiroler Volkspartei (SVP)*
sustained yield lumbering

swaddling
swine

tatting
*Tauglich*
tennis shoe death
*Teufel*
Teutonic
thickets
*Tirolerleber*
toilet training
*tragen*
transhumance pastoralism
transverse valleys
Treaty of St. Germain

vertical system
von Wolkenstein, Oswald
volcanic
votive

wainright
*Wampeler*
*Wetterglocke*
whetstone
whole house
wicket
*Wilden*

yodel